HOW AMERICA WON
WORLD WAR I

The US Military Victory in the Great World War—
The Causes, the Course, and the Consequences

ALAN AXELROD

Guilford, Connecticut

An imprint of Globe Pequot

Distributed by NATIONAL BOOK NETWORK

British Library Cataloguing in Publication Information available

Library of Congress Cataloging-in-Publication Data Is Available

ISBN 978-1-4930-3192-4 (hardcover)
ISBN 978-1-4930-3193-1 (e-book)

∞™ The paper used in this publication meets the minimum requirements of American National Standard for Information Sciences—Permanence of Paper for Printed Library Materials, ANSI/ NISO Z39.48-1992.

For Anita and Ian

Contents

Introduction

Wrong Turn in Sarajevo

ON JUNE 15, 1389, MURAD I, SULTAN OF THE OTTOMAN EMPIRE, LED an army of as many as forty thousand troops against perhaps thirty thousand Serbs under Prince Lazar Hrebeljanović, founder of "Lazar's state," in which medieval Serbs saw the hope for their former empire's resurrection. The two rulers and their armies met at Kosovo Field, northwest of Pristina, today the largest city in Kosovo. There the armies of Ottoman Islam and Serbian Christianity promptly annihilated one another nearly to the man and including both commanders, Murad and Lazar. Only because the Serbs could not muster enough men from among the civilian population to replace their catastrophic losses, the Ottomans under Murad's son, Bayezid, eventually conquered them and held them in subjugation until the sixteenth century.

The day of the battle, adjusted for the difference between the Old Style Julian calendar and the New Style Gregorian calendar, has been continuously celebrated by Serbs as Vidovan (St. Vitus's Day), a secular and sacred holiday that stirs profound emotion. And so it would have been celebrated in the city of Sarajevo, capital of Bosnia and Herzegovina, on June 28, 1914, were it not for the discordant note struck by the official visit of Archduke Franz Ferdinand and his wife, the Grand Duchess Sophie. The heir presumptive to the Austro-Hungarian throne, which had ruled Bosnia and Herzegovina since 1878, had deliberately chosen the great national holiday of its "colony" to make a highly publicized state visit.

Franz Ferdinand felt compelled to assert his imperial authority in a Balkan capital. Like his uncle, Emperor Franz Josef I, he was keenly aware that Austria-Hungary was an empire in jeopardy. Chronically wracked by violence, the Balkan Peninsula had just come through the convulsion of two costly wars: the First Balkan War of 1912–1913 and the Second Balkan War of 1913. The first pitted the Balkan states of Bulgaria, Serbia, and Greece against Turkey and resulted in the loss of most of Turkey's European possessions. In the second, Bulgaria squared off against Serbia, Greece, Romania, and Turkey. That war ended with Turkey losing even more of its European foothold. Not only did these conflicts fail to resolve the tensions in southeastern Europe, the fraying fringe of Austria-Hungary, but they also left the region burning with a new nationalism. Prior to the wars, the Balkan countries had been torn between Turkey and Austria (and then Austria-Hungary), the region's major powers. Now they sought independence, even as they forged a "pan-Slavic" ethnic bond with Russia, which eagerly offered itself as the defender of all who proclaimed themselves Slavs.

Russia's embrace of the Slavic Balkans was ostentatiously public, but within the Balkans themselves, the movement toward the creation of a single great Slavonic state was conducted covertly. In Serbia, at the time the most powerful independent state in the region, a secret society calling itself *Omladina* ("Youth") plotted a coup against the Serbian government for the purpose of taking the nation into a union with other Balkan states as well as parts of Poland, Moravia, Silesia, and Romania. On June 10, 1868, Omladina assassins dressed in formal black suits approached the carriage of Mihailo Obrenović—Prince Michael of Serbia—and shot him, his mistress, and her mother. Of the three, only the mistress survived. Some years later, agents of Omladina fomented a partially successful uprising against Serbian king Milan I, who abdicated in 1889 to his son, Alexander I, after adopting a liberalized constitution. Early in the morning of June 11, 1903 (May 29 by the Old Style Julian calendar still used in Serbia), Omladina men entered the Serbian royal palace, searched it, and found Alexander and his wife, Queen Draga, hiding in a secret chamber located behind a bedroom mirror. They executed the pair by gunshot and then mutilated, disemboweled, and hurled them through a second-floor palace window. The royal couple landed on a pile of garden manure.

In 1908, the Omladina renamed itself *Narodna Odbrana* ("National Defense"), and affiliated groups were formed in Slovenia, Istria, and in Bosnia and Herzegovina, where it was called *Mlada Bosnia* ("Young Bosnia"). In May 1911, Narodna Odbrana morphed into a secret society with a more sinister name, *Ujedinjenje ili Smert*: "Unity or Death." The Serbian parliament, in fear and trembling, called it the Black Hand. Its members were chiefly Serbian army officers, and its leader was a former Serbian colonel, Dragutin Dmitrievich, who adopted the nom de guerre, *Apis*, "The Bull." It was a sobriquet he had earned in 1903 as one of the bloody assassins of the Serbian royal couple. The police hunted him after that killing, found him, gunned him down, and then left him for dead. The Bull proved too strong for their bullets. He recovered, went into hiding, and then stepped up to leadership of the Black Hand.

Unsurprisingly, under Apis, the Black Hand was not so much a political or even an insurgent organization as it was a hit squad. Apis recruited his assassins mostly from among radical or radically inclined university students, and he especially singled out young men infected with the universal plague of the turn of the century—tuberculosis. Among the Bull's finds was one Gavrilo Princip. Gavrilo had been born on his father's farm in West Bosnia on June 13, 1894. At least, that was the date the local priest recorded in the parish register. When the cleric transcribed this date into the civil register, he suffered a slip of the pen, writing *July* instead of *June*. This error concerning an obscure record about an obscure boy would change history.

Gavrilo's father raised sheep, and he raised his son to shepherd them. This was not good enough for the boy's mother, however, who persuaded her husband to send Gavrilo to school. After his elementary education, the young man attended a business school in Belgrade. In the Serbian capital city, he boarded at the home of Danilo Ilic, a nationalist and pan-Slav who dreamed of uniting the Balkans in a great state free from Austro-Hungarian oppression. In Princip, Ilic found a ready listener and convert. Fired up, in 1912 Princip offered himself for enlistment in the Serbian army, which turned him down as obviously undersized and just as obviously consumptive. The rejection hit him hard. He became apathetic, lost interest in school, made no attempt to find employment, and looked in vain for a purpose beyond begging scraps of food and sleeping in doorways. To anyone who would listen, Princip spoke of revolution. One of the few who did listen to the ailing young derelict was nineteen-year-old Nedeljko Cabrinovic. Indeed, the two avidly traded fantasies of killing Archduke Franz Ferdinand, the Austro-Hungarian heir presumptive.

With the coming of spring of 1914 came rumors of the archduke's intended visit to Sarajevo. Invigorated, Princip, in company with Cabrinovic, recruited one of his boyhood friends, Trifko Grabez, to call on a certain Milan Ciganovic, hero of the Balkan Wars and possessed of a reputation for radical violence. Ciganovic welcomed the young men, spoke with them, and then told Apis about them. The Bull responded by giving Ciganovic four Belgian-made Browning FN M1910 nine-millimeter pistols, ammunition, six grenade-style bombs, and what he said were cyanide capsules—to be swallowed by the assassins in the event of imminent capture. In truth, the capsules were a fraud. They were filled with some inert watery fluid. The guns, bullets, and bombs were real enough, however.

Apis did not have high hopes for his lads. "There is an outside chance that they just might blunder into a success," he told an associate. "We might as well give them a try at it as any other."[1] Indeed, as professional killers, the four lads were neither experienced nor trained. Subsequent events would suggest that they didn't even possess any native aptitude for the task. In varying degrees, however, they did share one critical qualification. None of them expected to live much longer. All suffered from consumption. They had very little to lose.

Their assigned target was Archduke Franz Ferdinand, who would be accompanied on his marginally blasphemous and certainly offensive Vidovan tour of Sarajevo by his wife, the Grand Duchess Sophie. Franz Ferdinand, the nephew of the Austrian emperor, was thrust into the line of succession by the suicide of his cousin, Crown Prince Rudolf, and the death of his own father, from typhoid, in 1896. As for Sophie, she was nothing more than the daughter of a minor Czech noble and, therefore, in the eyes of Franz Josef I and his court, an unworthy consort for the heir presumptive. The problem was that Franz Ferdinand loved her madly. He would marry her even if he had to make the sacrifice the emperor demanded of him: renounce the right of his children to inherit the throne. The additional price? Suffer the slings and snubs of his uncle and virtually every other member of the court.

We don't know if sacrificing his children's birthright unduly disturbed Franz Ferdinand, but the hostility of the court surely took a toll. By nature an unpleasant, narrow, and intolerant man, Franz Ferdinand vented his rage against Serbia at every opportunity. He believed that the Serbian government—not insurgents within it—were goading the Bosnians to rebellion against the empire. He convinced himself that appearing in Sarajevo, on Vidovan no less, would thoroughly intimidate the Serbian-inspired nationalists. (Never mind that they were the very people who had slaughtered, mutilated, dismembered, and defenestrated the Serbian royal couple.) What is more, by making a formal state visit in company with his beloved Sophie, the people of Bosnia and Herzegovina as well as the imperial court of Austria-Hungary would be forced to acknowledge her as royalty.

Princip, Cabrinovic, Grabez, and Ilic, in addition to three others Ilic had brought into the plot, were deployed along three hundred yards of the Appel Quay, the principal avenue of Sarajevo. Because the archduke's timetable and route had been published in the local newspapers, the seven, armed variously with pistols and bombs, were certain they would not miss a close encounter. The first young man, positioned at the Cumuria Bridge, had a bomb; the second, a bomb and a Browning; the third, Cabrinovic, was armed only with a bomb. Ilic was next along the Quay; both he and another assassin had revolvers. Princip, holding a Browning, was second to last, just before Grabez. He was less nervous than he might otherwise have been, since his position as sixth in line gave him every reason to believe that the archduke would be dead well before his car reached him.

Franz Ferdinand was aware that he and his wife faced some danger, but he was convinced that an archduke of a great empire did not require an army to protect him in a city of his own empire. With the arrogance of groundless conviction, he ordered his military units to clear out of Sarajevo and stay out. He retained only a small cadre of bodyguards.

After arriving by train, the royal couple boarded an open-top limousine, designed to display to greatest advantage the archduke in the full-dress uniform of an Austro-Hungarian general officer, including a magnificent green-plumed hat. His wife was arrayed as a fitting complement in grandeur: plump in her white silk dress, red sash, flamboyant picture hat, and ermine-trimmed cape.

The motorcade passed Cumuria Bridge, its passengers quite unaware of the proximity of the first assassin. No wonder. The panic-stricken youth stood stock-still, unable to bring himself to hurl the bomb he carried. Cabrinovic, in the number-two position, did throw his grenade, but his timing was off and it bounced off the back of the archduke's limousine, rolled in front of the car following it, and exploded with enough force to damage the second vehicle and injure a number of spectators as well as members of the archducal entourage. Even Sophie felt the sharp sting of a tiny splinter that found its mark in her fleshy cheek.

The driver knew enough not to stop, but instead picked up the pace. As they watched the archduke's automobile sprint past them, both Ilic and the accomplice by his side were stunned into inaction. The same happened to both Princip and Grabez. The vehicle was moving too fast for thought or aim or action. Seven killers. Seven failures. Profoundly discouraged, Gavrilo Princip stole off to a table at an outdoor café. He sat down and ordered a coffee, the compact nine-millimeter weapon still heavy in his coat pocket.

Having glided almost harmlessly through a gauntlet of death, Franz Ferdinand and Sophie blithely attended a scheduled reception at the town hall. After this, however, the archduke ordered a change in the planned itinerary. He wanted to visit the local military hospital, to which those wounded by the bomb blast had been taken. This created a problem for his driver, who did not know the way to the hospital. He drove to the corner of the Appel Quay and Franz Josef Street. Then, bewildered, he made a sudden turn.

"What's this?" a military aide shouted to him. "We've taken the wrong way!"

Thoroughly rattled, the driver applied the brake and spun the wheel, hand over hand, hoping to negotiate a U-turn. Hemmed in by crowds that had gathered behind the car and were now in front of it, he had to slow to a crawl and, finally, stop. The limousine was broadside to the café-delicatessen of Moritz Schiller. Sitting disconsolately at an outdoor table, perhaps five feet from the archduke and the grand duchess, was Gavrilo Princip.

Princip later told police, "I recognized the heir apparent [*sic*], but as I saw that a lady was sitting next to him, I reflected for a moment whether I should shoot or not. At the same moment I was filled with a peculiar feeling and I aimed at the heir apparent from the pavement—which was made easier because the car was proceeding slower at the moment. Where I aimed I do not know. But I know that I aimed at the heir apparent. I believe I fired twice, perhaps more, because I was so excited. Whether I hit the victims or not, I cannot tell, because instantly people started to hit me."

It was 11:15 a.m., June 28, 1914, when Princip reached into his coat pocket, withdrew the small black pistol, and leveled it at virtually point-blank range. Catching sight of him, a policeman lunged at Princip, but an out-of-work actor named Pusara rushed the cop, shoving him out of the way. Princip squeezed off three rounds before the policeman regained his balance. By then, the assassin had turned to flee, and a bystander named Ferdinand Behr sought to facilitate his getaway by punching the officer in the gut. Clearly, there were more than seven residents of Sarajevo who had little use for the archduke. But instead of running, Princip stopped, seemingly transfixed as a man named Velic knocked the revolver out of his hand and other spectators fell upon Princip, landing blows and kicks.

The youth's first shot had passed through the car door, hitting Sophie in the abdomen. The second shot buried itself in the archduke's neck, clipping the carotid artery before lodging in his spine. There was a great deal of blood.

●

Except in small Serbian immigrant neighborhoods, mostly in industrial cities such as Pittsburgh, Chicago, Milwaukee, Cleveland, and New York—places where Vidovan was celebrated—June 28, 1914, was just another spring day in the United States. Most Americans probably could not have said just where Serbia was, much less the Bosnian city of Sarajevo. As for the Balkan Wars, few Americans were paying much attention. The assassinations in that obscure part of the world made international news, but the details were confusing. In fact, most Americans were confused and confounded by everything about Europe—the welter of alliances, the rumors of secret deals, the endless jockeying for diplomatic advantage, the numberless monarchs and princelings. Murky as all this was, affairs in the Balkans were murkiest of all.

No, Americans preferred their politics the way they liked their wars, cut and dried and in black and white. Politics was divided between Republicans and Democrats—end of story. As for the wars, the Revolution was lost by King George III and won by George Washington. War of 1812? Andrew Jackson beat the British in the end, at the Battle of New Orleans—enough said. US-Mexican War? Santa Anna lost—absolutely everything. Civil War? The South was crushed, even if they wouldn't admit it. Spanish-American War? A splendid American victory—and in practically no time at all! The Balkans were something else again. Unknown people fought for unknown reasons on a European continent that sensible folks left long ago for America. In fact, for most Americans, the significance of Europe was as a place to leave. What happened there on any given day had no discernible impact on this side of the wide Atlantic.

Now, even though he had died back in 1898, most adult Americans did know a thing or two about Germany's famed "Iron Chancellor," Otto von Bismarck—how he had essentially redrawn the map of Europe when he created the German Empire and how a lot of people credited him with making Europe a more peaceful place than it had been in, well, centuries. But, late in life, Bismarck himself had doubts. "If a general war begins," he remarked, "it will be because of some damn fool thing in the Balkans."[2]

●

In 1862, there was no German Empire. Back then, Otto von Bismarck was a foreign minister and minister president of Prussia. In these capacities, he addressed the Budget Committee of the Prussian Chamber of

Deputies, admonishing them that "the great questions of the time will not be resolved by speeches and majority decisions . . . but by blood and iron." He then guided his monarch, Wilhelm I, in prosecuting victorious wars against Denmark (1864), Austria (1866), and, most important of all, France (1870–1871). That Franco-Prussian War gave Bismarck a platform from which he rallied the disparate German states to unite around the core of Prussia and consolidate as an empire for the first time since the Middle Ages. This new imperial Germany fueled itself on coal mined from the Alsace-Lorraine, which France had to give up as a condition of the treaty it concluded after the humiliating defeat of 1871. Bismarck understood that Germany's annexation of this region would create lasting enmity with France, but Germany needed the coal and it needed a buffer between itself and its natural rival. So, the Iron Chancellor played all Europe like a chessboard, acting to isolate France from any potential allies by binding Russia and Austria-Hungary to Germany in 1873 with the Three Emperors' League, by which all three powers pledged to aid one another in time of war. When Russia withdrew from the League in 1878, Bismarck engineered the Dual Alliance with Austria-Hungary in 1879. The Triple Alliance, among Germany, Austria-Hungary, and Italy, came in 1882, and the next year Bismarck agreed to sign onto a pact between Austria-Hungary and Romania. With this, he succeeded in isolating both France and Russia from the rest of Europe. Of course, he understood that those two nations now had reason to join forces with one another, so he concluded in 1887 a secret "Reinsurance Treaty" with Russia, by which the German kaiser and the Russian czar agreed to remain neutral if either became involved in a war with a third party. The only exceptions to this Reinsurance Treaty were if Germany attacked France, or Russia attacked Austria-Hungary.

By weaving an increasingly intricate web of alliances, some public, some secret, Bismarck believed he had maneuvered Germany out of the possibility of a two-front war against an allied France and Russia, and he also believed that he had bound Europe in a set of relationships, all running through Germany, that pretty much guaranteed peace. "Let us put Germany in the saddle, so to speak," he famously quipped. "It already knows how to ride."[3]

Bismarck's Europe seemed to many the height of rationality, with the wise old man working the marionette strings tied to the continental nations. But when Wilhelm II ascended the throne in 1888, he brought with him a policy of much more rapid imperial expansion than what Wilhelm I had formulated under Bismarck. Seeing his careful diplomatic architecture endangered, the chancellor pushed back, and in 1890, Wilhelm II forced his resignation. Before the end of the year, the marionette strings began to fray. Russia chose not to renew the Reinsurance Treaty and gravitated toward the orbit of France, as Bismarck had feared it might. In 1894, Russia signed with France a formal military convention intended to oppose the Triple Alliance. France added to this a secret agreement with Italy, by which that nation agreed to remain neutral if Germany attacked France or even if France—to "protect its national honor"—attacked Germany. As such, Italy violated the Triple Alliance—without, however, informing Germany.

By virtue of its location between two vast oceans, the Atlantic and the Pacific, the United States enjoyed geographic isolation from the web of treaties the nations of Europe wove among themselves. Until the beginning of the twentieth century, the UK also isolated itself from continental Europe's machinations—not geographically so much as politically—by observing a strict policy of what its statesmen called "splendid isolation." This came to an end when, in 1902, Britain concluded an alliance with Japan meant to block German colonial overtures in the Pacific and in Asia in general. Two years later, the UK signed the Entente Cordiale with France, which was followed in 1907 by the Anglo-Russian Entente. Together, the 1904 and 1907 agreements created the Triple Entente among Britain, France, and Russia. In this way, even, before the opening decade of the twentieth century had ended, what had begun as an enmity between Germany and France following the Franco-Prussian War congealed into the division of all the major European powers into two opposed and very well-armed camps: Germany and Austria-Hungary on one side and France, Russia, and Britain on the other. Between these camps, Italy flitted fitfully.

•

"For God's sake," the Grand Duchess Sophie gasped to her husband the archduke, "what has happened to you?" With that, she crumpled against her husband's chest and into his lap. He cradled her head. "Soferl, Soferl, don't die!" he pleaded. "Stay alive for our children!"

But she was already gone.

By this time, a certain Count Harrach had climbed from the front seat of the open car into the back. Taking hold of the archduke, he asked, "Are you suffering, your highness?"

"It is nothing, it is nothing, it is nothing."

They were the last words of Archduke Franz Ferdinand.

At trial, Gavrilo Princip gave testimony the government of Austria-Hungary would use to make war on Serbia.

"I do not feel like a criminal," the youth said, "because I put away the one who was doing evil. Austria as it is represents evil for our people and therefore should not exist. . . . The political union of the Yugoslavs was always before my eyes, and that was my basic idea. Therefore it was necessary in the first place to free the Yugoslavs . . . from Austria. This . . . moved me to carry out the assassination of the heir apparent, for I considered him as very dangerous for Yugoslavia."[4]

There was never any question that Princip would be convicted. But those who assumed he would be executed for his crime, including Emperor Franz Josef I, were outraged by what happened at sentencing. The attorney appointed by the court to defend him argued that because the official *government* record gave his birthdate as July 13, 1894, instead of June 13, as recorded in the *church* record, Princip was only nineteen years old when he murdered the archduke and the grand duchess. At twenty, he would have been liable to execution. At nineteen, the worst he could get was twenty years.

No matter that tuberculosis put him under a death sentence beyond the power of any court to stay or commute, Count Leopold von Berchtold, Austria-Hungary's foreign minister, demanded a blood sacrifice. He had no evidence that Princip was an agent of the Serbian government.

On the contrary, the Black Hand was the enemy of the Serbian government and had been working to topple it for years. But Berchtold reasoned that if he could arrange to punish Serbia—severely—he would crush Bosnian nationalism and perhaps even derail the pan-Slavic movement.

Berchtold did not intend to start a European war, much less a world war. He wanted only to humiliate Serbia by bloodying it with a sharp, swift, contained war. He did not appreciate that in the interconnected Europe Bismarck had created, brief, local wars were no longer possible. Bound as they were by covenants both public and secret, if any nation began a war with even just one country, others would pile on. Heedlessly, Berchtold asked the emperor to authorize the full mobilization of the Austro-Hungarian army. Only after this was under way did he send a message to the German government, asking if Austria-Hungary could count on its support. By way of response, on July 5, 1914, Kaiser Wilhelm II invited Austria's imperial ambassador to lunch with him. The kaiser pledged that Germany would stand with Austria-Hungary even if it meant war with Russia, because he believed, even if Berchtold did not, that Russia, having promised to defend Serbia, would indeed defend Serbia. Those among Wilhelm's entourage who were present at the meeting were astounded by the impulsivity of the kaiser's pledge, especially given the prospect of going to war with Russia. They did not understand that, like just about everyone else, Wilhelm was quite confident that Serbia would accede to whatever demands Austria-Hungary made. There would be no war.

Days passed, and people talked of war while armies girded for battle. Across the ocean, in the United States, newspapers published the dispatches in their morning, afternoon, or evening editions. As each day passed, it seemed increasingly likely that good sense would prevail after all. Then, at six o'clock on the evening of July 23, Berchtold sent ten demands to Belgrade. All were humbling, but one was so humiliating that it amounted to a renunciation of nationhood. Berchtold demanded the prosecution of all the assassination conspirators. He inferred that there must have been more than Princip, and he demanded that Serbia turn over the investigation to Austria, whose officers were to be given free rein to operate within Serbia. Berchtold gave the Serbs forty-eight hours to reply.

Russian diplomats assured Serbian premier Nicholas Pashich that the czar would "do everything" to protect Serbia. At the same time, however, they begged Pashich to accept every demand—except the one that required absolute forfeiture of sovereignty. Accordingly, on July 25, the Serbian response was delivered. Nine of the demands were unconditionally accepted, but the government balked at allowing Austrian officials to operate independently within Serbia. That demurral was it all took. Berchtold put into motion a declaration of war.

Britain's foreign minister, Sir Edward Grey, offered mediation. While the kaiser was away on holiday, his ministers turned down the offer. Wilhelm returned to Berlin on July 27, and on July 28 Emperor Franz Josef I signed Austria-Hungary's declaration of war against Serbia. That was Russia's cue to partial mobilization of Russian army forces near the Austrian border.

Theobald von Bethmann-Hollweg, Germany's chancellor, was aghast. Wilhelm II wanted a war to expand his empire. But he did not want it now, before Germany was militarily prepared to win it. He sought, in effect, to retract what he had promised over lunch to Austria's imperial ambassador, and he endorsed Bethmann-Hollweg's frantic telegram to Count Berchtold, the Austrian foreign minister: "Serbia has in fact met the Austrian demands in so wide-sweeping a manner that if the Austro-Hungarian government adopted a wholly uncompromising attitude, a gradual revulsion of public opinion against it in all of Europe would have to be reckoned with."

Berchtold sent no reply.

Bethmann-Hollweg sent another telegram on the following day, sternly warning that Germany would not permit itself to be drawn into war just because Austria "has ignored our advice." Even Wilhelm II protested that Serbia's abject reply to Berchtold's demands "dissipates every reason for war."

Yet even as he tried to rein in Germany's ally Austria-Hungary, Bethmann-Hollweg sent Sir Edward Grey an inflammatory proposition. If England remained neutral, he proposed to him, Germany would refrain from annexing any territory of mainland France. (On July 31, Grey angrily rejected the proposal as "infamous.") To Russia, Bethmann-Hollweg sent warning that its partial mobilization was a provocation, and the Kaiser authorized the German navy to assume a war footing in the North Sea. Winston Churchill, at the time his nation's First Sea Lord, responded by mobilizing the British Grand Fleet.

On July 29, Austro-Hungarian gunboats began the bombardment of Belgrade, Serbia's capital. The Great War, as it would be called, had begun. Americans and their government looked on in horror and disbelief. They would soon scorn it as the "European War" and generally congratulate themselves on having nothing at all to do with it.

●

At first, in fact, it was easy to stay out of it. Nothing about the dispute—the casus belli, or cause of war—seemed clear-cut, let alone compelling. If anything, the rapid expansion of the war seemed mechanical, neither motivated nor governed by rational thought. It was all action and reaction. On August 30, Czar Nicholas II ordered the full mobilization of Russia's armed forces. Helmuth von Moltke, chief of staff of the German army, responded to this by picking up the telephone and ordering Field Marshal Franz Conrad von Hötzendorf, chief of staff of the Austro-Hungarian army, to "mobilize at once against Russia." This was incredible. Moltke was an army commander, not the kaiser, a head of state. Moreover, he was in command of the German armies, not those of Austria-Hungary. Yet Hötzendorf complied without question. Such was the nature of this war. Reason was abrogated, and obedience to any higher authority became a reflex.

That "higher authority" was not even necessarily a person. While Europe had been outwardly peaceful after the Franco-Prussian War and during some two decades of Bismarck's treaty making, the European states were steadily arming themselves and making plans for war. After the assassination of the archduke and grand duchess, Austria-Hungary shifted from its Plan B, the scenario for a local war against Serbia, to its Plan R, a general war against Serbia and Russia. Germany was governed by a plan that was first drawn up at the start of the century by Count Alfred von Schlieffen and had been repeatedly refined and modified. This so-called Schlieffen Plan prepared for precisely what Bismarck had aimed to avoid, a two-front war against France in the west and Russia in the east. Moreover, Moltke and everyone else in the German government and military assumed that every other major government operated from the same set of assumptions: that war necessarily meant an all-encompassing continental war. This assumption operated as a self-fulfilling prophecy. If a nation acted as if the war would be all-consuming, the war would consume all. Germany issued ultimatums to all possible combatants, demanding that Russia call off its general mobilization and that France dare not mobilize on pain of a declaration of war. Russia responded by rejecting the ultimatum, and France replied cryptically that it would consult its "own interests." Both responses Germany took as reasons for general mobilization, which was ordered on August 1.

That was the very day on which the German military committed itself to absolute adherence to the Schlieffen Plan, as if it were holy writ. Indeed, the Schlieffen Plan was not Germany's best plan. It was its only plan. It assumed a two-front war, against France and Russia, and reasoned that the French, whose military was more modern and more efficiently led, would mobilize more quickly than the Russians, who, though numerous, were poorly equipped and poorly led. Schlieffen calculated that Russia would take at least six weeks to mobilize effectively; therefore, the plan called for a quick offensive war against France and a simultaneous defensive war against Russia. France was to be invaded with overwhelming force and astounding speed while a much smaller army would be used defensively, to fend off a Russian invasion of eastern Prussia. Machine-like timing was paramount. France had to be neutralized before Russia could mount a full-strength, all-out offensive. With France crushed, troops would be transferred from the Western to the Eastern Front—and Russia disposed of. It was war fought on a schedule as unalterable as a railroad timetable.

●

What did the United States of America have to do with any of this? As far as anyone could tell, nothing.

Unlike the nations of Europe, the United States was unentangled by treaties binding its actions to foreign leaders and nations. Unlike some of the European belligerents, democratic America placed no value on lockstep obedience. Unlike the major belligerents, the US military had no plan for waging general offensive warfare, let alone a plan as meticulous as that of Count Schlieffen, a plan that demanded execution at once precise and slavish. Most of all, unlike the major combatants in Europe, the United States had not been arming for aggressive, offensive warfare on a large scale. In August 1914, Germany had 4.5 million men under arms; Austria-Hungary, 3 million; France, 4.02 million; Russia, nearly 6 million; Great Britain, just under 1 million. The US army consisted of only two hundred thousand men, active and reserves. It had the seventeenth-largest army in the world, a notch above that of Montenegro.

America was unprepared for war, and it didn't want a war. Elected to his first term in 1912, President Woodrow Wilson (figure 1) formulated a policy of strict neutrality, which we will explore in chapter 1. The

Figure 1. President Woodrow Wilson, December 2, 1912. NATIONAL ARCHIVES AND RECORDS ADMINISTRATION

overwhelming majority of Americans were delighted with this. Europe was a madhouse. Nothing about the war made sense. We were well out of it.

But that was before the Schlieffen Plan propelled the German army into Belgium and France. The plan did not call for a direct east-to-west frontal assault on France. Rather, it mapped out a "great wheel," a wide-turning movement northwestward through Flanders Plain (northeast of French territory), followed by a southwesterly arc swooping down into France from the north, hitting the French army's left flank and hooking around from behind. In all, five major German armies would sweep wide from the Alsace-Lorraine in an arc whose western leg would be deep inside France. Schlieffen put it this way to the field commanders: "Let the last man on the right brush the Channel with his sleeve."[5] The Schlieffen Plan hit the French army in the flank and the rear, where any army is most vulnerable. It also brought the war to France, ensuring that all the fighting would take place deep within that country and nowhere near Germany. If strategic retreat became necessary, it would be French, not German, territory that would be relinquished.

To succeed, the "great wheel" *had* to pass through Belgium, a neutral country. On August 2, the German government demanded free passage. Before King Albert could refuse, German divisions were already marching through Flanders. At three o'clock on the afternoon of August 3, Sir Edward Grey addressed the British Parliament to remind members of the 1839 Treaty of London, which bound the nation to defend Belgian neutrality. The "obligations of honor and interest" allowed no other choice, Grey warned. The British people were going to war. That very evening, Germany formally declared war on France, and as day slipped into twilight and twilight into night, Grey, at the window, took a friend aside. "The lamps are going out all over Europe," he said to him. "We shall not see them lit again in our lifetime." At dawn on August 4, Germany, having already invaded Belgium, declared war on the country. Britain responded with its own declaration. All of Europe was in eruption.

Americans were appalled. And yet, over the next few weeks, the velocity of that great German wheel was such that the whole question of what all this had to do with the United States of America seemed destined for irrelevance. For, by the end of August, the German army was on the very outskirts of Paris. The war would certainly be over before President Wilson and Congress even had to contemplate America's position with respect to it.

●

The Great War began when a chauffeur took a wrong turn down the wrong street in Sarajevo. On August 29, 1914, with the First and Second German Armies poised to attack and overrun Paris, the French commander in chief, General Joseph "Papa" Joffre, ordered the French Fifth Army to attack the flank of General Alexander von Kluck's First Army. This forced General Karl von Bülow to bring elements of his German Second Army to Kluck's aid, thereby interrupting the relentless rotation of the great wheel. Stalled in his effort, Bülow was exposed to French counterattack, and Kluck turned his First Army—which constituted the right wing of the entire German invasion, including the man whose sleeve was supposed to brush the English Channel—so that he could strike what he mistakenly believed was the exposed left flank of all that remained of the battered French army.

It proved to be the second wrong turn of the war—and Joffre knew just what to do. He put at the disposal of General Joseph Gallieni, the tough old military governor of Paris, the entire French Sixth Army. Far from being poised to annihilate the remains of the entire French army, Kluck found himself under desperate attack from a *fresh* army. The First Battle of the Marne was about to start. It would be called *Le Miracle de la Marne*, and would end in a decisive French victory that saved Paris, saved France, and doomed Europe to four years of war on whose Western Front, in France and Belgium, the opposing armies would annihilate each other as Murad I and Prince Lazar had done at Kosovo in 1389—albeit on a scale of time and devastation no one could have imagined earlier in 1914, let alone the fourteenth century.

Wilson, Congress, and the American people would be called on to make a decision after all. It would result in the death of 116,708 members of the US armed forces. It would cost $20 billion (1917 dollars; $334 billion in 2011 dollars). It would change the United States forever. But it would defeat Germany and the other Central powers. Immediately after the Armistice was signed in November 1918, an American journalist asked Paul von Hindenburg who won the war against Germany. The chief of the German General Staff, co-architect with Erich Ludendorff of Germany's Eastern Front victories and its nearly war-winning Western Front offensives, did not hesitate in his answer. "The American infantry," he said; the American infantry won the war. He made his response even more specific, telling the reporter that the final death blow for Germany was delivered by "the American infantry in the Argonne."[6]

The British and the French often disparaged the American contribution to the war, but they had begged for US entry into the conflict, and their stake in America's victory was, if anything, even greater than that of the United States itself. But the chapters that follow will not litigate the points of view of Britain and France. This book will simply accept as gospel the assessment of the top German leader whose job it had been to oppose the Americans directly: *The American infantry won the war.* And this book will tell how the American infantry did it.

The heart of *How America Won the Great War*, Part II, "The American Campaigns," is a narrative history of the US military on the Western Front and in Italy. Part I, "Safe for Democracy," tells the story of the nation's rapid journey from the American people's overwhelming embrace of neutrality to their sudden seizure by an intense, sometimes inspiring, but often very ugly war fever. Part III, "Marching into the American Century," explores the consequences of the American victory: how Woodrow Wilson's intention to make *this* war the "war to end all war" was twisted into an overture to a war yet more terrible, how the American mission to "make the world safe for democracy" actually made the world ripe for mass immolation and genocide, how America's role in saving the Western European democracies made the twentieth century the "American Century," and how and why that century came to so disquieting an end.

We will close with a backward glance over the first decade and a half of the twenty-first century and will look ahead to America's future in it. Will the United States' victories of 1918 echo into 2018 and beyond? If so, what will the world hear, and how will the world interpret it?

PART I
SAFE FOR DEMOCRACY

CHAPTER 1

Too Proud to Fight

DURING AUGUST 1914, AMERICANS WERE APPALLED BY THE VELOCITY of the "European War," and they had every reason to assume it would soon end with the surrender of France. Britain's foreign minister, Sir Edward Grey, was very much in the pessimistic minority when he told his friend during the twilight hours of August 3, 1914, that the lamps were going out all over Europe and that "we shall not see them lit again in our lifetime." Few—Europeans or Americans—imagined that they were seeing just the beginning of so dire and enduring a conflict. And in America, the operative phrase was decidedly "in Europe." In America, the lamps were all burning very brightly in August 1914, thank you very much.

Kaiser Wilhelm II always took pains to project an image of strength. Although he had fired Otto von Bismarck, the great chancellor under the first Wilhelm and his own father, Friedrich III, Wilhelm II was keen on presenting himself as the embodiment of Bismarck's famous phrase of 1862, that the "great questions of the time will not be resolved by speeches and majority decisions . . . but by blood and iron." In truth, however, Wilhelm II was weak and not very bright. He wanted a war that would further enlarge his empire, but he did not want it in 1914, when Germany was still very much in the process of building its military, especially its navy, which, the kaiser well knew, was much smaller than Britain's Royal Navy. But because he wanted a war, Wilhelm II would earn the unwanted title of sole instigator of the world war, and his nation would be forced to admit as much in signing the Treaty of Versailles years later.

The fact is that Wilhelm II got his war—prematurely—because he could not chew lunch and think at the same time. When on July 5, 1914, he pledged to Austria's imperial ambassador that Germany would stand by Austria-Hungary, even if doing so meant war with Russia, the promise seemed to emerge unbidden, like a well-fed belch. Having so casually purchased a war with a careless word, Wilhelm immediately suffered paroxysms of buyer's remorse. His chancellor, Theobald von Bethmann-Hollweg, sent Austria's Count Berchtold not one but two telegrams warning him not to make war on Serbia. The second message even included a half-hearted retraction of the kaiser's pledge of support.

But it did no good. Austria attacked Belgrade, and all Europe mobilized. What had begun was not the accidental war the brilliant American historian Barbara Tuchman described it as, in her classic *The Guns of August* (1962). From the German point of view, it was a desirable war—just far too premature. From the Austro-Hungarian point of view, it was an even more desirable war—provided it remained limited to crushing Serbia as an instigator of Balkan nationalism. That the war began much too soon and then, like the flashover that turns a modest blaze into a conflagration, spread in an instant far beyond Serbia to engulf most of Europe, made it all look to Tuchman and many other historians of her generation like an accident. It seemed too stupid to be anything else.

To many others who were present as the events unfolded, the eruption did not appear to be an accident at all, but the purposefully evil work of Wilhelm and his government of autocratic Huns. This, as we will see, is the acorn from which President Woodrow Wilson's mighty oak of a narrative of the Great War would later grow. But that process would take some time. In August 1914, Americans were inclined to credit another of the kaiser's promises, the pledge he made to his soldiers as they marched to war: "You will be home before the leaves have fallen from the trees."[1]

To most observers, including those following the action from the western shore of the Atlantic, the kaiser's promise seemed to have every prospect of being fulfilled. Following the Schlieffen Plan, the German army wheeled through Belgium and northern France before descending upon the flank and rear of the French army. By the end of August, German forces were on the outskirts of Paris. Victory before autumn suddenly seemed not only feasible but virtually inevitable. Helmuth Johann Ludwig von Moltke (1848–1916), chief of the General Staff in 1914, had served as deputy to his predecessor, Alfred von Schlieffen himself. He revered Schlieffen, and he regarded his namesake plan as sacrosanct. But Helmuth Johann Ludwig von Moltke lived and labored under two shadows. One was that of Schlieffen; the other was that of his own late uncle, Helmuth Karl Bernhard von Moltke (1800–1891), who, as field marshal in the Prussian Army, was the architect of the military victories in the wars that, under Bismarck, created the German Empire: the Second Schleswig War, the Austro-Prussian War, and the Franco-Prussian War. Schlieffen created a plan in which he was supremely confident. The elder Moltke gave Germany victories without fail. The younger Moltke, his nephew and keeper of the Schlieffen flame, would have done well to heed his uncle's most famous maxim: "No battle plan survives contact with the enemy."

On August 29, 1914, when all seemed lost to France, Joseph "Papa" Joffre, the French commander in chief who had led his nation's armies to this catastrophic brink, recognized a hiccup in the Schlieffen juggernaut. General Alexander von Kluck, commanding the First German Army, deviated from the sacred plan because he thought he saw an opportunity to finish off the French army. Joffre saw that this deviation exposed Kluck's flank. Accordingly, he ordered the Fifth French Army to attack. This, in turn, forced General Karl von Bülow to bring elements of his Second German Army to Kluck's aid, in the process interrupting his own army's advance. Relentless advance was the very essence of the Schlieffen Plan. Bülow now found himself stalled under French attack, and it became his turn to seek aid from Kluck. What began as a relatively minor deviation from the Schlieffen-mandated advance now metastasized into the collapse of the plan.

Alfred von Schlieffen had admonished field commanders to sweep forward such that "the sleeve of the last man on the right" would "brush the [English] Channel." This grand wheel would ensure the total envelopment of the French forces. In response to Bülow's need—a need that had developed in response to Kluck's need—Kluck abandoned the great wheel altogether and turned his First Army—which made up the right wing of the entire German invasion—to head sharply southeast.

His object was to attack what he believed was the exposed left flank not merely of the Fifth French Army, but what he thought was all that remained of the entire army of France. Kluck imagined he was not merely coming to Bülow's defense but also, in essence, ending the war.

Obese, elderly, slow-moving, and a passionate lover of good wine and even better food, General Joffre had spent the first month of the Great War losing it. At last, however, his finest hour had come. He saw what was happening, and he knew how to seize the opportunity presented by it. The entire German right wing, which had been bearing down on Paris, the prize whose capture would have ended the war, was now moving east of Paris instead of west, the direction from which the German invaders would have encircled and strangled the city into submission. Seeing his opening, Joffre handed over to Joseph Gallieni, the tough old general in command of the Paris garrison, the entire Sixth French Army. Gallieni's mission was to stand fast against Kluck.

For his part, General von Kluck was still looking forward to destroying the sad remnant of an all-but-beaten French military. Determined not to let the opportunity escape him, Kluck drove his First Army far in advance of the Second, thus dividing the German forces in the presence of the enemy—always a high-risk move. He did this quite unaware of the Sixth French Army buildup in and around Paris. This meant that he was also unaware that his action left von Bülow's Second German Army exposed to attack—*from* Paris itself, something no one, German or French, had anticipated.

From his vantage point at headquarters, receiving intelligence from all across the developing Western Front, Moltke realized what Kluck did not know. He saw that the French had just stood up an entire army and deployed it in and around the capital. If Moltke the Younger had been as bold and decisive as Moltke the Elder, he would have issued immediate orders to resume absolute adherence to the Schlieffen Plan, beginning with a move to protect von Bülow's right flank. But Moltke the Younger was not Moltke the Elder, and the order he issued failed to frame the urgency of the situation. Quite unaware of the context for the order and ignorant of the presence of the Sixth French Army, Kluck chose to obey what he judged to be the *intention* of the order without much altering the direction of his march. Rather than rush to assist the Second German Army, therefore, he resolved to continue his southerly drive, intent on disposing of what he believed was the last of the French army. In this way, Kluck deviated even further from the Schlieffen Plan. He crossed the Marne River, not only leaving the Second German Army in the lurch but exposing his own right flank just east of Paris. This happened to be precisely where the Sixth French Army had positioned itself.

Thus began the First Battle of the Marne (September 6–10, 1914). It arrested the German advance and, for this reason, was hailed as *le Miracle de la Marne* ("the miracle of the Marne"). Paris was saved—that was the miracle—but it was accompanied by a curse. Kluck's fateful turn multiplied a month of combat into four years of war on a Western Front along opposing lines of trenches running from the English Channel in the north to the French border with Switzerland in the south. For the next four years, gains and losses would be measured in meters—and blood.

THE RISE OF WOODROW WILSON

By the time of the Miracle of the Marne, eleven major powers were at war. Italy, eager to gain territory at the expense of Austria, would join the Allies in 1915, bringing the total to twelve. The United States, however, was separated from it all by an ocean and was obligated by none of the treaties that had pulled one European nation after another into the conflict. Certainly Woodrow Wilson, elected to the American presidency in 1912, seemed highly unlikely ever to involve the United States in Europe's war. Although he was a Democrat, he shared with Theodore Roosevelt, one of the two candidates he had defeated, a strong commitment to progressivism. Vice president under William McKinley, Roosevelt had ascended to the presidency in 1901, following McKinley's assassination by self-proclaimed anarchist Leon Czolgosz. He embarked on a dazzling program of progressive reform. Moreover, while he was a restless man of action and had personally fought in the Spanish-American War of 1898 as lieutenant colonel at the head of the famous "Rough Riders" cavalry regiment, Roosevelt successfully mediated an end to the Russo-Japanese War (1904–1905), for which he received the Nobel Peace Prize. Both he and Wilson were idealists, a title Wilson wore proudly, as he would make evident during the months leading up to the founding of the League of Nations.

In 1908, Roosevelt chose not to run for a second elected term, fearing that it would be seen as breaking with the two-term limit George Washington's example had created. (Roosevelt had served most of the slain McKinley's second term.) In 1908, he handpicked William Howard Taft as his successor. While Taft shared Roosevelt's progressive ideas, TR soon found Taft's tenure too conservative and regretted his own decision not to run. He contested Taft's Republican nomination for a second term in 1912. When the party nominated Taft anyway, Roosevelt helped to found a third party, the Progressive Party, and ran as its nominee. In 1912, TR came in second to Wilson, with the Republican incumbent Taft embarrassingly trailing in third place.

Wilson was indeed more progressive than Taft and arguably even more progressive than Roosevelt. Socially, however, he was less liberal than either. The son of a flinty Presbyterian minister, he studied at Davidson College in North Carolina, at Princeton, and at Johns Hopkins, from which he received a PhD in government and history. As of 2018, he remains the only US president to hold a doctorate. Wilson briefly practiced law but earned a lofty academic reputation for his distinguished political science texts. He found a home in academia, becoming a professor at Wesleyan University and then at Princeton University, which ultimately named him its president. Wilson simultaneously democratized Princeton and raised its academic standards and reputation. This willingness to reform outworn traditions was at odds with his own straitlaced demeanor and his decidedly illiberal attitude toward race relations. Born and raised in the Shenandoah town of Staunton, Virginia, he had lived through the Civil War. The experience of its devastation contributed to his general opposition to war as a means of resolving disputes. Yet, in some respects, Wilson remained an unreconstructed Southerner who advocated segregation. (When he was installed as US president, he even set about *resegregating* government offices by ordering separate dining facilities and washroom accommodations, even though these had been fully integrated for years.)

Wilson made the transition from academia and academic administration in 1910, when the corrupt New Jersey Democratic machine surprised everyone by tapping him to run for governor. On the face of it, he was an appropriate and imaginative progressive choice, a leader who had proved himself a remarkable administrator at Princeton and had earned a reputation as a popular presence in the community. The machine saw something even more important: a total political novice who was bound to be infinitely pliable.

The Democratic old guard was in for a shock. Wilson proved to be not only incorruptible but zealous, and no sooner did he enter office than he directed his reforms straight at the machine that had put him there. The people of New Jersey loved it, and Wilson very quickly commanded a national audience. Before completing his term, he was nominated by the national party to run against both Roosevelt and the incumbent Taft. He campaigned on an ambitious platform of progressive reform. Enactment of a progressive income tax had begun in 1909 during the Taft administration and required a Constitutional amendment, the Sixteenth, which was ratified on February 25, 1913, after Wilson's election but before he took office. As a progressive, Wilson was in principle diametrically opposed to political patronage, the lifeblood of corrupt machine politics. Nevertheless, he proved himself spectacularly adept at deploying patronage to get what he wanted—and in 1913, he wanted passage of the Revenue Act, which not only implemented the income tax authorized by the Sixteenth Amendment but lowered protectionist tariffs. The act passed the House on May 8 and the Senate on September 9. During this same year, on December 23, the Federal Reserve Act was passed, creating the Federal Reserve System and, among other things, authorizing it to issue Federal Reserve notes as legal tender. The next year, 1914, saw the strengthening of antitrust legislation with the Federal Trade Commission Act and the Clayton Antitrust Act and, in 1915, Wilson supported legislation that federally regulated working conditions for sailors, thereby establishing a strong precedent for federal enforcement of minimum standards for working conditions. In 1916, the Adamson Act (signed into law on September 3 and 5) mandated an eight-hour workday and overtime pay for interstate railroad workers, thereby setting a precedent for increasingly broad legislation mandating an eight-hour day and overtime. In the same month, the Keating-Owen Act sought to curtail children's working hours. Although it was subsequently ruled unconstitutional, the act created unstoppable momentum for more child labor legislation. Finally, 1916 also saw passage of the Federal Farm Loan Act, which provided low-interest credit to farmers.

Wilson's enlightened and hopeful progressive agenda offered a vivid counterpoint to the grim chaos of Europe during 1914–1916. Wilson was harvesting the fruits of peace, while Europe was picking the grapes of wrath. Wilson was pushing American democratic government to new heights, even as the "Central powers" of Europe—Germany, Austria-Hungary, the Ottoman Empire, and Bulgaria—were dragging down government-by-"aristocracy" to new and very bloody lows. Yet so relentless was the advance of Wilsonian reform that many voters were simply growing tired of the exhausting regime. Indeed, the prospects for Wilson's reelection in 1916 did not look particularly bright. His Republican opponent, Charles Evans Hughes, was also a progressive—he earned the endorsement of the Progressive Party—and very distinguished, having served as governor of New York from 1907 to 1910 and associate justice of the US Supreme Court from 1910 to 1916, resigning from the court to run for president. (He would rejoin the court in 1930 as chief justice, retiring in 1941.) Sufficiently alarmed by his competition, Wilson did not rest his reelection hopes solely on his record of progressive achievements but added to this a catchy campaign slogan that really caught on: "He Kept Us Out of War." In the end, the slogan allowed him to eke out a hard-won victory, 277 electoral votes to Hughes's 254, coming in at just under a popular majority with 49.2 percent of the vote versus 46.1 percent for Hughes.

AMERICA THE NEUTRAL

While "He Kept Us Out of War" was instrumental in Wilson's election to a second term, it is unusual as a campaign slogan in that it is a statement of past-tense fact rather than a promise for the future. Nobody seems to have commented on this, much less observed that past performance is no guarantee of a politician's future course. As a description of the Wilsonian first-term record, it is mostly accurate. On August 19, 1914, little more than midway through the Germans' execution of the Schlieffen plan's "great wheel" through France, President Wilson addressed the US Senate, delivering what has been widely called his "Declaration of Neutrality":

The effect of the war upon the United States will depend upon what American citizens say and do. Every man who really loves America will act and speak in the true spirit of neutrality, which is the spirit of impartiality and fairness and friendliness to all concerned. The spirit of the nation in this critical matter will be determined largely by what individuals and society and those gathered in public meetings do and say, upon what newspapers and magazines contain, upon what ministers utter in their pulpits, and men proclaim as their opinions upon the street.

The people of the United States are drawn from many nations, and chiefly from the nations now at war. It is natural and inevitable that there should be the utmost variety of sympathy and desire among them with regard to the issues and circumstances of the conflict. Some will wish one nation, others another, to succeed in the momentous struggle. It will be easy to excite passion and difficult to allay it. Those responsible for exciting it will assume a heavy responsibility, responsibility for no less a thing than that the people of the United States, whose love of their country and whose loyalty to its government should unite them as Americans all, bound in honor and affection to think first of her and her interests, may be divided in camps of hostile opinion, hot against each other, involved in the war itself in impulse and opinion if not in action.

Such divisions amongst us would be fatal to our peace of mind and might seriously stand in the way of the proper performance of our duty as the one great nation at peace, the one people holding itself ready to play a part of impartial mediation and speak the counsels of peace and accommodation, not as a partisan, but as a friend.

I venture, therefore, my fellow countrymen, to speak a solemn word of warning to you against that deepest, most subtle, most essential breach of neutrality which may spring out of partisanship, out of passionately taking sides. The United States must be neutral in fact, as well as in name, during these days that are to try men's souls. We must be impartial in thought, as well as action, must put a curb upon our sentiments, as well as upon every transaction that might be construed as a preference of one party to the struggle before another.[2]

It is a remarkable statement, aimed less at the international community than at the people of the United States. Moreover, far from being a legalistic document, it is a moral one, and far from constituting a declaration of isolation or isolationism, it calls for every citizen to be neutral in thought, word, and deed precisely so that the United States might play a role in determining the fate of the world. By remaining "impartial in thought, as well as action" the United States could hold itself ready, "as the one great nation at peace . . . to play a part of impartial mediation and speak the counsels of peace and accommodation, not as a partisan, but as a friend." Such international mediation Wilson saw as an American duty. With considerable wisdom, he also described neutrality as essential to "our" collective "peace of mind" as a "people . . . drawn from many nations, and chiefly from the nations now at war." A nation so constituted could easily become "divided in camps of hostile opinion, hot against each other, involved in the war itself in impulse and opinion if not in action." This could tear the nation apart.

On the face of it, the so-called Declaration of Neutrality was a simple and straightforward statement of the importance of maintaining neutrality "in fact, as well as in name" by rigorously striving to "be impartial in thought, as well as action," putting, where necessary, "a curb upon our sentiments," intense sentiments bound to be rife in a nation of immigrants. But the declaration also contained the kernel of its own eventual abrogation. Nothing could change the fact that Americans cherished a heritage from many lands. This was especially true in the 1910s, which were a high point of immigration especially from Europe. So when the time came to abandon neutrality and take sides, Wilson did not try to change the facts. Instead, he changed the conversation, turning it from warring nations to warring ideas, ideals, and values. When the time came, German Americans would not be asked to go to war against Germany

any more than French Americans or British Americans would be asked to fight on behalf of France or the UK. Instead, all Americans, regardless of the country of their origin or the origin of their parents or other fore-bears, would be asked to fight in defense of democracy (a great idea and a sacred moral value) and against the antidemocratic brutality of autocracy (a bad idea and an evil one).

As Wilson's declaration made clear, neutrality did not mean splendid isolation. In fact, international law and tradition did not prevent a neutral from participating indirectly and incidentally in a war. Neutrals were free to trade with the belligerents without risking compromise of their neutral status, as long as the trade did not unduly favor one side over the other. Since the United States was the greatest and most productive industrial power in the world, all sides turned to America to acquire military and other goods, including food. The European War meant a bonanza not just for American industrial companies but for American farmers as well—and, of course, for American financiers.

In theory, every one of the eleven or twelve major powers engaged in the war was a prospective customer for American-made goods and American-made money. In practice, however, it was actually quite difficult to avoid taking sides. In the first place, there were geography and logistics. The Allies were closer to America than any of the Central powers. Both Britain and France had extensive Atlantic coastlines with many ports. There was a risk to shipping at sea, especially from German U-boats, but there was no inland enemy territory to cross. The same could not be said for delivering to the Central powers. The mighty British Royal Navy set up a highly effective blockade of German ports and generally forced the German navy's High Seas Fleet to remain in German home waters or risk annihilation. Delivering the goods to Germany and its allies became increasingly difficult as the effectiveness of the naval blockade improved.

Then there was the political factor. The actions of the Central powers—especially as these actions were sensationalized and amplified by British (and to a lesser extent French) propaganda agencies—were making it increasingly difficult to remain balanced in deciding with whom to trade. Blaming Germany for "starting" the war was an oversimplification so gross as to be not just a distortion of the truth but downright wrong. Britain and France were both high-stakes colonial players on the world stage, and they had an interest in suppressing Germany's colonial ambitions—"suppressing" them by acquiring German colonial holdings for themselves. Even on the European continent, France especially had a compelling motive for going to war against Germany. As a result of the nation's ignominious defeat in the Franco-Prussian War of 1870–1871, Germany came into possession of Alsace and Lorraine. This was not only a severe blow to French nationalism but also left France without a sufficient domestic source of coal and coke, two commodities indispensable to industrial-scale manufacturing. The truth is that all eleven or twelve European powers had affirmative reasons for waging war. All of them owned a share of the conflict. But this was not the narrative either the Allies or the United States embraced. The way they told the story, Germany was the aggressor. As with everything else concerning Germany in the European War, there is some truth to this. Looked at from a short-range perspective, Germany did declare war on France and Russia without provocation, and, in faithful obedience to the Schlieffen Plan, Germany blithely violated Belgian neutrality and national sovereignty by invading the nation. Nor was the invasion polite and gentle. It was rough and highly destructive, and that was bad enough. To make matters worse, Allied propaganda magnified the transit through Belgium as an atrocity of "Hunnish" proportions. Variations on the phrase "poor, brave little Belgium" were disseminated throughout the United States—mainly by British agents. Soon, Germany was transformed in the American mind and imagination from the land of Kant, Beethoven, and Goethe into a horde of brutish, butchering "Huns."

Finally, the Allies not only appeared to be better people than the Central powers but they were also more creditworthy. This was true from the beginning of the war and only became increasingly the case as the British blockade became more effective. As shortages drove up prices, sources of funding to the Central powers became fewer and far more expensive. Inexorably, then, the flow of trade and credit between the United States and Europe increasingly veered toward the Allies. This, in turn, made it highly desirable that the Allies win the war. For the losers would surely be saddled with massive reparations and would be in no condition to pay their bills and repay their loans.

The British Spin

In the predawn of August 5, 1914, hours after Britain declared war, a British cable tender, a ship designed to service and repair the transatlantic cables that carried so much vital traffic between Europe and the United States, steamed out on a very different mission. It deliberately severed five German overseas cables, which passed from the lower Saxon seaport of Emden through the English Channel to Vigo in Galicia, Spain, thence to Tenerife in the Canary Islands, and onto the Azores, its last landfall before striking out for the United States. Clearly, the British understood that they had at least one great advantage in global warfare. One way or another, Germany's transatlantic communications passed through land they controlled. The British Isles were the first landfall for submarine cables coming into Europe and the last anchor point for cables leaving Europe.

Severing the cables cut direct German communications to the world beyond Europe, including the United States. This left indirect communication routes, which used cables that were not merely anchored on the UK coast but passed overland through British systems. This meant that British intelligence agents could tap into the lines and intercept messages through them. Although the Germans took the precaution of encrypting these indirect messages, British codebreakers quickly broke the German diplomatic ciphers and were freely reading most German signals to their embassies. As we will see in the next chapter, this capability would pay a spectacular dividend early in 1917, in the form of the infamous Zimmermann Telegram. More immediately, however, it was the great reduction in the volume of German transatlantic communication resulting from simply cutting the cables that gave the British the greatest advantage in controlling the information that reached America. True, the Germans often treated the civilians of occupied nations harshly, even brutally. This gave Allied—especially British—propagandists plenty of material to work with, but experts in the British Foreign Office developed a veritable cottage industry devoted to exaggerating and sensationalizing stories of

German atrocities. The British used their monopoly on direct transatlantic communications to flood the data channels of the day with their version of the truth.

British-produced atrocity stories focused on the most violent acts committed by the German and Austro-Hungarian armies, putting special emphasis on the medieval barbarity of "the Hun." Distribution channels for this propaganda included books, newspapers, pamphlets, sketches, posters, films, lantern slides, postcards, and even cartoonlike illustrations on such items as plates, cups, and medals. Some propaganda came in the guise of official government reports that presented the sensational material as bona fide evidence of routine German violations of the Hague Conventions of 1899 and 1907, which laid down the rules of "civilized" warfare and specifically enumerated certain practices as war crimes. Both Germany and Austria-Hungary were signatories to the conventions. The British government did not rely on faceless bureaucrats to front their reports, but used well-known and highly respected individuals. In the 1915 *Report of the Committee on Alleged German Outrages*, for example, credit is given to a committee "Appointed by His Majesty's Government and Presided Over by The Right Hon. VISCOUNT BRYCE, O. M., &c., &c., Formerly British Ambassador to Washington."[3]

The Bryce report includes eyewitness accounts from victims as well as perpetrators, but the methods of investigation employed typically fall far short of accepted legal standards. The Bryce document recounts a collapse of German discipline during the retreat from the First Battle of the Marne and mentions "evidence of burning of villages, and the murder and violation of their female inhabitants. . . . In this tale of horrors hideous forms of mutilation occur with some frequency in the [witness] depositions, two of which may be connected in some instances with a perverted form of sexual instinct." The report mentions the frequent "cutting [off] of one or both hands," apparently by cavalry troops wielding their sabers while storming through a town. In other instances, however, "the motive may have been the theft of rings." What the report committee also finds are "many well-established cases of the slaughter (often accompanied by mutilation) of whole families, including not infrequently that of quite small children." Interestingly, the Bryce report backs off somewhat, conceding that "there are cases tending to show that aggravated crimes against women [by German soldiers] were sometimes severely punished [by German officers themselves]. . . . These instances are sufficient to show that the maltreatment of women was no part of the military scheme of the invaders, however much it may appear to have been the inevitable result of the system of terror deliberately adopted in certain regions."[4] Why dial back the sensationalism in this way? Perhaps because it was the truth, or perhaps because such a concession on the part of the report committee preempted accusations of outright fabrication. Another motive may have been to illustrate the ungovernable barbarity of the individual German soldier, whose brutality was beyond their officers' ability to control.

In addition to official reports, atrocity stories became fodder for undisguisedly sensational newspaper articles, popular books, and even public exhibitions. Typically, the emphasis was on the depiction of "German *Kultur*," by which German writers meant superior German civilization but Allied propagandists revealed to be civilization reduced to the level of barbarism. As the war progressed, propaganda often pitted the mad obscenities of *Kultur* against the virtuous values of English, French, and, later, American civilization.

The problem for the Germans was that their actions, policies, and behavior supplied more than a kernel of truth around which the sensational accounts could be shaped. Any German denials were easily undercut. German forces really did violate rules and concepts of "civilized" warfare. They used aircraft to bomb London and other British towns, and they used poison gas on the battlefield, which was an explicit violation of the Hague Conventions. The most highly publicized early instance of German chemical warfare was at the Second Battle of Ypres (Belgium, April 22–May 25, 1915). By the time of that battle, the German army had amassed 168 tons of chlorine, which it deployed using gas "projectors" (essentially pumps and hoses or pipes) fed from 5,730 chemical cylinders north of Ypres. When the Allies subsequently protested, Germany countered that the Hague convention banned chemical *artillery shells*, not the deployment of the agent through the use of projectors. This legal quibble hardly improved the German image, yet the fact is that the

British and the French also used gas throughout the war, and, in fact, the French were the first to use chemical agents—tear gas—back in August 1914. Attaching chemical weapons to the Germans is an example of propaganda built on more than a grain, but less than a full foundation, of truth. Indeed, "poison gas," like other German "atrocities," was enveloped in a mythology out of proportion to the underlying facts. Chemical weapons were terror weapons, their emotional impact far greater than both their tactical and strategic effect.

NEUTRALITY STRESS TEST: THE FINAL VOYAGE OF RMS *LUSITANIA*

By the second year of a war that in 1914 had seemed destined to be over in a matter of months, practically everything that Germany did was viewed in the neutral United States through the lens of British propaganda. This included operations on the high seas. Both the German and the British navies devoted far more effort to disrupting one another's seaborne commerce than they did to directly fighting each other at sea. At the very outbreak of war, Britain used its naval superiority to set up a blockade of Germany, a nation served by just two trade routes: one via the English Channel and the Dover Straits; the other around the northern tip of Scotland. The British heavily mined the Dover Straits, retaining only an extremely narrow lane of passage, which made it easy to intercept ships. The seas north of Scotland, however, were vast and called for large patrols to create an effective blockade.

And it *was* effective. More than three thousand vessels were intercepted and inspected. Outward-bound trade from Germany was completely halted. Historians still debate the overall impact of the blockade on the war, but there is no disputing that it brought great hardship on the German people. In 1915, Germany's imports were 55 percent below their 1914 levels, and exports were more than halved. The supply of imported raw materials, including coal, nonferrous metals, and nitrogenous fertilizers, was largely cut off. Food staples such as grain, potatoes, meat, and all dairy products became so hard to come by that, as 1916 drew to a close, Germans were subsisting on a variety of "ersatz" products including *Kriegsbrot* ("war bread" made from rye) and powdered milk. Food riots became common in Germany as well as Austria-Hungary (especially in Vienna and Budapest). The winter of 1916–1917 saw the German potato crop fail, forcing the people to make do with unpalatable Swedish turnips. To this day, that winter is remembered as the *Steckrübenwinter* ("turnip winter").[5]

To be sure, the British blockade did interdict a good deal of war materiel. Mostly, however, it blocked food and fuel (coal) shipments and therefore largely waged war against civilians. Yet virtually no one in the neutral United States questioned the morality of the blockade. They did, however, criticize—often with righteous and heartfelt outrage—the German U-boat attacks on the British merchant marine and the commercial shipping of other nations. On October 20, 1914, the British merchant steamship *Glitra* was torpedoed, and on January 30, 1915, two Japanese liners, *Tokomaru* and *Ikaria*, were sunk. Americans and others noted that, whereas the attack on the British vessel had been preceded by a warning—the German submarine surfaced before attacking—which gave passengers and crew time to evacuate, the Japanese ships were torpedoed without warning, the U-boats not surfacing beforehand. This was widely regarded as a violation of basic tenets of civilized warfare. Heedless of such criticism, on February 4, 1915, Germany announced that it would regard the waters around the British Isles as a war zone in which all Allied merchant ships would be targeted and in which the safety of no ship, of any nation, would be guaranteed.

The British blockade and German "unrestricted" submarine warfare— that is, submarine attack without warning—were desperate responses to a Western Front war that had become deadlocked. Unable to make a breakthrough from the trenches, both sides looked for alternatives that might tip the balance in their favor. Both sides saw naval warfare as a vehicle of attrition that might accomplish what the land battle could not. The German generals especially demanded the relentless application of unrestricted submarine warfare—even though the practice was developing into a serious propaganda liability. The danger here, as German diplomats recognized, was that the United States would be moved to end its neutrality. As German secretary of state Gottlieb von Jagow had pleaded to his nation's admiralty back in 1914, "Unrestricted U-boat war would in any event mean the breaking of diplomatic relations with the United States, and, if American lives are lost, would finally lead to war. . . . If we take up unrestricted U-boat warfare, the attitude of all neutral Powers will be changed against us and we shall have to calculate upon establishing new fronts. Germany will in such case be looked upon as a mad dog against whom the hand of every man will be raised for the purpose of finally bringing about peace."[6] For the United States, freedom of navigation of the high seas and freedom of trade were well-recognized rights of neutral nations and were essential to national sovereignty. Beyond these political and moral principles, however, the export trade had become economically vital to American business and financial interests during this war. Both the American people and American commercial interests were increasingly outraged by the German menace to trade.

Built at a cost of £1.2 million and launched in 1906, Cunard's *Lusitania* (with its sister ship, *Mauretania*, also launched in 1906) was the fastest, largest, and most luxurious liner making the transatlantic crossing. Yet it was by no means exclusively a civilian ship. Its construction had been subsidized by the British admiralty, which also shared with Cunard its operating costs. The admiralty openly carried the vessel on its official lists as an "auxiliary cruiser." It was, in effect, a hybrid civilian passenger vessel and naval warship. Cunard fitted out the liner with gun mounts, hidden beneath its wooden decks. Its power plant was below the water line, as specified for a ship of war, and its forward coal bunkers were usable as powder magazines. All of these features were designed for quick conversion to a warship, but, even as a passenger vessel, despite British government claims to the contrary, the *Lusitania*, on its 201st crossing from New York bound for Liverpool, on May 1, 1916, carried some 4,200,000 rounds of rifle cartridges, 1,250 empty shell cases, and 18 cases of nonexplosive fuses, all of which were listed on its manifest.[8] Not listed on the manifests was a probable cargo of gun cotton (nitrocellulose). There were also consignments of "fur" sent from Dupont, the American explosives manufacturer, and "butter" addressed to the Royal Navy Weapons Testing Establishment in Essex, England.[8]

On April 22, 1915, after the ship arrived in New York, the German embassy published an announcement—a paid advertisement—in fifty US papers, including every paper in New York City, as follows:

NOTICE!

TRAVELLERS intending to embark on the Atlantic voyage are reminded that a state of war exists between Germany and her allies and Great Britain and her allies; that the zone of war includes the waters adjacent to the British Isles; that, in accordance with formal notice given by the Imperial German Government, vessels flying the flag of Great Britain, or any of her allies, are liable to destruction in those waters and that travellers sailing in the war zone on the ships of Great Britain or her allies do so at their own risk.

IMPERIAL GERMAN EMBASSY

Washington, D.C., 22 April 1915.[9]

As of May 1, when the *Lusitania* embarked from New York bound for Liverpool, the British Admiralty had decoded German radio communications that gave the position of U-boats operating south of Ireland. The captain of the *Lusitania* was not informed, however, nor was he told that the British cruiser HMS *Juno*, which had been assigned to escort the liner through the always-perilous waters off the southern Irish coast, had been withdrawn. The reason for the admiralty's silence and the withdrawal of the naval escort has never been disclosed. Still, the passengers and crew aboard the *Lusitania* could take some comfort in knowing that German U-boats working close to the British Isles had been operating hitherto under "Cruiser Rules," which meant that they gave warning and provided time for evacuation before attacking. What was not known, however, was that the use of so-called Q-ships by the British—well-armed Royal Navy vessels disguised as merchant vessels—had prompted orders from the German admiralty giving U-boat captains full discretion in deciding whether or not to surface and warn before attacking.

On May 7, when Kapitänleutnant Walter Schweiger saw the *Lusitania* through the periscope of his submarine, U-20, he chose to attack without warning. Schweiger fired a single torpedo, which penetrated *Lusitania's* hull slightly forward of the wheelhouse at 2:20 in the afternoon, as the ship passed about ten miles off Old Head of Kinsale, southwest Ireland. The impact created an immediate explosion. It was, however, the second explosion, moments after the impact, that proved catastrophic. (Some historians believe this second explosion is proof of the presence of more explosives on board than what was listed in the manifest. Others attribute it to the explosive bursting of steam pipes on contact with cold saltwater as the ship flooded below decks.) The liner listed suddenly and severely to port, making it nearly impossible to launch the lifeboats. Only six of the forty-eight it carried were successfully deployed. Some remained on their davits. Others fell, capsized, and broke apart in the water.

Just eighteen minutes after the torpedo struck, the *Lusitania's* bow dug into the seabed of the shallow coastal waters, the stern lingering above the surface before it, too, slid under the waves. The loss of life was staggering. Of 1,962 passengers and crew, 1,198 were lost. Among these were 128 Americans. As the ship attracted the rich and famous, some of the rich and famous were among the dead, including (among US nationals) the popular inspirational writer and publisher Elbert Hubbard, Broadway impresario Charles Frohman, and the fabulously wealthy Alfred Vanderbilt.

First reports of the sinking immediately raised outrage and anti-German sentiment in the United States to a fever pitch. But news stories appearing within forty-eight hours of the sinking revealed that the *Lusitania* had been carrying munitions, and William Jennings Bryan, President Wilson's secretary of state, who was both a pacifist and an advocate of strict neutrality, wrote on May 9, "Germany has a right to prevent contraband going to the Allies, and a ship carrying contraband should not rely upon passengers to protect her from attack. It would be like putting women and children in front of an army." Vice President Thomas Marshall echoed him by pointing out that "when a person boarded an English vessel he was virtually on English soil and must expect to stand the consequences."[10]

"Colonel" Edward M. House, a Texas politician who was President Wilson's most trusted advisor—and an ardent Anglophile—thought differently, urging in a cable to the president that the time had come for "intervention" in the war, which, he argued, "will save rather than increase the loss of life." He counseled the president that "America has come to the parting of the ways, when she must determine whether she stands for civilized or uncivilized warfare. Think we can no longer remain neutral spectators."[11]

But Wilson's vantage point was in Washington, not London, and he did not sense that the American people were sufficiently angry to go to war. Heeding the advice of Joseph Tumulty, his chief advisor on domestic affairs, the president made a speech (which had been scheduled long before the *Lusitania* tragedy) in Philadelphia, where he articulated his position—and what he intended to be America's position—in language that seemed tailor-made for scorn by the likes of Theodore Roosevelt as well as British and French government officials and others itching to get America into the European War. Wilson told his audience that "there is such a thing as a man being too proud to fight—there is such a thing as a nation being so right that it does not need to convince others by force that it is right."[12] At the same time, Wilson composed a stern diplomatic note to Berlin, demanding an end to attacks on merchantmen and calling for financial reparations for the *Lusitania* sinking. Wilson declared that submarine attacks on passenger vessels violated "sacred principles of justice and humanity" and warned that the United States would do whatever was necessary to enforce its rights as a nation as well as the rights of its citizens. Secretary of State Bryan found the note inflammatory, and he suggested that Wilson should balance it with a note to the British government to condemn its blockade as an illegal attempt to starve the civilian population of Germany. President Wilson rejected Bryan's idea.

In the meantime, Wilson received no explicit reply to his note from Berlin. What he did not know is that Kaiser Wilhelm II had been persuaded by his advisors to order U-boats to refrain from attacking large passenger liners without warning. Wilson did not know this because the kaiser's order was kept secret. Presumably, the hope of the German government was that the United States would take note of the German change in policy and would respond favorably to that, without the kaiser having to admit that he had made a concession. If this was the hope, it was forlorn. Germany received no recognition for changing its policy, and Wilson was criticized by both those who sought to remain out of the war as well as those who wanted to enter it. As for William Jennings Bryan, on June 9, he resigned in protest from the Wilson cabinet.

Despite the kaiser's order to stop attacking passenger liners without warning, on August 17, the British-registered SS *Arabic* was sunk, resulting in more American deaths and a new US protest. The Germans now promised to ensure the safety of passengers before sinking any more liners but then torpedoed and sank the SS *Hesperia*, on September 18, again without warning. After this, at the insistence of worried German diplomats, the German navy agreed to suspend U-boat activity in the English Channel and west of the British Isles. The danger of raising the temperature of war fever in the United States receded.

WILSON OFFERS MEDIATION

Since the outbreak of the war in 1914, Colonel House had served as President Wilson's informal expert on the conflict and his unofficial envoy to London and Paris. Wilson specifically asked him to assess the receptivity of the Allied leaders to a mediation effort that would be personally led by Wilson. After all, Theodore Roosevelt had been very successful in mediating between Russia and Japan to end the Russo-Japanese War. Unfortunately, Wilson greatly overestimated House's skill as a go-between. The garrulous Texan lacked the sophistication to navigate the arcane realm of European diplomacy. In his talks with British foreign secretary Sir Edward Grey, whose cordiality quite disarmed him, House allowed himself to be played. Wilson had asked House to sound Grey out on a US mediation effort. What he got instead was the House-Grey Memorandum of February 22, 1916. A supremely ambiguous document, it declared that the United States would offer itself to all parties as a disinterested mediator, but it also—gratuitously—stipulated that the United States might enter the war on the side of the Allies if Germany rejected the offer of mediation. At the same time, the memorandum further stipulated that the right to initiate US mediation rested with Great Britain. In other words, if *Germany* rejected mediation, the United States *might* enter the war. If *Britain* rejected the mediation, there would be no consequence.

This, of course, was hardly a disinterested role for the United States. Moreover, while the memorandum could be interpreted as an effort to initiate binding mediation, it could just as readily be interpreted as the first step toward American entry into the war—against Germany.

In the end, the memorandum was never implemented. As the presidential elections of 1916 approached, President Wilson decided it was best to suspend his peace initiative with its implied threat to enter the war. For the purposes of reelection, he wanted to broadcast to the American people the unambiguous message, "He Kept Us Out of War." Besides, at the urging of Chancellor Bethmann-Hollweg, Germany's military leaders formally agreed to postpone renewal of a pending declaration of unrestricted submarine warfare. Wilson read this as a hopeful sign that his diplomatic note was finally having an effect.

REELECTED

Woodrow Wilson's reelection margin of victory was too narrow for him to claim a mandate for or against war. Perhaps for that reason, he further delayed taking any direct action toward peace. For one thing, the victory that Germany, with its ally Bulgaria, had achieved over Romania emboldened the kaiser's government to make a peace proposal of its own—on its own terms. Moreover, the militarists had worn down Bethmann-Hollweg, who declared that if the new German proposals were rejected, the Imperial Navy could resume unrestricted submarine warfare. No, Wilson thought, now was not the time to resume an American push for peace.

Predictably, Bethmann-Hollweg's terms, presented on December 12, 1916, were quite outrageous. The German government demanded annexation of the Belgian fortress town of Liège as well as a border strip of Belgium in addition to sections of the occupied portion of northeastern France. The Allies rejected the proposal, of course. But now Wilson felt obliged to step in. On December 18, he invited all the combatants to clear the air by stating their "war aims." Perhaps a clear understanding of everyone's objectives would provide a place to start negotiation. Whether or not at the behest of Wilson, however, Robert Lansing, who had replaced William Jennings Bryan as secretary of state, secretly suggested to the Allies that they offer terms as unreasonable as those proposed by

Germany. The Germans smelled a rat and charged collusion between Wilson and the Allies. While they still agreed to begin negotiations, they refused to change their own demands. Within a month's time, by the middle of January 1917, Wilson's attempt at mediating peace collapsed and was abandoned. The war continued, and 1917 opened with the United States still a neutral.

CHAPTER 2

Tipping Point

THERE WERE NO NATIONAL POLLS IN THE UNITED STATES IN 1916, AND so there are no reliable figures on how Americans felt about the European War in general, let alone how they felt about the prospect of the United States participating in it. About eight months into the conflict, in 1915, *Literary Digest* polled 367 American writers and editors, of whom 105 favored the Allies and 20 the Germans, but 242 called for Wilson's policy of absolute neutrality to continue.[1] In the end, the most reliable indicator of American sentiment as of November 1916 was the reelection of Woodrow Wilson—narrow though his victory was—which was based in large measure on his campaign slogan, "He kept us out of war."

In April 1917, days after he asked Congress for a declaration of war against Germany (the other Central powers, including Austria-Hungary and the Ottoman Empire, were not included), Wilson appointed a former muckraking journalist, George Creel, director of an agency to be called the Committee of Public Information (CPI)—essentially the first propaganda ministry of the United States. In his aptly titled insider history of the CPI, *How We Advertised America*, Creel explained that his was no easy task, saying, "It is to be remembered that during the three and a half years of our neutrality the land had been torn by a thousand divisive prejudices, stunned by the voices of anger and confusion, and muddled by the pull and haul of opposed interests."[2] Creel was in a position to know, because the man who was now in charge of infecting America with war fever— creating "a passionate belief in the justice of America's cause that should weld the people of the United States into one white-hot mass instinct with fraternity, devotion, courage, and deathless determination"—had written, less than a year earlier, *Wilson and the Issues*, a campaign pamphlet that included a righteous defense of Wilson's increasingly maligned "too proud to fight" neutrality policy.[3]

To form the necessary "one white-hot mass," Creel decided that he had to stir in Americans what he called a "war-will." It sounded like a crude imitation of Nietzsche. Creel defined it as "the will-to-win," which, in a democracy, "depends upon the degree to which each one of all the people of that democracy can concentrate and consecrate body and soul and spirit in the supreme effort of service and sacrifice. What had to be driven home was that all business was the nation's business, and every task a common task for a single purpose." That he had to instill this sentiment *into* the American people implies that it did not exist in early 1917 anymore than it had in 1916. Creel understood that his task was to create the universal "conviction that the war was not the war of an administration but the war of one hundred million people"[4] (figure 2).

In 1916—and even as late as April 1917, the month that the United States declared war—achieving such unity of sentiment and purpose was far from inevitable. Indeed, it hardly seemed likely. The United States was home to the largest population of Germans (many first- and second-generation immigrants) outside of Germany. As late as the end of 1916, numerous German American *Bund* organizations were raising funds for German civilian relief and even specifically to support the kaiser's war effort. Add to the first- and second-generation German immigrant community the Irish. They had no special affection for Germany, but many of them enthusiastically approved of anyone willing to kill the English, who had oppressed Ireland for some seven hundred years. Among the mass of Americans who were not inclined to favor one side or the other—who were, in fact, neutral—it simply made no difference who won and who lost just as long as the United States was not immersed in the bloodbath.

Whatever the numbers, it is clear that, in 1916, most Americans wanted no part of the European War. And this was just as well, since the US military was hardly prepared to go to war. The statistics are startling: in August 1914, the French army consisted of 4.02 million men; the German army, 4.5 million; the Austro-Hungarian army, 3 million, and

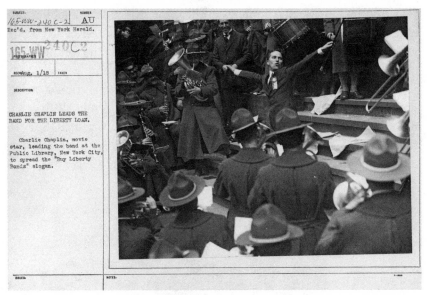

SUBJECT: /65-WW-240 C-2 NUMBER: AU
Rec'd. from New York Herald.

165 WW 240C2
PHOTOGRAPHS

REC'D Aug. 1/18 TAKEN

DESCRIPTION

CHARLIE CHAPLIN LEADS THE
BAND FOR THE LIBERTY LOAN.

Charlie Chaplin, movie
star, leading the band at the
Public Library, New York City,
to spread the "Buy Liberty
Bonds" slogan.

ISSUED: NOTES:

Figure 2. The US government borrowed the money it needed to go to war, and much of the borrowing was from the people of the United States, who contributed to a series of "Liberty Loans" by buying Liberty Bonds and Liberty Stamps. Celebrities such as Charlie Chaplin, pictured here leading a band on the steps of the New York Public Library on Fifth Avenue, exuberantly pried open the public's purse. *NEW YORK HERALD* PHOTOGRAPH, NATIONAL ARCHIVES AND RECORDS ADMINISTRATION

the Russian army, 5.97 million. The British had a professional and reserve force of 975,000—although they could raise far more by conscription. The UK also possessed the largest and most powerful navy in the world. By comparison, the United States had, by 1916, a Regular Army of some 133,000 men, a force smaller than that of Serbia. It was a force so small that General Peyton C. March accurately described it as "scarcely enough to form a police force for emergencies within the territorial limits of the United States."[5]

Indeed, on March 15, 1916, when President Wilson ordered Brigadier General John J. Pershing to lead a 10,000-man "Punitive Expedition" into Mexico in pursuit of the revolutionary and social bandit Pancho Villa (who had crossed the US-Mexican border to raid Columbus, New Mexico, on March 9), the US Army's inadequacies became acutely apparent, especially since Wilson decided to deploy as many as 100,000 troops to patrol the US-Mexico border, an order that required the mobilization of some 70,000 National Guard units. Augmenting the Regular Army with the guardsmen and some 130,000 reservists raised the total strength of US land forces to 330,000 in 1916.

Congress, not the president, used the Punitive Expedition as a pretext for enacting a sweeping military authorization. While Wilson had not asked for it, he did not oppose it. Signed into law on June 18, 1916, the National Defense Act of 1916 provided for substantial increases in the Regular Army and created a federal National Guard (figure 3;

Figure 3. A US National Guardsman. NATIONAL ARCHIVES AND RECORDS ADMINISTRATION

hitherto, the National Guard had been under state control, commanded by the governors, until specifically called up), a federal Army Reserve, and the Reserve Officer Training Corps (ROTC).

As was the case with Great Britain, the US Navy was better prepared than the army. In 1916, it had 67,000 officers and sailors to man 300 ships and 130 shore stations. Nevertheless, on August 29, another legislative initiative, the Naval Act, called for building up a "Navy second to none," to include twenty-six battleships and battle cruisers, fifty destroyers, and a quantity of support craft. Not even mentioned in the Naval Act was another force controlled by the Department of the Navy, the US Marines, who, in 1916, numbered just 10,000. It was a force so small that President Theodore Roosevelt came close to disbanding it in 1908 and 1909.

Although President Wilson signed both military expansion acts in 1916, he had opposed authorization for increased military spending back in December 1914. In February 1917, about two months before he asked Congress for a declaration of war, Wilson continued to give full-throated approval to anything that looked like actual mobilization for war, calling America the "champion of peace" and telling Congress and the nation, "I am not now preparing or contemplating war or any steps that lead to it."[6]

Despite Wilson's ambivalence and an enduring public reluctance to enter the war, among politicians, the ranks of interventionists grew. By mid-1915 and early 1916, mostly Republican activists, including former president Theodore Roosevelt, former secretary of war Henry Stimson, and Senator Henry Cabot Lodge, spearheaded a "preparedness movement," which amounted to a low-level military mobilization without presidential approval (see figure 4). Also included among the vanguard of this movement was the financier J. P. Morgan, who was one of numerous American moneymen who had extended monumental loans to the Allies (mostly to Britain) and were now intent on protecting their investment. Partisan promotional and lobbying organizations, including the National Security League, the National Civic Foundation, and the Navy League, were formed with the mission of preparing the nation for what members believed was the inevitable and imminent entry of the United States into the European War.

Figure 4. Preparedness movement—department store employees do their prewar calisthenics. NATIONAL ARCHIVES AND RECORDS ADMINISTRATION

The preparedness movement oscillated between, on the one hand, a realistic view of the dangers of isolationism and an idealistic outlook on America's obligations as a world power, and, on the other hand, the worst kind of jingoism, xenophobia, and nativism. The movement applied considerable pressure to President Wilson, moving him through righteous opposition to entry into the war, to ambivalence about it, to a cautious inclination to intervene, and, finally, to asking Congress to go to war. Still, in 1915–1916, Wilson feared that the focus on preparedness would derail his ongoing program of progressive domestic reforms, and he also believed that, by maintaining its neutrality, the United States was preserving itself as an honest broker available to mediate a peace. Wilson's 1916 campaign writer, Creel, denounced the preparedness frenzy as "manufacturing hysteria." He wrote, "Novelists and short-story writers, quick to realize that their sex stuff was no longer in demand, turned quickly to 'patriotism,' and thundered denunciations of America's sordidness, with now and then a touch of the elaborately sarcastic by comparing the United States to Liberia." Creel's prime target, however, were war profiteers. "The issue, in its very essence," he wrote, "is empire versus democracy. The question that the people of the United States are called upon to answer is this: Are we to continue as a democratic people, holding to our ancient faith in liberty and justice as great governing principles, or are we to turn America over to a group of financiers, denationalized by greed, drunk with a dream of imperialism, and blind to every domestic need?"[7]

As we saw in chapter 1, the sinking of the *Lusitania* on May 7, 1915, turned up American war fever—at least for a short time. While it failed to move the mass of Americans to clamor for immediate intervention, the sinking gave early impetus to the preparedness movement. On August 10, 1915, Leonard Wood, commanding general of the army's Department of the East, joined forces with prominent New York attorney and social figure Grenville Clark to create a special reserve military training center in Plattsburgh, New York. Thanks to Clark, who recruited ninety-nine socially prominent and influential figures, the so-called Plattsburgh movement quickly caught on. It was a training camp aimed primarily at attracting young captains of industry, executives, and professionals, many of whom were not only listed on the Plattsburgh muster rolls but also in *Who's Who*. Plattsburgh was intended to deliver rudimentary military training to prepare a class of military officers of the "right sort"—socially speaking.

By the end of 1915, the Plattsburgh movement had expanded, and several camps were opened. The movement was privately funded, but the War Department pitched in with funds that it—not the president or Congress—controlled. The army also detailed some of its officers and drill sergeants to duty in the camps. By the summer of 1916, the movement had unofficially trained forty thousand young men. Passage of the National Defense Act of 1916, however, dealt the Plattsburgh movement a sharp blow, by putting preparedness—especially officer training—firmly into the hands of the new federal National Guard. While the legislation diminished the relevance of Plattsburgh, it did not kill it. Indeed, the movement survived World War I itself and remained active during the interwar period and even into the 1940s as the Military Training Corps Association (MTCA).

Although President Wilson mildly opposed the Plattsburgh movement, by the fall of 1916, even as the general election approached and

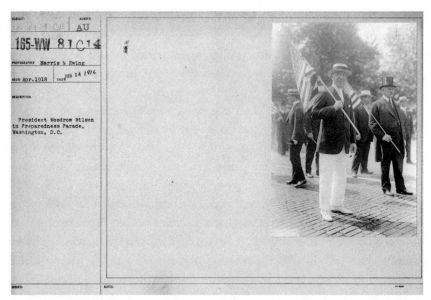

Figure 5. President Woodrow Wilson marches in a "preparedness parade" in Washington, DC, on June 14, 1916, a little less than a year before the United States declared war on Germany. NATIONAL ARCHIVES AND RECORDS ADMINISTRATION

even as he continued to run on "He kept us out of war," Wilson increasingly voiced support not only for preparedness (figure 5) but even for pro-war activists. He began to publicly associate readiness for war with Americanism, going so far as to declare, "We do not covet peace at the cost of honor."[8]

●

By the close of 1916, the European War had killed nearly four million. All the belligerents suffered. In 1914, which saw five months of fighting, from August through December, France lost 200,000 or more soldiers. The British Expeditionary Force (BEF), consisting of some 120,000 men, suffered a catastrophic 50 percent casualty rate, killed or wounded. In the Russian army, at least 400,000 had been killed by the end of 1914. The German and Austro-Hungarian armies each lost about 200,000 killed in the first five months of the war. In years two and three, 1915 and 1916, every Allied attempt at an offensive not only failed but failed with catastrophic losses. On the Western Front, 150,000 British and 268,000 French soldiers were killed in 1916. Germany lost 143,000 killed that year. The southern front, pitting Italy (which entered the war in August 1915) against Austria-Hungary along the Isonzo River, was the scene of futile slaughter, not only of soldiers but of civilians in the Italian-Austrian border region. Along the Isonzo, disease, starvation, and privation claimed even more lives than shells and bullets. Deadliest of all the theaters, however, was the Eastern Front, where the Germans, although outnumbered, cut down poorly equipped, poorly trained, and poorly led Russians by the hundreds of thousands.

The Russian army was also being attacked from the inside. In February 1917, during the first of the year's two Russian Revolutions, the czar's Petrograd garrison mutinied, forcing Nicholas II to abdicate, and thereby ending the three-hundred-year-old Romanov dynasty. For a time, the revolutionary factions, including the Soviets, remained grimly committed to a "defensive" war against Germany, but when the Bolsheviks, led by Vladimir I. Lenin, took power after the October (1917) Revolution, the provisional Soviet government and the Central powers concluded an Armistice on the Eastern Front, which led to the newly installed Bolshevik government negotiating a "separate peace" with the Germans by the Treaty of Brest-Litovsk, signed on March 3, 1918.

•

On the brink of 1917, the Allies were at a very low point. With Russia out of the war, Germany could focus on the Western Front. The Central powers, chiefly Germany, already held vast tracts of Allied territory. Yet, like the Allies, the Central powers were losing huge numbers of men. Aware of this, the Allies fought on.

Although most of Britain's professional army of 1914 was dead, thanks to conscription, the strength of the British army on the Western Front stood at about 1.2 million men by the end of 1916 and was increasing. France had summoned to Europe almost all of its colonial troops, so, despite catastrophic losses, it now fielded 2.6 million men. In all, at the start of 1917, the Allies managed to deploy just under 4 million men on the Western Front. Against this force, the Germans had 2.5 million.

And yet, Germany seemed to have the edge.

Although they fought on, both Britain and France were suffering severe crises of confidence. Field Marshal Sir John French, who had led the BEF to the continent in 1914, was removed in December 1915 and replaced by Sir Douglas Haig, who was promoted to field marshal. Under Haig's command, more British lives would be lost than under any other military leader in the history of the nation. At the same time, the British civilian establishment was shaken when Prime Minister H. H. Asquith was forced to create a coalition government in May 1915. It held together until December 1916, when a new coalition was formed under David Lloyd George, who was far more hawkish than Asquith.

In December 1915, the French cabinet was purged, and Aristide Briand, long a vociferous critic of the Allies' Western Front strategy and nemesis of General Joseph Joffre, was restored as prime minister, a post he had briefly held in 1913. Strangely enough, that same month Briand formally named Joffre commander in chief of the armies and backed his proposal to defend Verdun—a complex of fortified positions centered on the city of Verdun in northeastern France—regardless of cost. By the end of 1916, however, Briand, stunned by the absence of progress on the Western Front, replaced Joffre with Robert Nivelle, the most dynamic, not to say bloodthirsty, of the commanders at Verdun.

The change of command came too late, however, to save Briand's premiership. In March 1917, a month before Nivelle launched the offensive that would be named for him and a month before the United States declared war, Briand was out for the same reason that he had removed Joffre: failure to break the Western Front deadlock.

●

From the perspective of the United States, the Allies by the end of 1916 could be viewed as either in desperate need of American help or as a lost cause scarcely worth helping. But then a new variable was thrown into the equation.

It is absolutely accurate to say that the European Allies were losing the war by the end of 1916. But it is also just as accurate to say that the Central powers were losing by that time. The Western Front had brought stalemate in the form of a war of attrition. As a military term, *attrition* means wearing an enemy away through sustained action or attack. The root meaning of the word, however, is not military. Attrition is the wearing away by friction. Sand a piece of wood, and you wear it away. The action, of course, also wears away the sandpaper, which eventually must be discarded. Similarly, on the Western Front, both sides were being worn away. It was only a question of which side would be discarded first—or not quite *only*. There was another question: Would *both* sides be worn away? That is, would they beat each other to death?

Faced with this existential situation, the German naval staff and high command pressed the kaiser to reauthorize unrestricted submarine warfare. By the end of 1916, the high command no longer thought US entry into the war was a matter of *if* but a matter of *when*, and the generals were projecting "when" at five months. The German admiralty presented statistics indicating that, if the German navy could sink six hundred thousand tons of Allied shipping in each of these next five months, US entry would be rendered moot because Britain would have been forced to surrender. And its surrender would in turn force France to sue for peace. Persuaded by the arguments he heard, Kaiser Wilhelm II issued an order on January 9, 1917, directing the navy to resume unrestricted submarine warfare on February 1.

President Wilson responded on January 22 with an appeal he must have known would fail. He called for international conciliation based on "peace without victory." It is a measure of the Allies' prevailing desperation that the British government sent Wilson a secret message agreeing to accept his mediation, even on these incredible terms. Publicly, Austria-Hungary also indicated its willingness to listen to the president's peace proposals. And on January 31, 1917, German chancellor Theobald von Bethmann-Hollweg responded by reasserting his nation's earlier, unreasonable terms—slices of Belgium and slices of France—but he nevertheless invited President Wilson to persist in offering mediation. Following this invitation, Bethmann-Hollweg concluded by announcing that unrestricted submarine warfare would indeed recommence the next day, February 1.

The SS *Pickhuben* was a German passenger liner built in 1890. In 1895, it was renamed the SS *Georgia*, and it plied the Atlantic for the

Hamburg America Line. The outbreak of the European War in 1914 caught the *Georgia* in the port of New York. The vessel was interned by order of the US government, which sold it on April 16, 1915, to the Housatonic Steamship Company, which renamed it the *Housatonic* and converted it into a freighter. A British firm out of London chartered the *Housatonic* on February 23, 1916, for the term of the war, and it was operated between the United States and Britain until February 3, 1917, when it was stopped twenty miles southwest of Bishop Rock off the Isles of Scilly by the German U-boat *U-53*, commanded by Kapitänleutnant Hans Rose. Although Rose now had authority to attack without warning, he instead surfaced and sent an officer and two seamen to board the ship. The trio brought the *Housatonic*'s American captain, Thomas A. Ensor, back to the *U-53* for questioning. In response to Ensor's explanation that he was carrying wheat, Rose ordered him to abandon ship. "You are carrying food to the enemy of my country," he explained.

After his men had appropriated the *Housatonic*'s supply of soap (a precious commodity in wartime Germany), Rose's boarding crew opened the seacocks to scuttle the *Housatonic*. They then returned to the *U-53*, and Rose administered the coup de grâce with a single torpedo. In answer to Captain Ensor's plea, the *U-53* towed the ship's two lifeboats toward the English coast. Sighting a British trawler, Rose fired his deck gun as a signal and cut the lifeboats loose. The boats were soon intercepted by the trawler, which safely transported the entire crew of the *Housatonic* to Penzance.

That same day, Woodrow Wilson cited the sinking of the *Housatonic* as the reason for severing diplomatic relations between the United States and Germany, even though Rose had given both warning and aid to its crew. On February 26, President Wilson asked Congress for the authority to arm US-flagged merchant vessels and to take other military measures to protect American commerce. He called this a policy of "armed neutrality." With it, what had been an unofficial, grassroots preparedness movement finally became US government policy.

●

The Punitive Expedition, launched against Pancho Villa on March 16, 1916, was called off on February 7, 1917, without having apprehended

Villa. It did, however, succeed in doing two things. First, it prompted Congress to pass the National Defense Act of 1916; second, it put a potentially hostile, revolution-wracked Mexico in the forefront of American popular consciousness.

On January 16, 1917, the German foreign secretary, Alfred Zimmermann, sent a coded telegram, via the German ambassador in Washington, DC, to the German minister in Mexico:

We intend to begin on the first of February unrestricted submarine warfare. We shall endeavor in spite of this to keep the United States of America neutral. In the event of this not succeeding, we make Mexico a proposal of alliance on the following basis: make war together, make peace together, generous financial support and an understanding on our part that Mexico is to reconquer the lost territory in Texas, New Mexico, and Arizona. The settlement in detail is left to you. You will inform the [Mexican] President of the above most secretly as soon as the outbreak of war with the United States of America is certain and add the suggestion that he should, on his own initiative, invite Japan to immediate adherence and at the same time mediate between Japan and ourselves. Please call the President's attention to the fact that the ruthless employment of our submarines now offers the prospect of compelling England in a few months to make peace. Signed, ZIMMERMANN.[9]

The ambassador duly presented Zimmermann's proposal to the government of Mexican president Venustiano Carranza: a German-Mexican alliance by which Mexico would declare war on the United States in return for a German pledge of military support in a Mexican campaign to retake the territory it had lost in the Texas War of Independence of 1836 and the US-Mexican War of 1846–1848. He also passed on the request that Carranza invite Japan to join the anti-American alliance. In all this, the German objective was less to injure the United States than to ensnare the nation in an armed conflict with not one but two nations. Thus preoccupied, the Americans would be in no position to join the Allies in the European War.

Delusional though it was, the Zimmermann proposal was founded on some historical precedents. In 1906, Kaiser Wilhelm II had tried to recruit the United States as an ally in a racist crusade against what the kaiser called the "yellow peril." As part of this, he circulated to the American press fabricated accounts of Japanese imperialist activity in Mexico. While some papers ran with these tales, President Theodore Roosevelt was unimpressed, and the invitation from Germany came to nothing. Now desperate, the German foreign ministry thought of a new role for both Mexico and Japan. Indeed, Germany had been for some time covertly active in turbulent Mexican politics. When a revolution/civil war broke out in Mexico in 1910, Germany attempted to trade arms in exchange for permission to establish a naval base in the country. Military intervention by President Wilson in the form of the US occupation of Veracruz during April–November 1914 blocked the execution of these plans, but after the outbreak of the European War later in 1914, Germany covertly supported the coup d'état of General Victoriano Huerta against Carranza, the presidential leader favored by the Wilson administration. Again, the objective was to keep the US military too busy to send troops to Europe. When the Wilson government foiled German efforts by arresting and imprisoning Huerta in Texas, Germany gave secret aid to Pancho Villa.

Though no lover of Woodrow Wilson, President Carranza understood that Germany was playing him, and he turned the proposal down flat. That was bad enough for the German government, but far worse was the fact that British agents had been monitoring all German diplomatic cable traffic—and they knew how to decrypt it. A decryption of the Zimmermann Telegram was handed to Walter Hines Page, US ambassador to the UK, who wasted no time in transmitting it to President Wilson. A number of recent historians have tended to see Wilson as actively favoring entry into the war by this point in his presidency. Nevertheless, he was not quick to respond to the intercepted message. The first word out of the executive branch came from Secretary of the Interior Franklin K. Lane on March 31: "We can stand Germany's arrogance no longer."[10]

If we are to credit (and not all historians do) the recollection of Wilson's longtime friend Frank Cobb of the *New York World*, the American president was feeling great stress. Cobb remarked that he had never seen the president "so worn down." He quoted Wilson as remarking that entry into the war would attack the American soul with a "spirit of ruthless brutality [that] will enter the very fiber of our national life, infecting Congress, the courts, the policeman on the beat, the man in the street. Conformity will be the only virtue. And every man who refuses to conform must pay the penalty." Cobb's recollections imply that Wilson, on the verge of taking the nation into a horrific war, believed that democracy in America would have to be abridged, perhaps permanently damaged, in order to mobilize for and prosecute a war the president justified as a struggle to make the *world* "safe for democracy."[11]

●

In *Wilson and the Issues*, the 1916 reelection campaign pamphlet he had been hired to write, Creel undertook the unenviable task of arguing that the president who "kept us out of war" had not failed to prepare the American military for war. In fact, on April 2, 1917, when President Wilson prepared to address a special joint session of Congress to ask for a declaration of war against Germany, he must have known very well that the United States was far from ready to fight in the greatest armed struggle the world had ever seen. Woodrow Wilson began delivering his war message at 8:40 that evening. Some historians believe that, even as the first words left him, he inwardly believed that he would never actually have to send troops to Europe. With both sides suffering the effects of attrition, the American president may well have hoped that the mere threat of an industrial giant, prosperous and peaceful, entering the war would be sufficient to tip the Central powers over the edge of endurance, and they would sue for peace.

If this sounds like an unwarranted speculation, because no political leader of Wilson's intellectual caliber could cling to so wild a hope, consider the following. On April 6, four days after Wilson's war message, after hearing testimony concerning appropriations needed to deliver an army to France, Senator Thomas S. Martin of Virginia, chairman of the Senate Finance Committee, a senator who had just voted to approve the declaration of war, exclaimed in disbelief, "Good Lord! You're not going to send soldiers over there, are you?"[12]

Joseph Tumulty, who acted as Wilson's private secretary, confidant, and advisor on domestic issues, provided a much-cited picture of a president who was far from living on hope.

Tumulty recalled that, at about 10:00 p.m., having returned to the White House after delivering the war message, Wilson slumped in a chair at the conference table in the empty cabinet room. The president looked into Tumulty's eyes. Reflecting on the thunderous applause that had greeted his call to war, Wilson said to him, "Think what it was they were applauding. My message today was a message of death for our young men. How strange it seems to applaud that." With that, Tumulty wrote, Woodrow Wilson buried his head in his hands and sobbed uncontrollably.[13]

As with Cobb's recollections, some historians suspect that Tumulty, who was openly worshipful of his boss, mythologized the moment. Perhaps Wilson cried, perhaps not. Perhaps, having delivered the speech, he felt severe pangs of ambivalence. Perhaps not. In the war message itself, which was widely considered the finest speech of a chief executive celebrated for his speeches, there was not a trace of doubt. The case Wilson made for war was ideological and idealistic. "There is one choice we cannot make; we are incapable of making," he told Congress. "We will not choose the path of submission!" He spoke of fighting "for the ultimate peace of the world and the liberation of its people," for "the world must be made safe for democracy."[14]

For a public figure, Woodrow Wilson was a notoriously private man. Some believe that he was goaded to war by British propaganda, by taunts from figures like Theodore Roosevelt and Republican hawks, and by Wall Street, which was quite heavily invested in the Allied cause. Some believe that the president really had been pushed to his moral limits by accounts of "Hun" atrocities on land and, on the sea, treacherous U-boat attacks that had cost American lives. Others believe that the Zimmermann Telegram, for all its ignorant arrogance, was the proverbial last straw. Germany's inciting nations to war against the United States could not go unanswered.

It is likely that some or all these motives were active in Wilson's mind and heart. But subsequent events, particularly at the end of the war, indicate that one motive reigned above all the others. Wading willingly into the blood of the Western Front would confer an unprecedented advantage on the United States. Wilson must have seen that the belligerents were like two prizefighters who had fought each other to the very verge of a knockout. Bring in a fresh fighter, and the contest would be quickly ended. To be sure, there would be costs, not the least of which was "death for our young men" and risk to democracy. But the rewards for the United States would include instant elevation to the stature of a world power. Such a rise for the nation would bring to its president a seat at the table around which the other powers would gather, come the victory, to create a new world order. And if the United States fought this war to the utmost, giving all that it had—if this country was recognized as having tipped the balance toward victory—then he, Woodrow Wilson, would have more than a place at the table of great powers. He would have the seat at the head of that table. He would be positioned to guide the whole world toward what he called a "scientific peace," a peace built on a rational conception of the good and the just. "Sometimes people call me an idealist," Wilson would declare in the increasingly bitter aftermath of the war. "Well, that is the way I know I am an American. America, my fellow citizens—I do not say it in disparagement of any other great people—America is the only idealistic nation in the world."[15] If his America could win the war, Woodrow Wilson possessed the unapologetic audacity of his idealism to believe himself capable of transforming the atavistic cataclysm of what had begun as the European War into a truly Great War, a world war, the war that the writer H. G. Wells called "the war to end war."[16]

CHAPTER 3

Regimenting the Public Mind

WOODROW WILSON ENTERED THE WAR AS AN IDEALIST. HE DISAVOWED the motive of material gain for the United States—although industrial and banking interests stood to profit mightily from an Allied victory. He claimed to want no new territories. What he envisioned was an opportunity to end war itself, end it once and for all, replacing kinetic responses to international disputes with intellectual solutions. Wilson also argued that Germany posed a threat to civilization, creating a situation in which the world had to be made safe for democracy.

Of all Wilson's reasons for going to war, only those in the last sentence even approached an existential motive—something like a clear and present threat to the United States. For the most part, Wilson was proposing entering the war, this horrifically bloody and thus far futile war, for the purpose of defending ideas and ideals. As he presented it, the European War was a war of choice for the United States, rather than a war of necessity.

History would show later in the twentieth century that, when faced with imminent danger—for example, the massive destruction of the Pacific fleet in Pearl Harbor on December 7, 1941—it would be fairly easy to unite the American nation in response. The matters of life and death at issue would hit home. Confronting an ideological challenge, however, presented a more daunting task. Wilson understood that the nation had to accomplish two major objectives and do so quickly. One was to create a huge army, bigger, even, than that with which it had fought the Civil War. The other was to unite the American people behind the war effort. To an outside observer, the first task would have appeared the more daunting. The United States was something like a fifth-rate military power, a half million men in varying states of readiness going up against three or four million battle-hardened soldiers of the Central powers on the Western Front. What Wilson understood, however, was that the second task was actually the harder of the two, especially in a democracy populated by what had long been called (at least since the 1890s) "hyphenated Americans." Of greatest concern, of course, were the German Americans and the Irish Americans. How would German Americans feel about waging war on their onetime homeland or the homeland of their parents or grandparents? How would Irish Americans respond to a military alliance with the oppressor England? But even nonhyphenated Americans were hardly in the bag. Untouched by the European carnage and enjoying the economic prosperity of a nation exporting unprecedented quantities of food and materiel to the Allies, why would they want to give up their sons, brothers, and husbands to the prospect of grave injury or death in a foreign land? Why would they choose to take on that risk themselves?

Woodrow Wilson decided that he had to create overwhelming popular support for the war and do so very quickly. Strangely, the initial impulse of this apostle of democracy, who had sworn an oath to uphold a Constitution that included a guarantee of freedom of speech, was the passage of a draconian censorship law. The man who talked him out of this approach—at least partially—was his 1916 campaign writer, George Creel.

Shortly after his reelection, Wilson proposed to reward Creel for his campaign work by appointing him assistant secretary in one of the cabinet posts. Creel was not interested, but, in March 1917, with war clouds gathering, he wrote to the president pleading that he eschew censorship. Creel had a better idea, he said. In a private brief to Wilson, he wrote that with "America's youth sailing to fight in foreign lands, leaving families three thousand miles behind them, nothing was more vital than that the people's confidence in the news should not be impaired." Rigorous censorship would "inevitably stir demoralizing fears in the heart of every father and mother and open the door to every variety of rumor." He conceded that freedom of the press was often abused, but "even these abuses are preferable to the deadening evil of autocratic control."[1]

To this idealistic argument against censorship, Creel added three pragmatic reasons to avoid it. First, censorship would prove all but impossible to police, let alone enforce. Second, while censorship laws might intimidate the smaller newspapers, they would have little effect on the biggest and most influential. This, he argued, was the case in Europe. Third, censorship would inevitably grow, "slipping over [from protecting military secrets] into the field of opinion," thereby infringing on free speech and freedom of the press. Creel concluded that suppressing "independent discussion" in wartime was corrosive because "the people did not need less criticism in time of war, but more. Incompetence and corruption, bad enough in peace, took on an added menace when the nation was in arms."[2] Instead of censorship, Creel proposed a "voluntary agreement that would make every paper in the land its own censor, putting it up to the patriotism and common sense of the individual editor to protect purely military information of tangible value to the enemy." Creel argued that news was not the threat; lack of information was. Without reliable information, rumor would take over. Without information, the public morale would inevitably decline. "*Expression*, not *suppression*, was the real need." The objective should not be to stop potentially dangerous news and other communication, but to inundate every media outlet with positive communications useful to the Allied war effort.[3]

Expression—the steady flow of information—would not be strictly domestic, but would be directed toward "an even greater task beyond our borders." The "war-weary peoples of England, France, and Italy" required the rejuvenating benefit of a "message of encouragement," whereas "the peoples of the neutral countries [had] to be won to our support, and the peoples of the Central Powers to be reached with the truth." Creel wanted to disseminate propaganda on a global scale and through every medium—not "propaganda as the Germans defined it," but "propaganda in the true sense of the word, meaning the 'propagation of faith.'"[4]

Obviously, Creel explained to the president, supplying authoritative information was no fit task for a "Board of Censors." What was needed was a new agency, one that would fight to win what Wilson himself had called "the verdict of mankind." The agency must have the power to "reach deep into every American community, clearing away confusions," and it must "seek the friendship of neutral nations" while breaking "through the barrage of lies that kept the Germans in darkness and delusion."[5]

In Creel, Wilson decided that he had his man. The war message was delivered on April 2, Congress declared war on April 6, and on April 14, 1917, Wilson created "a Committee on Public Information, to be composed of the Secretary of State [Robert Lansing], the Secretary of War [Newton Baker], the Secretary of the Navy [Josephus Daniels], and a civilian who shall be charged with the executive direction of the Committee. . . . As Civilian Chairman of this Committee, I appoint Mr. George Creel."[6] As fast as this sequence was, standing up the "CPI" would be even faster. Within weeks, it became the biggest propaganda program any nation had developed to that time.

●

The CPI—which the public usually called the "Creel Committee"— was supposed to be a source of official, and therefore accurate and truthful, information. To a surprising degree, it was just that, yet Creel also had to fit himself and the CPI within what became a very strict censorship regime.

It started with legislation of a kind and severity not seen since John Adams had signed into law the infamous Alien and Sedition Acts of 1798, with their frankly unconstitutional restrictions on free speech and peaceable assembly. A version of the Espionage Act was introduced in the House and Senate on February 5, 1917, four days after Germany announced the resumption of unrestricted submarine warfare and two days after Woodrow Wilson severed diplomatic relations with Germany. Called the Webb-Overman Bill, it would have punished by imprisonment of up to twenty years and fines as high as ten thousand dollars anyone who in wartime and without lawful authority should "collect, record, publish, or communicate" certain types of information, which the bill broadly and vaguely defined as of a military nature or otherwise "directly or indirectly, useful to the enemy." Even more draconian was the provision of this same dire penalty for the communication or publication of "false reports or statements" or "reports or statements likely or intended to cause disaffection in, or interfere with the success of, the military or naval forces of the United States." A version of the bill passed the Senate, but it died in the House upon the adjournment of the lame duck session of the 64th Congress on March 4.[7] More bills followed, and with each new legislative proposal, newspaper editors became more outspoken in defense of freedom of the press and objection to censorship, yet the public, fearful of enemy agents, tended increasingly to welcome restrictive legislation. Newspaper editors generally admitted the necessity of strong laws to expose, arrest, and punish spies—for the nation was soon gripped by spy hysteria, with some papers wildly claiming that one hundred thousand German agents were at work in America but they decried portions of the bill that would censor the press.

As one version after another of the Espionage Bill was debated, the nation's papers voiced opposition to censorship. "America will never submit to the suppression of information to which the people are plainly entitled," the *Philadelphia Public Ledger* cried out. "The American people are not accustomed to wearing muzzles," said the *Hartford Courant*.[8]

In the end, however, it was the editors, not the people, who protested, and on May 15, 1917, the Senate passed a version of the Espionage Bill without an amendment *explicitly* authorizing press censorship. The House followed, and the Espionage Bill was signed on June 15, 1917. The people thought of it as an antispy law, but its language was breathtaking.

Title I, Section 3, of the law forbade anyone from making or conveying "false reports or false statements with intent to interfere with the operation or success of the military or naval forces of the United States or to promote the success of its enemies." It outlawed any "attempt to cause insubordination, disloyalty, mutiny, refusal of duty, in the military or naval forces of the United States" or to "willfully obstruct the recruiting or enlistment service of the United States." Punishment for violating these proscriptions included a fine of up to ten thousand dollars and/or imprisonment for up to twenty years.[9] Before the end of the war, the US Department of Justice would use Title 1, Section 3, to prosecute some two thousand cases—very few of them for spying as such. And while it was true that the law did not mention censorship, Title XII barred using the US mails from transmitting any material that violated other provisions of the act. This ensured government control (via postal inspectors) over magazines and other subscription matter that were customarily mailed. Additionally, the Trading-with-the-Enemy Act of October 6, 1917, authorized censorship of all messages—published or personal—that passed between the people in the United States and those in any foreign country. The transmission of transatlantic news was included—and therefore subject directly to the outright censorship that Creel (a member of the censorship board created by the act) disavowed.

On May 7, 1918, the Espionage Act was amended in a manner so far-reaching that the *amendment* was (and still is) usually referred to as the Sedition *Act* of 1918. The amendment expanded Title I, Section 3, of the Espionage Act by applying the ten-thousand-dollar fine and twenty-year prison term to anyone who might "make or convey false reports, or false statements, or say or do anything . . . with intent to obstruct the sale by the United States of bonds . . . or the making of loans by or to the United States, or whoever shall wilfully utter, print, write, or publish any disloyal, profane, scurrilous, or abusive language about the form of government of the United States, or the Constitution of the United States, or the military or naval forces of the United States, or the flag . . . or the uniform of the Army or Navy of the United States, or any language intended to bring the form of government . . . or the Constitution . . . or the military or naval forces . . . or the flag . . . of the United States into contempt, scorn, contumely, or disrepute . . . or shall wilfully display the flag of any foreign enemy." In addition, strikes, labor slowdowns, and even the mere incitement or advocacy of "any curtailment of production in this country of any thing or things . . . necessary or essential to the prosecution of the war" were outlawed under severe penalty.[10] As with the original Espionage Act, the Sedition "Act" stirred little public objection.

●

George Creel persuaded Woodrow Wilson to authorize the CPI as an agency to create, promote, disseminate, and generally *manage* expression rather than simply *suppress* expression. Creel's objective was less to prevent dangerous information from leaking than it was to create among the people a unified war-will. The thing is, by the time CPI was in full operation, the nation had changed. Having reelected a president because he had "kept them out of war," the people were nevertheless soon caught up in war hysteria. Creel discovered that his task was less to rally the public than to manage the press. He had believed that the big job facing him would be to recruit the press in support of a grand appeal to the people. Instead, he discovered that he could count on the people to back his efforts to manage the press by enlisting the media's cooperation in avoiding anything that might raise questions or create doubt about the war. In return, the CPI would provide the media with an endless stream of news stories to satisfy the appetite of a people who, it seemed, were as hungry for propaganda as they were for news.

Creel set out to fashion the CPI into a mammoth, all-encompassing press agency—essentially, a one-stop shop to which reporters, writers, and editors could go for *all* the news they needed. Authorized on April 14, 1917, the CPI exploded into, before the end of the year, a plainclothes army of more than one hundred thousand people. The purpose of this army was to enable a nationwide program of voluntary media censorship by flooding all press outlets with news from official or officially approved sources in a comprehensive effort to control the war information that reached the public.

Mostly, he did it alone. Secretary of the Navy Josephus Daniels and Secretary of War Newton Baker essentially ceded their authority to him and devoted themselves to other duties. Secretary of State Robert Lansing distrusted Creel and was concerned that, as neither a uniformed nor elected civilian, this cheap journalist (in Lansing's view) was in a position to abridge the prerogatives and operations of the cabinet, including those of the Department of State. But as Lansing accurately wrote in his *War Memoirs* (1935), "I do not think the change to a 'one man' office was distasteful to Mr. Wilson, as he had great confidence in Creel's ability and personal loyalty."[11] James R. Mock and Cedric Larson, authors of *Words That Won the War: The Story of the Committee on Public Information 1917–1919* (1939), pointed out that neither Daniels nor Baker nor even Lansing objected when Creel took off from the CPI's "primary job of directing the release (or sometimes the suppression) of news of the American people at war" and "moved into the far less restricted field of opinion management," what we today call public relations. He and those he hired for the CPI "invented new techniques and perfected old ones, and first to last built up a stupendous propaganda organization," the purpose of which was "to make President Wilson's theories known to every village crossroads in this country and in remote corners of foreign lands."[12]

Creel saw himself and his agency as far more than the nation's cheerleader. A cheerleader urges victory for the sake of victory. Creel proclaimed himself a propagandist—by which he meant a propagator of the faith. His mission was to win victory for Woodrow Wilson's ideologically established gospel of democracy. Creel's propaganda was aimed at heightening public consciousness to create a set of ideologically based beliefs, individual by individual, yet with perfect uniformity.

While it was true that enthusiasm for the war ran surprisingly high by April 1917, cultivating a sophisticated degree of uniform ideological understanding across the American population was a tall order indeed. Mock and Larson invited their readers to imagine the situation of a Midwestern family living "on a quarter-section of farmland a dozen miles from the railroad, telegraph, and post office. The nearest daily newspaper was published at the far end of the next county, seventy-five miles away. No through road passed near their farm, they had seen pavement only a few times in their lives, and they had no phone. Normally they paid scant attention to public affairs. Their only aim in life, so it seemed, was to bring in the golden harvest."[13] *These* were the people that the CPI had to reach and educate in the intellectual principles of Wilsonian democracy. Obedient to Wilson's will, Creel wanted to generate not merely support for the war but genuine understanding of it—that is, as Woodrow Wilson understood it.

Creel set out to transform the American mind by ensuring that every item of war news Americans saw, wherever encountered, was not just officially approved but precisely the same information that millions of their fellow citizens were getting at the same moment.[14] The stories that appeared in the nation's newspapers were the work of many hands, but all of those hands ultimately worked for the CPI. There was not a single significant media outlet that failed to carry a CPI message. In addition to newspapers and magazines, county fairs, movies, classrooms, post office walls, churches, synagogues, union halls—virtually every physical interface with the public—were venues for a CPI message. The result was a torrent of news and other information. Brainwashing? Not really. The reporters and writers for the CPI were professional journalists who engaged in reasoned, rational exposition and argument made overwhelmingly powerful by dint of sheer volume, repetition, and ubiquity.

●

While leadership of America's new ministry of propaganda flowed from George Creel and George Creel alone, he rapidly assembled a large and extraordinary apparatus to aid him. "Putting the Committee on Public Information together," Creel later wrote, "was like asking the Babylonians to build a threshing machine, for there was no chart to go by." This, he argued, was an advantage. "Starting from scratch seemed a hardship at the time, but on looking back, I see it as my salvation. With the organization put together man by man, I knew it from top to bottom and could keep an eye and hand on every division."[15]

If the United States went to war with a tiny army—compared to those of the European combatant nations—it also went to war with nothing even remotely resembling a propaganda ministry. For the first several weeks of operation, the CPI did not even have an office. Everyone worked out of the US Navy Library. Secretary of War Baker lent Creel the services of Douglas MacArthur (figure 6), at the time a young major in the Regular Army, who located space for the CPI at 10 Jackson Place, once the dwelling of either Daniel Webster or John C. Calhoun (tradition is divided on the identity of the occupant), across the street from the White House. As the agency grew, a second and third Jackson Place dwelling were commandeered, as was space in the Treasury Building.

The growth of the propaganda ministry was explosive—almost literally. Historians Mock and Larson, who had access to all of the living principals, including Creel, warned their readers that "no one" could "draw a definitive outline of [CPI's] work" or growth. It exploded into existence. "A 'come at once' telegram would be dispatched to some journalist, scholar, or public figure, he would catch an afternoon train; and presto! the next dawn would break on a brand new unit of the CPI."[16]

Figure 6. Douglas MacArthur as a brigadier general during the defense of the Champagne-Marne. He served at the time with the 42nd "Rainbow" Division and would win his third Silver Star during the campaign. NATIONAL ARCHIVES AND RECORDS ADMINISTRATION

Among the very first to receive such a telegram was Arthur Bullard, editor of *The Outlook* (a magazine focusing on social and political topics) and the author of *The Diplomacy of the Great War* (1916). Next came Ernest Poole, a crusading Progressive journalist best known for his 1915 novel *The Harbor*, which portrayed life and death on the rough Brooklyn waterfront. Harvey O'Higgins, Edgar Sisson, W. L. Chenery, and Charles Hart also came aboard in the first days. Canadian-born O'Higgins was a muckraker whose works included *The Beast* (1910), a sensational exposé of the social environment of city-bred children, and *Under the Prophet in Utah* (1911), a sensational exposé of the Mormon Church.[17] Sisson left the editorship of *Cosmopolitan* to work for the Creel Committee. Chenery left *Collier's*. Charles S. Hart left a $10,000-a-year post as advertising manager of *Hearst's Magazine* to work for the CPI at $3,900 a year. They saw themselves—and were—patriots, who left the cushy private sector for the sake of the war and worked day and night to get the CPI up and running by the end of its very first week of existence.

Creel established the CPI first and foremost as the source of guidance for the voluntary press censorship program. He composed an authoritative policy, printed it on a ten-by-twelve card, and distributed to the nation's editors:

WHAT THE GOVERNMENT ASKS OF THE PRESS

The desires of the government with respect to the concealment from the enemy of military policies, plans, and movements are set forth in the following specific requests. They go to the press of the United States directly from the Secretary of War and the Secretary of the Navy and represent the thought and advice of their technical advisers.

This was followed by an eighteen-point list of proscribed items, ranging from "Advance information of the routes and schedules of troop movements" to "Information that would disclose the location of American units or the eventual position of the American forces at the front" to "Information of the locality, number, or identity of vessels belonging to our own navy or to the navies of any country at war with Germany" to "Information of the laying of mines or mine-fields or of any harbor defenses" to "Information of the transportation of munitions or of war material."[18] It was all eminently reasonable, and the list was designed to convey the message that censorship really did apply to areas that were military secrets, not to opinion and analysis. This said, Creel saw to it that all opinion and analysis would be supplied by the CPI.

Although the development of the CPI was an improvisation, it was not without at least an outline of a plan. Creel's first imperative was to create, issue, and win approval for the rules of voluntary censorship. After this, "the next step, obviously, was the fight for national unity." For Creel, this meant forming public opinion, which, in turn, implied a necessary preparation: "before a sound, steadfast public opinion could be formed, it had to be *informed*. Not manipulated, not tricked, and not wheedled, but given every fact in the case." The object was to avoid creating the impression that the war was "the war of the administration or the private enterprise of the General Staff," but was, rather, "the grim business of a whole people." Creel believed he had to give every man, woman, and child "a feeling of partnership." To do this, he would "put trained reporters in the War Department, the Navy, and every other agency connected with the war machine."[19] Among the earliest activities of the CPI, therefore, were recruiting and deploying the journalists who made up the first major unit of the CPI, the Division of News. Next came the creation of the Division of Pictorial Publicity, after the celebrated graphic artist Charles Dana Gibson (creator of the iconic "Gibson Girl") walked into CPI headquarters on or shortly before the morning of April 17, 1917, with a poster he wanted to contribute. Creel welcomed the contribution and immediately pressed Gibson into service to recruit an entire army of famous artists for the production of many more paintings and posters (figure 7). Later that very afternoon, Creel was visited by another walk-in, Donald Ryerson, who presented his plan for putting speakers in the movie theaters of Chicago. Before he left Creel's office, Ryerson had been given a brief to assemble a national organization to be called the Four Minute Men. It would become the most visible and vocal of the CPI's operations.

The Four Minute Men were a cadre of select volunteers—some seventy-five thousand strong—who gave four-minute speeches on topics the CPI supplied to them. Although they spoke in a number of venues,

Figure 7. Artist and illustrator James Montgomery Flagg was best known for his "I Want You" poster featuring Uncle Sam, but this seductive image may well be his World War I recruitment masterpiece. NATIONAL ARCHIVES AND RECORDS ADMINISTRATION

the most popular were in the nation's movie theaters. They delivered their talks during the four minutes it took a professional projectionist to change the reels of a feature film. Although the topics were furnished by the CPI, the speeches were composed and delivered by the volunteers, who were mostly men prominent in the community—influencers, often successful merchants, lawyers, physicians, and businessmen. The topics dealt with all aspects of the war and were intended to get the community involved in bond purchases, in growing vegetable gardens, in sharing accurate war information, and otherwise supporting the war. During 1917–1918, some 7,555,190 speeches were given in 5,200 communities.

The Four Minute Man program moved Creel to also create a Speaking Division, which enlisted professional speakers already experienced on the Chautauqua educational speaking circuit. Creel persuaded Arthur Bestor, president of the Chautauqua Institution, to run the new division.

Within mere days of Creel's meetings with Gibson and Ryerson and his call to Bestor, he met with Herbert Houston, publisher of *Our World*; William H. Rankin, another editor-publisher; Thomas Cusack, who owned a major billboard advertising company; and William H. Johns, an advertising executive. They proposed that Creel purchase huge amounts of advertising space in newspapers and magazines and on billboards. Johns promised to fill it all very productively, and so Creel hired him to create and to lead the CPI's Division of Advertising.

By war's end, CPI was divided between two main sections, the Domestic Section and the Foreign Section. An Executive Division, headed by Creel, planned, initiated, and coordinated all CPI operations. Within the Domestic Section were the Division of News, which issued some six thousand major releases published in about twenty thousand newspaper columns per week. Additionally, the *Official Bulletin* was created. The first official daily newspaper of the United States government, it was intended as a record of the nation's participation in the war.[20]

Before April 1917 ended, a Foreign Language Newspaper Division was established. Its role was to monitor every foreign-language newspaper in the United States and to translate CPI publications into foreign languages. The historian Guy Stanton Ford, dean of the Graduate School of the University of Minnesota, came on board to create the Division of Civic and Educational Cooperation, which commissioned, edited, and published 105 books and pamphlets, mostly by eminent scholars. These were distributed through schools and colleges, achieving an incredible circulation of seventy-five million. The division also issued a sixteen-page newsletter, *The National School Service*, which circulated to some twenty million households.

The Picture Division, established in October 1917, managed the production and distribution of war-related still photographs. The Bureau of War Photographs, created somewhat later, served essentially the same function. Established along with the Picture Division in October 1917 was a Film Division, which initially did nothing more than distribute motion pictures produced by the US Army Signal Corps. Later, it spawned an Educational Department and Scenario (script) Department and began making original motion pictures.

A Bureau of War Expositions organized, mounted, and circulated, nationwide, exhibits of the weapons of war as well as battle trophies captured by US forces. A Bureau of State Fair Exhibits also displayed weapons and war trophies, but mainly promoted food conservation programs to aid in the war effort.

The CPI's Division of Industrial Relations, which was created late in the war, was intended to secure the ongoing cooperation of labor. Its work was soon taken over by the US Department of Labor, but the CPI continued to run an American Alliance for Labor and Democracy, which was headed by no less a figure than Samuel Gompers.

The CPI's Division of Syndicate Features enlisted leading novelists, popular essayists, and short-story writers to contribute syndicated feature material to the nation's newspapers and magazines, reaching, by Creel's estimate, some twelve million readers each month.

A Division of Women's War Work created and distributed news stories and other information relating to the role of women in the war effort (figure 8). Personnel in this unit also wrote some fifty thousand personal letters in response to questions posed by the wives and mothers of servicemen.

SUBJECT.
165-WW-171-19   AU
165-WW-171 19
Cen. News Photo Ser.
PHOTOGRAPHER
May --1918   --1918
REC'D   TAKEN

DESCRIPTION:

GIRL WAR FARMERS WIN PRAISE
OF FARMER WHO EMPLOYS THEM.

"The best help I've ever had,"
is the way farmer Hankinson
of Mercer, N.J. describes
the contingent of farmerettes
of the Women's Land Army of
America who has been working
on his land for five weeks.
The young ladies most of
them are college trained girls
answered the call of farmer
Hankinson for girl farm hands,
laid down their books, or
forsook the drawing room and
started on the trail to the
farm. Dressed in overalls and
leggings old shoes and broad
brimmed hats, the city girls
successfully attacked the problems of spring life of the
farm from chopping wood and
pruning trees, to milking cows.

(continued on reverse)

Figure 8. Women's war work: "Farmerettes" of the Women's Land Army work the bucksaw at the Hawkinson Farm, Mercer, New Jersey. "The best help I've ever had," the farmer commented. Women filled in for men across the home front.
NATIONAL ARCHIVES AND RECORDS ADMINISTRATION

An important CPI unit was the Division of Work with the Foreign Born, established in May 1918 to promote the patriotism of various national and ethnic minorities living in the United States. It was part of the CPI's Foreign Section, which also operated a Wireless and Cable Service to prepare and transmit news dispatches to practically every country in the world; a Foreign Press Bureau, directed by Ernest Poole, which supplied CPI press agents stationed abroad with a steady stream of feature articles and photographs to be offered to foreign newspapers and magazines; and a Foreign Film Division, which managed the export of movies from the Division of Films (under the Domestic Section).

●

The CPI devoted a great deal of attention to "Work with the Foreign Born," partly to ensure the transformation of "hyphenated Americans" into Americans, but also out of concern for the safety and security of new and established immigrants, especially those from the Central powers countries.

The US government declared, on April 16, 1917, all males older than fourteen who were still "natives, citizens, denizens, or subjects" of the German Empire to be alien enemies. The following year, this designation was extended to women fourteen and older. Alien enemies were prohibited from owning firearms, aircraft, or "wireless" (radio) transmitters and receivers. They were prohibited from making any verbal or printed attacks on any aspect of the US government. They were subject to restrictions concerning where they might take up residence, and they could be moved to any location designated by the president. Alien enemies were not permitted to leave the United States without permission and were required to register with the government and to carry a registration card on their persons at all times.

All persons of German or Austrian descent were looked on with suspicion. In some places, they were discriminated against by local businesses, including banks. Some communities initiated boycotts of their businesses. Sometimes, individuals and families were attacked or even lynched. Anyone who spoke English with an accent or who spoke German—or any other foreign language—in public was suspect. Indeed, a number of states passed laws prohibiting the speaking of German in public. In Iowa, Governor William L. Harding, issued the so-called Babel Proclamation on May 23, 1918, which outlawed the public use of *all* foreign languages. This was the culmination of a statewide anti-German movement that had begun on November 23, 1917, when the Iowa State Council of Defense ordered the abolition of German-language courses in public schools. Not only were German-language instructors on the state payroll dismissed but all German textbooks were burned. At the same time, Iowa towns and streets were renamed. Berlin Township became Hughes Township; Muscatine's Bismarck Street became Bond Street; Hanover Avenue, Liberty Avenue; the village of Germania in Kossuth County was rechristened Lakota.

Governor Harding announced that the Babel Proclamation would have the full force and effect of law. He dismissed protests that it violated the First Amendment by saying that the "official language of the

United States and the State of Iowa is the English language. Freedom of speech is guaranteed by federal and state constitutions, but this is not a guarantee of the right to use a language other than the language of this country—the English language." All conversation in public places, on public conveyances, and over the telephone was required to be conducted in English, and English only was to be spoken in churches—although the proclamation was silent on the subject of Latin in the Catholic liturgy and made no mention at all of worship in synagogues.[21]

Creel bucked the extreme xenophobia by printing various CPI pamphlets and other publications in German, Yiddish, Italian, Hungarian, Russian, Chinese, and other languages common among foreign-born groups. He also recruited foreign-speaking Four Minute Men. Despite criticism of these efforts, he persevered in them.

●

The foreign-born and "alien enemies" were not the only Americans whose civil liberties were infringed in the name of more effectively prosecuting a war to save democracy. The right to protest and dissent was sharply curtailed, and government agents cracked down on members of the radical labor movement. Any disruption of war production was viewed as approaching the level of treason and giving aid and comfort to the enemy.

Communists and Socialists were targeted for persecution and prosecution, but no group was more squarely in the government's crosshairs than the Industrial Workers of the World (IWW) or "Wobblies," the "one big union" that organized unskilled labor. In September 1917, 165 IWW leaders were arrested on charges ranging from treason to the use of intimidation in labor disputes. Of these, 101 were tried together in April 1918, including IWW head William Dudley "Big Bill" Haywood. The trial lasted five months before ending in guilty verdicts for all defendants. Haywood and fourteen others each received twenty-year prison sentences, and all defendants were fined a total of $2,500,000.

The trial broke the back of the IWW. It also triggered rumors that the IWW had been infiltrated by pro-Germans. In July 1917, a group of armed vigilantes rounded up about 1,200 IWW agricultural laborers in Arizona, packed them into cattle cars, shipped them to New Mexico, and abandoned them in a remote desert area. They were subsequently rescued by US soldiers, who led them to a detention facility, where they remained for months, without trial or hearing, until they were unceremoniously released.

•

If the account of *New York World* reporter Frank Cobb is to be trusted, on the eve of asking Congress for a declaration of war, President Woodrow Wilson predicted that the experience of fighting the European War would attack the American soul with a "spirit of ruthless brutality [that] will enter the very fiber of our national life, infecting Congress, the courts, the policeman on the beat, the man in the street. Conformity will be the only virtue. And every man who refuses to conform must pay the penalty."[22]

Wilson's prediction, at least as Cobb reported it, was all too accurate. The great irony of America's experience in the war to "make the world safe for democracy" was that, for the duration of the US participation in the conflict, democracy within the United States was virtually suspended.

Chapter 4

From Over Here to Over There

"AMERICAN EXCEPTIONALISM" IS A PHRASE TO WHICH AMERICAN POLI-
ticians are especially partial. It describes a notion that because, as a nation
founded on a set of ideas, the history of the United States is different
from that of other countries, the United States itself is therefore different. The phrase was unknown at the time of World War I, but back then
its definition would have been far simpler than it is in today's politically
fraught climate. As most people saw it early in the twentieth century,
America was indeed exceptional, but chiefly because of its geography.
Huge, spanning an entire continent, America was nevertheless physically
isolated. A friendly neighbor lay to the north, a more troublesome but
much weaker neighbor to the south, and vast oceans formed the nation's
western and the eastern borders. No wonder the United States military
never contemplated, much less prepared for, an overseas campaign. For
geographical reasons, such a mission never seemed even remotely likely.

Yet, during the opening years of the twentieth century, the United
States, following its victory in the brief Spanish-American War of 1898,
was beginning to see itself as what it was in fact becoming: a world
power. As part of this national evolution, the US Army was slowly
undergoing reforms intended to modernize the force and put it on
par with the militaries of the great European powers. It was, however,
by no means a rapid process. The overwhelming nature of the victory
against Spain tended to obscure the fact that, while the navy had performed admirably, the army stumbled badly in its effort to mobilize a
substantial force for overseas service. Deploying an army in the distant

Philippines was daunting, but even crossing the relatively short distance from the southeastern United States to Cuba and Puerto Rico created confusion and delay. Had Spain been a more formidable opponent, the American landings on these islands would have been disastrous. Yet while there was movement toward modernization within the military, the political policy of the United States called for studiously avoiding what President Washington had called "entangling alliances" with European nations. Thus, the military modernization from 1899 to 1917 focused on improving defensive capability, with the US Navy figuring as the first line of defense and the army concentrating on improving its arsenal to keep abreast of technological developments. It is to the credit of the nation's naval leaders that, at sea, increased emphasis was put on acquiring more modern firepower in the form of bigger guns. Land commanders, however, were slower to upgrade the basic infantry and artillery weapons, but they did make some progress.

●

Development of high-velocity, low-trajectory, clip-loading rifles designed to deliver a high rate of sustained fire made the US Army's Krag-Jørgensen rifle, standard since 1892, obsolete. Recognizing this, the Regular Army, in 1903, began receiving the improved bolt-action, magazine-type Springfield rifle. The Spanish-American War had revealed the weakness of the standard rod bayonet, which proved too flimsy in modern combat. In 1905, the army replaced it with the much tougher knife bayonet, and in 1911, it supplemented this close-quarters weapon with the new .45-caliber Colt single-action, semi-automatic M1911 pistol, which vastly outperformed the standard .38-caliber revolver.

Of all the advances in infantry weapons, the most consequential was the machine gun. It had evolved from the Gatling gun, which had come into prominence at the end of the Civil War, and was now the extraordinarily deadly modern machine gun with which the European armies of World War I were equipped. Possession of this weapon became the table stakes for combatants in the Great War. The machine gun gave a two-man team firing from a trench the capability of killing a hundred attackers—perhaps even more. The weapon ensured that, in the trench warfare that dominated the Western Front, the defenders would always have the advantage—at least if given a sufficient supply of machine guns and gunners and ammunition to serve them. Between 1898 and 1916, the US Congress appropriated a parsimonious average of $150,000 per year to procure machine guns. This provided each Regular Army regiment (the authorized strength of which was one thousand men and officers) just four weapons—a spectacularly insufficient number. With the onset of the preparedness movement in 1916, Congress allocated a healthy twelve million dollars to upgrade the equipment of the US Army. In an extraordinary display of military bureaucracy, however, the War Department delayed spending the funds until 1917, when the slow-moving weapons board finally decided which weapons were appropriate for the American land forces.

Even while World War I was being fought during its first two years, contemporary commentators were calling it an "artillery war." At the Battle of Verdun (February 21–December 18, 1916), for example, the Germans and the French fired as many as sixty million shells during the ten months of the principal action. The United States was very slow to develop modern shells. One reason was that the army did not have the advanced field weapons to use them. While the US Army had a well-developed Coastal Artillery arm, which served the massive weapons permanently mounted in the emplacements of the nation's coastal forts, the newest field artillery piece the army had was the 1902 three-inch gun, which was fitted with a modern recoil mechanism. In an age of strong steel and high explosives, problems of range and detonation were being solved rapidly, but the physics of recoil took longer to work out. Each time a field gun recoiled, it moved, which meant that it had to be "re-layed" (re-aimed). To the degree that the effects of recoil could be mechanically reduced, the gun could be fired more rapidly, since there would be less need for re-laying the piece. By 1903, American manufacturers were producing enough of the three-inch guns to equip most of the artillery batteries of the Regular Army—but the Regular Army was small, between 133,000 and 166,000 men. Moreover, the European armies not only had far more artillery but they had it in a wide variety of designs suitable to a broad array of applications, including the high-tra-

Figure 9. American doughboys man a French thirty-seven-millimeter gun on the parapet of a second-line trench. Most of the artillery Americans used during the war were French weapons. NATIONAL ARCHIVES AND RECORDS ADMINISTRATION

jectory mortars and howitzers, which were most effective for attacking enemy trenches and other fortifications (figure 9).

Motorized transportation became important in World War I, but the US Army of 1917–1918 was still largely horse-drawn. In any case, American troops overseas were expected to make use of vehicles supplied mainly by the French—some of which were imported from US manufacturers. Of greater significance was the degree to which the US military was behind all of the European powers in the field of aviation. It is one of the ironies of innovation in the early twentieth century that the nation in which powered, heavier-than-air flight was invented should fail to make much progress beyond the Wright Brothers prior to World War I. The US military had no aircraft capable of going up against even obsolescent European models. Consider that, between 1908 and 1913, the United States spent an estimated $430,000 on military and naval aviation.

During this period, France and Germany each spent $22 million; Russia, $12 million; and Belgium—Belgium!—$2 million.[1]

●

The US Army did make important organizational and administrative reforms following the Spanish-American War. Elihu Root, President William McKinley's secretary of war, instigated change when he realized that the army, whose mission after the Civil War had been primarily to police the Indians in the West, was not up to the task of maintaining order in newly acquired overseas possessions. Root boldly redefined the mission of the US Army from a kind of frontier constabulary to a force charged with prosecuting modern wars. He revised the organization of the army with an eye toward more closely integrating the Regular Army (including reserves), militia, and volunteers. Root perceived the chief weakness in the organization of the army to be the minimization of the secretary of war's authority. All command decisions were the sole province of the army's commanding general, whereas the secretary controlled only administrative and financial matters. Root replaced the commanding general with a chief of staff, who functioned as the advisor to and executive agent of the president and secretary of war. Within the army itself, Root created the General Staff, a group of senior officers responsible for preparing military plans. Finally, Root instituted an Army War College, responsible for educating the most senior officers. Acting on its own initiative, the army revamped the rest of its educational system, creating the General Staff and Service College at Fort Leavenworth, Kansas, as well as the Signal School, the Field Artillery School in 1911, and the School of Musketry. In 1910, Major General Leonard Wood became chief of staff and reorganized the Army General Staff to focus its mission on planning.

Along with reform of the Regular Army's internal organization, planners turned their attention to reorganizing the reserve forces. Once again, Root assumed the lead, presenting to Congress in 1901 a program to reform the National Guard. The result was the Militia Act of 1903, which, superseding the Militia Act of 1792, recognized the National Guard as the nation's principal militia force. The act also brought the

Guard's organization and equipment on par with that of the Regular Army. In 1908 and 1914, additional legislation gave the federal government greater control of the National Guard, which had hitherto been under the exclusive peacetime authority of the states.

Reform was also applied to the field organization of the army. In peacetime, the largest field unit was the regiment. The Spanish-American War demonstrated the need for larger, more self-sufficient units capable of combined-arms (infantry, artillery, cavalry) operations. In 1910, the General Staff created a plan for the establishment of three permanent infantry divisions, which would be composed of Regular Army and National Guard regiments.

In the end, it was the Punitive Expedition in pursuit of Pancho Villa in 1916 that constituted a crash training course for elements of the Regular Army and National Guard. The campaign against Villa also required intensive training of those Regular Army and Guard troops who served on the Mexican border, and the entire experience yielded a cadre of seasoned soldiers around which the army that fought World War I would be formed.

•

The Punitive Expedition and the Mexican border troubles were not the only active military preparedness programs going. As discussed in chapter 2, the Plattsburgh movement was giving young business and professional men an opportunity for preliminary preparation as "officer material." By early 1916, President Wilson, while continuing to insist on the complete neutrality of the United States, not only called for enlarging and modernizing the US Navy but began discussing something approaching universal military training for civilians. Even earlier, in September 1915, within the Wilson cabinet itself, Secretary of War Lindley M. Garrison had recommended more than doubling the size of the Regular Army, increasing federal funding for the National Guard, and establishing a new four-hundred-thousand-man trained, "ready" reserve separate from the Guard and under direct federal control. The Senate took notice, but the House objected to competition with the National Guard, and President Wilson remained lukewarm to Garrison's entire initiative.

Frustrated, Garrison resigned, and Newton D. Baker, the progressive mayor of Cleveland, Ohio, a man without any military experience, became the new war secretary.

Baker did not push for anything like the expansion Garrison had advocated, but he did support reform, and the National Defense Act of 1916 authorized a modest increase in the peacetime strength of the Regular Army as well as a much more substantial wartime increase. As discussed in chapter 2, the National Guard was authorized at more than four hundred thousand men—a fourfold increase—and was bound more closely to the federal government in that it was legally required to respond to a presidential call-up. Previously, such a call-up came from the president via the state governors, who could, in theory, refuse the presidential request. An Enlisted Reserve Corps was established for the Regular Army, along with an official Reserve Officers' Training Corps (ROTC) program at colleges and universities.

The National Defense Act of 1916 also took a step toward truly modern warfare in an industrial age. It gave the president authority not only to place orders for materiel and munitions but also to compel industry's compliance. After passing the law, Congress created a civilian Council of National Defense, whose members were industrialists and labor leaders, to manage the economic aspects of military mobilization. In this way, American civil society was subtly put on a war footing, and the commitment to neutrality accordingly was eroded.

●

British propaganda, which amplified accounts of German atrocities, and the Zimmermann Telegram served to edge America toward war. Aside from Woodrow Wilson's ideological rationale for US entry into the fray—to "make the world safe for democracy"—the proximate motive for a declaration of war was Germany's resumption of unrestricted submarine warfare. Allied ships carrying American passengers and US-flagged vessels alike were being attacked. Given this cause for war, President Wilson could have decided to launch a naval campaign against the submarines instead of committing troops to the Western Front, which is what the Allies were begging for. There was certainly an argument to be made for the navy-only approach, since the US Navy was far better prepared for war than the army. The problem was that nobody in the government—or the public—was enthusiastic about this limited approach, and so the complete US military went to war, which meant that the entire nation went to war.

The propaganda offensive conducted by George Creel's CPI generated a great deal of voluntary enlistment. Some of this, doubtless, was due to patriotism, and even more was the result of an appeal to a sense of manly adventure. As the Creel drumbeat grew ever more insistent, however, social pressure was added to the motives for enlistment. Those young men who failed to enlist risked being branded as "slackers"— selfish and cowardly shirkers of their duty to their country, their families, and their God.

Former president Theodore Roosevelt was among those who led the call for volunteers. When he appealed to President Wilson to allow him to command an entire division of US Volunteers, Wilson felt that his wartime leadership was being challenged, and he made the bold decision to eliminate the US Volunteers as a separate organization and instead resort to conscription. Through Secretary of War Baker, he ordered Judge Advocate General Enoch H. Crowder to draw up legislation for a Selective Service Act. Crowder was personally opposed to conscription, but he was a very good soldier and delivered to Baker a complete document within just twenty-four hours of his order. Congress offered significant opposition to conscription, with House Speaker Champ Clark, a Democrat from Missouri, proclaiming that, to the people of his state, "there is precious little difference between a conscript and a convict."[2] It required several votes before Congress finally passed the Selective Service Act of 1917, 397 to 24 in the House, and 81 to 8 in the Senate. The act was signed into law on May 18, 1917. Under its provisions, 23.9 million men were registered over the next two years, of whom 2.8 million, most between the ages of twenty-one and thirty, were actually drafted. Added to the voluntary enlistees, by Armistice Day 1918, this number created an army of 4.5 million (see figure 10).

Doubtless the draft increased voluntary enlistment. Knowing that they were subject to conscription, many young men preferred to get the social credit for preemptively volunteering. A vocal minority, however, not only persisted in opposition to US entry into the war but also protested the draft. There was widespread fear among public and government officials alike that bloody draft riots, such as those that broke out during the Civil War in both Northern and Southern cities, would recur. These fears proved unfounded, however, and there was no mass protest violence. As for legal challenges to the draft, all were overturned by the US Supreme Court, which affirmed the constitutionality of conscription. Moreover, protesters were largely cowed by provisions in the Espionage and Sedition Acts that levied heavy fines and long prison sentences on those who spoke out against the war effort or attempted to interfere with recruitment or the draft. Yet, even with war fever raging, instances of draft evasion were fairly common. Some three million men of draft age are believed to have successfully avoided registration. Most were never discovered, let alone prosecuted. Moreover, of those who did register and were called up for service, 338,000—12 percent of draftees!—did not report for induction or deserted almost immediately upon arrival at training camps.

Both military and civilian police units staged periodic "slacker raids," in which they rounded up evaders and deserters. These operations almost certainly violated the Fourth Amendment, since young men were randomly stopped by officers and agents, who, absent probable cause, demanded to see their draft registration cards. Approximately half of the 338,000 outright delinquents were apprehended in slacker raids.

Not everyone who sought to avoid service did so by simply breaking the law. A total of 64,693 draft registrants identified themselves as conscientious objectors, requesting exemption from service on religious or, in some cases, political grounds. Some 20,000 of these claims were rejected. Of this number, 16,000 men relented and served as combat soldiers, but roughly 4,000 absolutely refused to bear arms. Of these, 1,300 accepted unarmed service in the medical corps or in other noncombatant roles. Most of the rest were "furloughed" for farm labor. A hard core of 540 were court-martialed and imprisoned.

Figure 10. James Montgomery Flagg's artwork for his iconic "I Want You" recruiting poster. The popular poster was inspired by a British recruiting poster featuring Lord Kitchener instead of Uncle Sam. WIKIMEDIA

•

Registering many millions and drafting 2.8 million was a gargantuan task. Thanks to the introduction of the federal income tax via the Sixteenth Amendment, which was ratified in 1913, the national bureaucracy was becoming adept at tracking its citizens. But it is one thing to induct an army, subject the incoming horde to the most rudimentary of medical examinations, and tell them when and where to report for duty, but altogether another matter to actually turn these civilians into soldiers.

Since the United States had not come into the war with a large standing army, it was immediately faced with the daunting task of housing millions. The first priority was to construct sixteen cantonments—temporary billets—for existing National Guard units. Since guardsmen were already part-time soldiers, they were expected to be among the very first sent to France. The cantonments, which offered shelter mostly in tents, were set up in the South, where winters were sufficiently mild to allow large numbers of men to be accommodated under canvas. Additionally, sixteen new wooden barracks facilities were constructed in or adjacent to existing bases, mainly in the north. These were intended to accommodate the first wave of civilian recruits, who would need to undergo longer periods of training. In the interest of saving time, construction contracts were let not on the normal basis of competitive bidding but, under the direction of Colonel I. W. Littell, commander of the Division of the Quartermaster Corps, on a "cost-plus" basis by which the chosen contractor received 6 to 10 percent above the actual costs of completing a given project on time. It was expensive, and the results were barely livable. But Littell did manage to build his spartan cantonments and barracks on time. One of the prime rites of passage in the transformation of civilians into soldiers was the shocking transition from the comforts of home to the miseries of camp life.

In addition to sheltering its new troops, the United States had to clothe them. Stocks of uniforms chronically ran behind demand, but no soldier was sent off to war without the olive-drab, choke-collar uniform of the US Army. They were, however, initially sent overseas without helmets. They wore high-crowned, broad-brimmed felt campaign hats or folding "overseas caps." The European Allies insisted on the necessity of helmets, and US troops were soon outfitted in British "wash basin" helmets. In fact, once properly helmeted, the US infantry uniform would prove to be among the most practical for trench fighting and continual exposure to the elements, let alone the hazards of combat.

In camp, all recruits received "basic training," which consisted of as much as six months of physical conditioning and drill (essentially the art of marching in slavish obedience to command) in addition to acquiring the rudiments of rifle handling, maintenance, and marksmanship, as well as hand-to-hand fighting, including bayonet training (figure 11). Soldiers who had certain skills in civilian life, various degrees of aptitude demonstrated during basic training, or who simply had good or bad luck were selected for specialist training in the weaponry of modern industrial warfare. This included the operation of machine guns, artillery training, and training in chemical warfare. In addition, troops were trained in vehicle

Figure 11. A British sergeant major (left) instructs a doughboy in the art of the bayonet attack at a training session at Camp Dick, Texas, sometime in 1917. NATIONAL ARCHIVES AND RECORDS ADMINISTRATION

maintenance and repair, wired telephone and wireless radio communications, and other specialties—ranging from preparing meals to collecting and identifying corpses for burial.

An army of more than four million required approximately two hundred thousand officers of all grades. In April 1917, when the army went to war, it did so with about six thousand officers in the Regular Army and an additional fourteen thousand in the National Guard. The additional officers required were commissioned directly from the enlisted ranks and even from certain civilian occupations and professions. College graduates, whether they had attended ROTC or not, were often inducted directly as officers. About a third of the US World War I officer corps were commissioned directly from civilian life.

As for the US Military Academy (West Point), although it turned out very fine officers, it did so in very small numbers. To supply the enormous wartime need for officers, a special Officer Training Corps (OTC) was created. Promising enlisted personnel were tapped for the OTC, where they were subjected to three months of special training, from which they emerged as newly minted second lieutenants. About half of the officer corps of the World War I army were products of the OTC and were contemptuously dubbed "ninety-day wonders."

In the case of both enlisted men and officers, the stateside training they received was, on their arrival in France, immediately deemed inadequate by the European Allies. All troops were therefore given additional training after arriving in France, mostly under French military tutelage. In addition, to the extent possible, they were "blooded" (introduced to combat) in so-called quiet sectors, portions of the Western Front that saw the least intense action. This was intended to ease their entry into full combat by making them more confident and effective frontline troops (figure 12).

By the time he reached France, the civilian was a "doughboy." This is what the US infantryman of World War I was called. It was a term that had been used as far back as the US-Mexican War of 1846–1848, but it became universally identified with the World War I soldier. Although a very common term, its origin is both obscure and subject to debate. Some say it is a reference to the soldiers' large brass uniform buttons, which

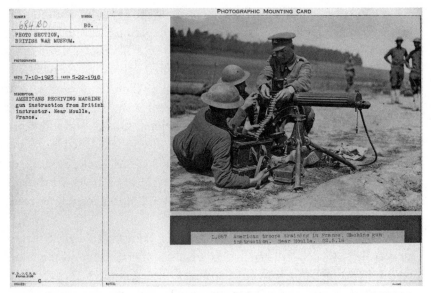

Figure 12. American doughboys receive machine-gun instruction from a British army sergeant-instructor, near Moulle, France. BRITISH WAR MUSEUM

were thought to resemble "doughboys," bread dough that has been rolled thin and deep fried. Others believe it came about during the war with Mexico, when soldiers were perpetually covered with the chalky dust of the trail, which gave them the appearance of being coated in flour or unbaked dough. While the term was used by cavalrymen to disparage infantrymen, it was universally—and, by civilians, affectionately—applied to all US troops in World War I (figure 13).

●

The army of 1917–1918 was racially segregated. There was a slight degree of integration in the navy, but less than had been the case in the Union navy during the Civil War. During World War I, the only shipboard jobs open to blacks were as cooks, mess boys, and stewards. In the army, African Americans were disproportionately assigned to labor details—although African American soldiers who saw combat were often keen to distinguish themselves. Two all-black infantry divisions were raised during the war; one of them, the 95th, served under French command (figure 14).

"I know a girl at home who looks just like you

Figure 13. "I know a girl at home who looks just like you" reads the handwritten caption on this sketch of a doughboy in France by Cyrus Leroy Baldridge, an illustrator who served as an artist for *The Stars and Stripes*, the army's official newspaper. WIKIMEDIA

Figure 14. "Negro draftees ready for service. Lexington, Kentucky." NATIONAL
ARCHIVES AND RECORDS ADMINISTRATION

Women also served in narrowly defined roles during the war. The
army accepted women into its ranks only as nurses to serve in the US
Army Nurse Corps, which had been created in 1901. By December 1917,
424 regular nurses and 3,600 reserve nurses were serving. By the Armistice, this number had grown to 3,500 regular nurses and 18,000 reservists. The US Navy recruited about eleven thousand women as nurses and
as clerks and typists (figure 15).

●

With the long-hoped-for US entry into the war now a reality, the British and the French sent delegations to the United States to hammer out
plans for America's participation in the war. Astoundingly, the two delegations not only arrived separately but had no common agenda to present
to their new ally. The first order of business for each of the two European

Figure 15. Women were permitted to join the US Marine Corps to perform noncombat duties, thereby freeing up more men for service at the front. NATIONAL ARCHIVES AND RECORDS ADMINISTRATION

allies was to secure new US loans. Both the French and the British delegations were sufficiently realistic to understand that no great American force would be coming across the Atlantic immediately, but Marshal Joseph Joffre, of the French delegation, suggested that a single American division be sent right away—just to bolster decaying French morale. As for actually deploying American manpower as it became available in significant numbers, the two European allies had very different ideas.

The French made it clear that they would help train the arriving US units, but they believed that, ultimately, the Americans should fight as an independent army. In contrast, the British proposed the speedy mobilization of a half million American troops to land in England, where they would not only be trained and equipped by the British, but wholly absorbed into the British Army.

There were practical advantages to simply incorporating the new manpower into the British or French armies. It was easier and faster to expand an existing military body than to create a new one. Building an independent US force in Europe would require time and a lot more troops. Both time and transport ships were in critically short supply, and the situation on the Western Front was desperate. On the other hand, it was unlikely that the American people would allow their sons' fate to be put in the hands of foreign powers. Issues of national pride and sovereignty, not to mention the professionalism of the US Army officer corps, were at stake. Even more important, as President Wilson saw it, if the US contribution to the war effort were rendered essentially invisible, the American government, in the person of the president, would be unable to claim a leadership role in creating the peace that would follow victory. Wilson accordingly rejected unconditionally the British proposal of absorption. He agreed to Joffre's recommendation to send a division to France immediately and to accept French help in training. Work started immediately to assemble a division of four regiments in two brigades, a total of 17,700 men, of whom 11,000 were infantrymen.

Even before he took the United States into the war, President Wilson had planned to put Major General Frederick "Fearless Freddie" Funston in command of what was to be called the American Expeditionary Force (AEF). A hero of the Spanish-American War, Funston was a commander of great skill, daring, and popularity. He was also a workhorse, who drove himself relentlessly. Wilson liked that. It was the rare moment that found Frederick Funston relaxing, as he did on February 19, 1917, in the lobby of the St. Anthony Hotel in San Antonio, Texas, listening to the house orchestra glide through "The Blue Danube Waltz." "How beautiful it all is," Funston remarked. He then grabbed at his chest, collapsed, and died, at age fifty-one, of a massive heart attack.[3]

Funston's sudden and unexpected death gave Major General John J. Pershing (figure 16), commander of the Army's Southern Department at

Figure 16. General John Joseph "Black Jack" Pershing, commanding officer, American Expeditionary Force. WIKIMEDIA

Fort Sam Houston, Texas, the opportunity of a lifetime. He was asked to select the four infantry regiments that would make up the first division to be sent to France. He picked the most battle-ready—the 16th, 18th, 26th, and 28th Infantries—and added the 6th Field Artillery. All required many new recruits to attain full strength. As a result, by the time the 1st Expeditionary Division sailed for France on June 12, under Brigadier General William L. Sibert, two-thirds of its personnel were raw recruits. As expected, Secretary of War Newton D. Baker announced the selection of Pershing as overall commander of the AEF. While Funston had been the president's first choice, there were still five other major generals more senior than Pershing. The most capable of them, former chief of staff Leonard Wood, was simply too old, and the others were not considered as capable as Pershing.

The new AEF commanding officer wasted no time in putting together his headquarters staff, which consisted of Major James G. Harbord (as AEF Chief of Staff), Major Fox Conner (G-3, Chief of Operations), and Captain Hugh Drum. On May 28, Pershing and his entire headquarters staff of 191 left for England and then France. In addition to coordinating with their Allied military counterparts, Pershing and his staff committee inspected ports and railroads to begin arranging for transportation and lines of communications. On June 26, the advance elements of the 1st Division joined Pershing and his staff in France. The troops were billeted in the Gondrecourt area of Lorraine, about 120 miles southwest of Paris, where they began a rigorous training regimen. Equally important, Pershing acceded to the wishes of French authorities that he detach a battalion of the 16th Infantry to march through Paris on the Fourth of July. The sight of the fresh young American troops did greatly lift popular spirits, and when the parade ended at Picpus Cemetery, the burial place of Lafayette, the French hero of the American Revolution, Colonel Charles E. Stanton, one of Pershing's quartermaster officers and a fluent French speaker, delivered an address on behalf of the AEF commander. The speech is forgotten, but its ending well remembered. "Lafayette, we are here!" Stanton proclaimed. It was the perfect thing to have said, moving the French and the American people and reminding both of the long-held bond between the two nations.

•

Few generals were ever given the combination of responsibility and free rein that Wilson, through Baker, gave Pershing.

"I will give you only two orders," the secretary of war told the general, "one to go to France and the other to come home. In the meantime, your authority in France will be supreme."[4]

Pershing and his staff spent the summer of 1917 laying the foundations for the AEF. Their planning and decision-making is discussed in the next chapter, but it is important to note here that the staff scrambled to establish a separate American zone of operations and lay out training areas within it. Pershing wanted the arriving elements of the AEF to be able to get to work rapidly. His objective was to build a core of seasoned soldiers and well-trained recruits around which the entire AEF could be built. He chose an area in Lorraine, which provided good training space, but also offered proximity to the Longwy-Briey iron fields and the coal deposits of the Saar, valuable French territory held by the Germans. This, Pershing thought, would give the American forces a prime objective for an initial offensive—once they were sufficiently trained.

The result of the American staff's studies and planning was the General Organization Project, which guided the AEF's organization throughout the war. Among many other things, the Project outlined the contours of a million-man field army comprising five corps of thirty divisions. Pershing and his staff were doing nothing less than innovating the first truly modern American army. It was a complex combined-arms organization, which deployed infantry, heavy artillery, engineers, cavalry, antiaircraft, signal, and support units together in an integrated fashion unprecedented in earlier American military formations.

By the end of August, the organization of the AEF was a settled matter, and now Pershing was faced with laying out a long-term strategy. This was constrained by some hard truths. First, Allied losses had been so heavy in 1917 that the British and French (it was believed) would be unable to launch any major offensive in 1918—even with the Americans now in the war (figure 17). It seemed impossible to get enough

US troops in France and battle-ready before early 1919. The strategy for 1918, therefore, would be largely defensive—meeting and overcoming any German offensives—while perhaps executing some limited offensive operations, such as reducing the St. Mihiel salient, a strong German position that bulged into the Allied lines at St. Mihiel in the Meuse department of northeastern France. Pushing this salient back—reducing it—would reclaim for the Allies territory from which future advances into Germany could be made.

●

But 1918 and 1919 seemed a long way off. In the meantime, Pershing and his headquarters staff laid the cornerstone of the AEF's organization and operation, everything from training, tactics, troop strength, and shipping to a grand strategy for final victory. As for shipping, the army pressed into service every available vessel, including chartering passenger liners, converting seized German ships that had been interned in US ports at the outbreak of the war, and borrowing a large number of vessels from the European Allies. Every one of the two million Americans who shipped out to France did so aboard vessels that crossed and recrossed from New York, New Jersey, and Newport News, Virginia. The mobilization effort pushed the US military to new limits. In France, the harbors of Bordeaux, La Pallice, Saint Nazaire, and Brest were used as points of entry from which troops disembarked from the incoming vessels to board French trains to the front. American military engineers built eighty-two new ship berths and nearly a thousand miles of railroad track to accommodate the influx of troops, which reached an average of ten thousand a day by June 1918.

We can only imagine General Pershing's thoughts as he watched the trickle of men grow into a flood. What Pershing believed imperative to victory and the effective use of the American forces was a single-minded insistence on maintaining the integrity and independence of his army. His officers and men would cooperate closely with the British and the French, but they would serve under an American flag. This, at least, was his vision, and sustaining it through the end of the war would prove to be a battle in itself.

TEACHING THE YOUNG IDEA HOW TO SHOOT
American Officers at a forward Ordnance 'Shop'.

Figure 17. This newspaper engraving is captioned "Teaching the Young Idea How to Shoot–American Officers at a Forward Ordnance 'Shop'" in a British sector.

CHAPTER 5

Black Jack

John Joseph Pershing

NOT SINCE ULYSSES S. GRANT IN THE CIVIL WAR AND, BEFORE HIM, George Washington in the Revolutionary War was an American military commander given more responsibility than John Joseph Pershing. No American general had ever led so large a force into combat— ultimately more than two million men—and no American president ever gave an American general greater autonomy. "I will give you only two orders," Woodrow Wilson's secretary of war told Pershing, "one to go to France and the other to come home. In the meantime, your authority in France will be supreme."[1] Indeed, in contrast to James K. Polk in the US-Mexican War, Abraham Lincoln in the Civil War, Franklin Roosevelt and Harry S. Truman in World War II, and Lyndon Johnson and Richard M. Nixon in the Vietnam War, President Wilson put the prosecution of America's role in the Great War entirely in the hands of Pershing, whom he never questioned, criticized, or praised. Wilson entrusted victory to Pershing and seems never to have doubted that Pershing would bring him victory.

●

Pershing was born on September 13, 1860, in Laclede, Missouri, and grew up a farm boy but attended a local elementary school that catered to gifted students. After graduating from high school in 1878, Pershing became a teacher at a school for local African American children. While still teaching, he went on to the State Normal School (today Truman State University) in Kirksville, Missouri, from which he graduated in 1880 with a bachelor of science degree in scientific didactics. Two years after this, he applied for admission to the US Military Academy. Like Omar Bradley of World War II fame, young Pershing was less interested in West Point as a gateway to a military career than as an opportunity for a free college education. He graduated in 1886 and was commissioned a second lieutenant in the 6th Cavalry, with which he saw service in the culmination of the wars with the Plains Indians. He learned a hard lesson about the cruelty of war when he was assigned to search out and round up fugitives from the Wounded Knee Massacre (December 28, 1890).

Young lieutenant Pershing kept one foot planted in academics. From 1891 to 1895, he was professor of military science at the University of Nebraska, serving there as commandant of cadets. He rose from second to first lieutenant in 1892—the pace of promotion in the peacetime army was glacial—yet he was sufficiently uncertain about remaining in the army to take time out to earn a law degree. In 1895, he left the University of Nebraska to assume command of a troop of the Tenth Cavalry. In the segregated US Army of the period, this was a famous regiment of African American troopers—"Buffalo Soldiers," they were called—all under the command of white officers. It was from this assignment that Pershing earned his Black Jack nickname, which had been sanitized for evolving societal norms from the original "Nigger Jack." He wore both versions as badges of honor.

In October 1896, Pershing was appointed aide to Major General Nelson A. Miles, who had been appointed commanding general of the US Army the year before. This was Pershing's introduction to the very highest level of army command; however, in June 1897 he returned to West Point as an instructor in tactics, leaving this post in April 1898 to rejoin the 10th Cavalry as its quartermaster. He served with this unit in the Spanish-American War at the Battles of El Caney and San Juan Hill (July 1–3, 1898), distinguishing himself in combat. As one commanding officer said of him, he was, under fire, "as cool as a bowl of cracked ice."[2]

"Ice" was doubtless what many thought of when they dealt with Black Jack Pershing. The social activist and popular novelist Dorothy Canfield Fisher had first met Pershing when he was teaching at the University of Nebraska, where her father was chancellor. She met him again years later, during World War I, in France and was struck by his manner, which she found "hard, intent, stern, like a doctor called to a sickroom." Pershing's AEF subordinates saw him much the same way: "cold, hard-bitten, unreasonable, petty, rigid." He came down hard on "the slightest sign of sloppy housekeeping in billets," and he took "harsh notice of muddy shoes or headgear not set right." In fact, his "men found him forbidding and menacing. Most soldiers were afraid of him and were sometimes too nervous to answer coherently when questioned about the quality of their meals." Laurence Stallings, a junior AEF officer who, after the war, collaborated with Maxwell Anderson on the 1924 World War I play *What Price Glory?*, remarked on his hard eyes and set thin lips. He called him the "Iron Commander." As another writer, the journalist Heywood Broun, commented, "They will never call him 'Papa' Pershing. . . . He can read a man's soul through his boots or his buttons."[3]

●

Unscathed in battle, Pershing was stricken with malaria during his Cuban service and invalided home in August 1898 to recover. He was then sent to longer-term convalescence behind a desk at the War Department. This led to his appointment as chief of the Bureau of Insular Affairs, the War Department division that oversaw civil administration of US territories, from September 1898 to August 1899, when he requested an active-duty posting to the Philippines. Pershing served on northern Mindanao from December 1899 to May 1903, where he was engaged in the pacification of the Moros, members of the Muslim population of the islands, who resisted American authority. He employed a combination of respectful negotiation and harsh military tactics to suppress the so-called Moro Rebellion. On one occasion, under his command—but not by his order—US soldiers publicly buried some Moro fighters in the same grave with a dead pig, a severe affront to any faithful Muslim. This led to an urban myth, perpetuated by Donald Trump (first as candidate and then as president) that Pershing personally executed forty-nine "Muslim terrorists" with bullets dipped in pig's blood and then set the fiftieth free to spread the word about what had been done.[4]

Pershing returned to Washington and staff duty shortly before his marriage to Helen Francis Warren on January 25, 1905. From March 5, 1905 to September of 1906, Pershing was stationed in Japan as a military attaché and observer in the Russo-Japanese War (1904–1905). The assignment turned out to be a breakthrough opportunity for Pershing's career. It brought him into contact with President Theodore Roosevelt, who, greatly impressed with Captain Pershing, caused his promotion—in a single leap over many, more senior, officers—to brigadier general on September 20, 1906.

From December 1906 to June 1908, Pershing was back in the Philippines, commanding a brigade at Fort McKinley, near Manila. He then accepted an appointment as military commander of Moro Province in the Philippines in November 1909 and served in this most demanding post until early 1914, during which time he continually conducted small-scale operations against recalcitrant Moro rebels.

●

In April 1914, Pershing was assigned command of the 8th Brigade, in San Francisco, but, with civil war raging in Mexico, he was almost immediately dispatched to Fort Bliss, with headquarters in El Paso, Texas, on the Mexican border. On August 27, 1915, he received a telegram with the news that his wife and three daughters—Mary (age three), Anne (age seven), and Helen (age eight)—had all died of smoke inhalation when fire swept through their quarters at the Presidio in San Francisco. Francis Warren, Pershing's six-year-old son, survived. Although those who knew him believed that he was devastated, Pershing also exhibited that crushed-ice temperament others had recognized. He dutifully attended the four funerals at Lakeview Cemetery in Cheyenne, Wyoming (where his wife's family lived), and then returned to Fort Bliss with his son and with his sister May, who had volunteered to help look after the boy. He plunged back into his duties as commanding officer, even as condolences from prominent figures continued to pour in.

Among those who sent sympathetic telegrams was Francisco "Pancho" Villa. Less than a year later, on March 9, 1916, this famous—or infamous—revolutionary and social bandit ordered four of his subordinates, Francisco Beltrán, Candelario Cervantes, Nicolás Fernández, and Pablo López, to lead a party of some five hundred men in a raid against Columbus, New Mexico, which was garrisoned by elements of the US 13th Cavalry Regiment. The raiders burned a swath of the town and killed seven or eight troopers (sources vary) as well as ten civilian residents before withdrawing back across the border. President Wilson responded to the raid by sending ten thousand troops under Pershing into Mexico in pursuit of Villa. This so-called Punitive Expedition began on March 14, 1916. At the cost of 15 US soldiers killed, 28 wounded, and 3 missing, the expedition managed to kill 169 Villistas (soldiers loyal to Villa) and 82 Carrancistas (soldiers loyal to Mexican president Venustiano Carranza), wounding or capturing a few others, before the mission was ended on February 7, 1917. Villa evaded his pursuers.

●

The pursuit of Villa had been called off in part because it proved fruitless, but even more because of the growing likelihood of going to war against Germany. As explained in chapter 4, Frederick Funston was Woodrow Wilson's first choice for command of the AEF in the coming war, but his sudden death on February 19, 1917, thrust Pershing into the forefront of consideration. He was summoned to a single brief interview with the president, who, acting on the advice of other senior army commanders, summarily appointed Pershing to command the AEF on May 10, 1917. At this point, Pershing was a major general (two stars). To underscore the magnitude of his new assignment, he was once again given a leapfrog promotion to full general (four stars), the first Regular Army officer appointed to this rank since Philip Sheridan in 1888.

His mission was as staggering in its dimensions as that of George Washington's in that he was ultimately responsible for creating an effective fighting army. He was charged with leading the organization, training, and supply of a force that was being grown from about two hundred thousand men to some four million—of whom more than two million would serve overseas as part of the AEF. Pershing went into war fully understanding that he actually had two wars to fight. There was, of course, the Germans—"the Hun"—a force that had not only held out against the combined French, British, and Russian armies but had, though badly depleted, gained the upper hand against them. The second enemy was the high command of both the British and French forces. Both Wilson and Secretary of War Baker had given Pershing absolute authority over the AEF, and they supported his insistence that the AEF operate as an independent American army under American command. As mentioned in chapter 4, while the French were initially in agreement that the AEF needed to operate as an independent army, the British wanted a half million American soldiers to be, for all practical purposes, absorbed into the BEF. Pershing stood firm against this—and he prevailed. Quite soon, however, both the British and the French would be clamoring for American forces to be committed to battle well before they were ready in sufficient numbers to operate cohesively as more than mere replacements and certain cannon fodder. Almost up until the Armistice of November 11, 1918, Pershing would have to resist the piecemeal use of the AEF by the Allies. Even so, he would find himself compelled to make some compromises.

One was made even before he departed for France with his headquarters staff from Governors Island in New York Harbor in May 1917. As Black Jack, Pershing had not only commanded African American troops but he had come to respect them as tough fighting men, especially during the concluding phase of the Plains Indian war. He was outspoken in his admiration—yet, before he departed, he resolved not to advocate for their full participation on the battlefield in France. They would be consigned, as they had been since the Civil War, to segregated units and reserved mostly for logistics, support, and labor assignments rather than deployed as frontline troops. Clearly, Pershing did not want to pick a fight with the mass of white America or with the president, an unreconstructed Southerner when it came to matters of racial segregation.

●

Pershing bowed to the French request to make some show of American force as quickly as possible—not to the Germans, but to the people of France. A portion of the Sixteenth Infantry paraded through the streets of Paris soon after Pershing and his headquarters party arrived. Although it was Pershing's aide, Colonel Charles E. Stanton, who spoke the memorable line, "Lafayette, we are here," General Pershing made certain that he was photographed saluting the grave of the marquis.

From August 1917 through October 1918, Pershing directed the American buildup in France. In view of limitations of transport and time required for training and supply, Pershing sent the War Department a report that no more than 420,000 men could be ready to fight by the end of 1917 and no significant US force could be sent into combat before February 1918. It was a test of Pershing's character that he was able to cling to reality under the tremendous pressure of his desperate Allies. By the end of 1917, the British and French armies had suffered combined casualties of 5.8 million killed and wounded. German losses during that period were 3,349,000 killed and wounded.

On December 13, 1916, Joseph "Papa" Joffre, who had taken the French armies into World War I, was replaced by Robert Nivelle as commander in chief of the Armies of North and Northeast. Nivelle had no compunction when it came to spending men. In contrast to Joffre, who favored what he called a strategy of "biting" at the enemy in the hope of nibbling it away, Nivelle favored all-out offensives, including the Anglo-French "Nivelle Offensive," which began on April 9, 1917, when the British attacked Arras in the northeastern corner of France. The battle began well but bogged down by the middle of May at the cost of 158,000 British Empire troops. At the same time, Nivelle launched his own portion of the offensive with 1.2 million men on the BEF's right flank. From the start, the result was disaster, and, by the end, 187,000 French *poilus* had been killed or wounded. Nivelle did manage to capture some 21,000 German prisoners, but total German losses, including those prisoners in addition to killed and wounded, were 163,000, and Nivelle had made almost no advance against the German front. The French government and the French people sunk into despair and desperation. Worse, during the first three weeks of May, the French army was increasingly paralyzed by mass mutiny, which eventually affected sixteen French army corps.

Pershing was fully aware that the Allies had ample reason for their desperation. He believed that the failure of the Nivelle Offensive and the widespread mutinies did make it likely that the Germans would, sooner or later, break the stalemate on the Western Front. He saw that the Allies were running short of men, and he understood that the incoming Americans could stiffen their thinning ranks. Pershing even accepted that throwing in American soldiers as quickly as possible and putting them under British and French command would stave off Allied defeat. But, far more important, he understood that throwing away his soldiers like that would not win the war.

Pershing had a plan for victory, not merely for the delay of defeat. The plan required that he build an army of one million men *before* sending a single American soldier into combat. Moreover, this million-man combat force had to fight as an independent American unit. It could not be diluted and diminished by absorption into the Allied ranks. Whatever else Pershing achieved in the Great War, his first victory was ensuring that the AEF would not be frittered away in a vain attempt to merely postpone defeat.

Most historians who write about Pershing go no further than describing his determination to defend the integrity of the US forces. In fact, his strategic thinking was more complex than this. Even as he fought for autonomy, he worked earnestly with his British and French counterparts to create what they, on their own, had failed to achieve—productive unity of command, the concept that the Allies on the Western Front would operate under the final authority of a Supreme War Council headed by a single commander. It was the great paradox of Pershing's arrival that he was willing to incur the ire of both the British and the French by refusing to squander his forces to help them even as he promoted the creation of the Supreme War Council in November 1917 to forge a single great instrument of battle out of three disparate armies.

●

While General Pershing worked to coordinate with the Allies, he ensured that his AEF would have an ample sector in which to operate both independently and in coordination with the British (figure 18) and the French. Pershing ordered his staff to make a reconnaissance of the Lorraine region, south and southwest of Nancy. This sector was well positioned to receive supplies and incoming troops, and it offered promising potential as ground from which a decisive AEF offensive could be launched once the buildup was complete. The reconnaissance team recommended that the AEF assume the section of the Allied line from St. Mihiel to Belfort and that principal training areas be laid out in and around Gondrecourt and Neufchâteau. Pershing's choice of sector was also influenced by a French recommendation to place US troops in

Figure 18. American troops marching through London, cross Westminster Bridge, with the Houses of Parliament in the background. NATIONAL ARCHIVES AND RECORDS ADMINISTRATION

the eastern half of the Allied line. After all, the BEF needed to remain on the Allied northern flank, so that it could guard the Channel ports, which not only were the logistical link between Britain and the Continent but were a line of retreat and escape, should the Germans finally make a decisive breakthrough on the Western Front. As for the French, it was imperative that they be positioned to protect all approaches to Paris, the heart and soul of France; this position was on the BEF's right flank. What, then, was left for Pershing but Lorraine? It now, therefore, became the Allied southern flank.

●

Once General Pershing was satisfied with the position of the AEF along the Western Front, he and his staff turned to the tactical organization of the force. Pershing himself wanted the AEF to be positioned for major offensive operations aimed at achieving what the British and French had, in three years of fighting, failed to achieve: a sustained, war-winning breakthrough. His idea was to drive the enemy from the trenches and force a sudden transition from a war of stalemate to a war of movement in which, Pershing was convinced, the American army would prevail.

Again, paradoxically, Pershing's General Organization Project, according to which he and his staff proposed to build the million-man field army of five corps of thirty divisions, as discussed in chapter 4, was much less about mobility than about creating staying power for prolonged combat. This meant that Pershing was less interested in making many separate attacks than in mounting a truly massive offensive for a penetration that would be both deep and broad. Whereas the British, the French, and, for that matter, the Germans had tended to throw everything they had against one another in the hope of achieving an overwhelming breakthrough, Pershing created formations that allowed for lead units to be continuously relieved by units advancing from behind. This degree of depth was lacking in the plans of the other two Allies. Pershing's idea of an offensive was less to pierce the enemy line and advance through it once than to apply constant pressure against the enemy. Eventually, the dam would fail and burst, the trench war would become a war of movement, and the movement would be out of France and into Germany.

Pershing's thinking represented a historic innovation for the US Army. For most of its existence, the American army was organized on a regimental model drawn from the days of Napoleon and even earlier. From the regiment, Pershing stepped up to the division, which he established at a strength of 25,484 men. This made the US division twice as large as the French and British divisions. More importantly, Pershing's AEF introduced the modern corps and the modern field army. Organizational units of this size enabled the degree of coordination necessary to create sufficient depth to sustain the pressure of a massive offensive.

The AEF organization plan for a field army called for a headquarters of about 150 officers and men. Within the army, each corps would have an even larger headquarters, of about 350 officers and men. Both the field army and the corps would have their own combat arms that operated independently of the attached divisions. Each corps was directly assigned a brigade of heavy artillery and an engineer regiment as well as cavalry, antiaircraft, signal, and support units. The field army would have its own artillery organization of twenty-four regiments as well as large engineer, military police, and supply units. Each corps would also include some 19,000 support troops, and each field army would have 120,000. This was an aspect of planning for sustained offensive combat operations, as were base divisions organized to feed the field armies with a steady stream of trained, combat-ready replacements. Initially, the replacements would come from the base divisions, but as the war continued, the base divisions would accept incoming troops from the United States, oversee their training, and then feed them forward to the front lines.

●

With the mechanics of sustained offensive combat established, Pershing's staff formulated a strategic study, which it delivered in September 1917. It was a comprehensive outline of the prospects going forward of the war in Europe. The staff analysts agreed that Allied losses had been so heavy in 1917 that the British and French would be incapable of launching any major offensive in 1918—even (Pershing believed) with the Americans now in the war. The staff also concluded that it would be impossible to get a US force of offensive strength into France and battle-ready before early 1919. The strategy for 1918, therefore, would be defensive—meeting and overcoming any and all German offensives—while perhaps executing some very limited offensive initiatives, such as reducing the St. Mihiel salient, a strong German position that bulged into the Allied lines at St. Mihiel in the Meuse department of northeastern France. Pushing this salient back—reducing it—would reclaim territory from which future advances could be made.

For 1919, the AEF planners proposed a grand, war-winning offensive along the entire Western Front. While the British and French targeted German communication and economic objectives in the north, the AEF would press northeast from Lorraine along the Metz-Saarbrücken axis. This would be a forty-five-mile advance northeast from Nancy, which, in due course, would sever the two railroads running from Strasbourg to Metz and to Thionville. At the same time, French forces would cut rail lines north of Metz, thereby cutting off the German forces from supply via Lorraine. Moreover, the German left wing would be cut off from the right wing, thereby forcing the Germans to begin a withdrawal from positions in France and Belgium.

The US advance against Metz was intended to be the spearhead of the Allies' entire final Western Front (map 1) operation. General Pershing was offering a plan by which the United States would create the victory that had eluded France and Britain since 1914. As Pershing saw it, the US Army would not let itself be used as a stopgap. The only acceptable role for the American forces was to win the war.

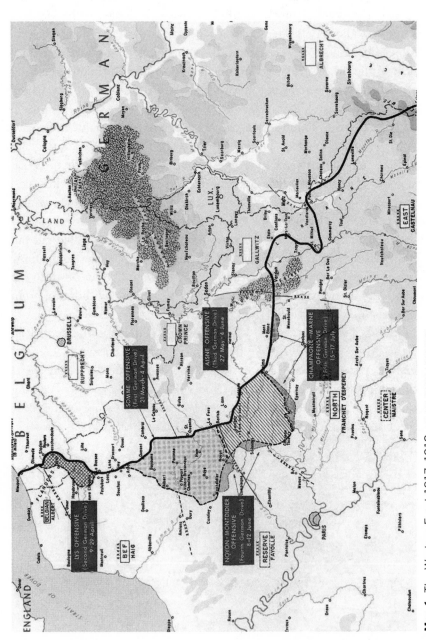

Map 1. The Western Front 1917–1918. US MILITARY ACADEMY

Part II

The American Campaigns

CHAPTER 6

First Blood

Cambrai and the Somme Defensive, November 20–
December 4, 1917, and March 21–April 6, 1918

DURING WORLD WAR II, GENERAL GEORGE S. PATTON JR. ENFORCED
on his great Third Army the doctrine that every soldier—from cook
to line infantryman—was, first and last, a rifleman. An army is tradi-
tionally divided into a "tooth" and a "tail." The frontline combat troops
whose business it is to engage the enemy directly are the tooth, and
the support and logistics troops, who perform the myriad rear-echelon
functions that enable the frontline army to live and to fight, are the tail.
Patton held that in any large and desperate clash of army against army,
the distinction between tooth and tail did not apply. Everyone was and
had to be a warrior.

CAMBRAI: AN UNLIKELY BAPTISM OF FIRE
In World War I, the Battle of Cambrai (November 20–December 4,
1917) proved this doctrine (which Patton would articulate years later)
to General John J. Pershing and the growing body of soldiers that
was the AEF. Troops of the AEF fought at Cambrai for the first time
in World War I. The units involved were never intended to be frontline combat soldiers. They were elements of the 11th, 12th, and 14th
Regiments of Engineers, which, in response to the pleas of British
commander in charge Sir Douglas Haig, were attached to the British
Third Army in the Cambrai area (map 2). They were railroad engineers,

assigned to lay track and organize the rail transportation of a new weapon in the Great War: the tank.

Few senior military officers had much faith in this armored novelty. Indeed, the Germans, who had developed a number of advanced weapons and who would design some of the greatest tanks of World War II, lagged behind both the British and the French in tank development, fielding only one model, the A7V, in all of World War I. But, in Britain, the tank had one very highly placed champion. In January 1915, Winston Churchill, at the time First Lord of the Admiralty, recommended to Prime Minister H. H. Asquith that a "committee of engineering officers and other experts" be convened to develop "special mechanical devices for taking trenches." This, Churchill argued, was the only way to break the Western Front stalemate of trench warfare. After just six months, in June 1915, a lieutenant colonel of engineers, Ernest D. Swinton, drew up a set of requirements for an armored fighting vehicle capable of overcoming entrenched machine guns. He specified that the machine have the ability to scale a five-foot ledge, span a five-foot trench, have a range of twenty miles, weigh about eight tons, and accommodate a ten-man crew to operate two machine guns and one field gun. The army wasn't at all interested, but Churchill took on the project on behalf of the Royal Navy and referred to the vehicle accordingly as a "landship." The prototype, dubbed Little Willie, made its debut on September 19, 1915. A larger model followed. Christened by the Royal Navy HMS *Centipede*, the larger tank was better known as Big Willie or, strangely enough, Mother.[1]

Mother performed none too well, but marginally well enough to enter production as the Mark I. Equipped with caterpillar tracks instead of wheels, the Mark I could conquer most obstacles and span most trenches. It was mostly impervious to small-arms fire, including the machine gun— unless a lucky shot happened to strike one of its fuel tanks. The Mark I would be deployed at Cambrai, Haig desperately hoping that it would be instrumental in breaking through the German trenches.

●

Field Marshal Haig badly needed a victory. Under the Second Army (commanded by Sir Herbert Plumer), the Battle of Messines (June 7–14,

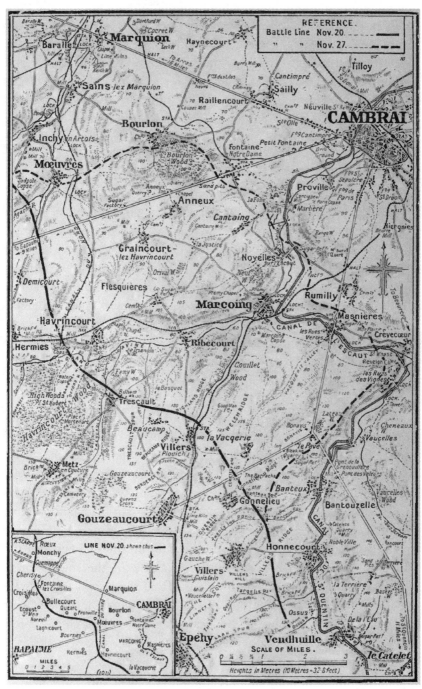

Map 2. Cambrai Area, 1917. WIKIMEDIA

1917) in Flanders had been deemed a victory. Although costly—24,562 British casualties versus about 25,000 on the German side—it drove the Germans off their high-ground position and forced them to rush reserves up from the Arras and Aisnes fronts. This took significant pressure off the French, who fought on the portion of front that was to the south of the British positions. Most important at Messines, the Germans were unable to mount a counterattack. Contrary to the usual dismal pattern on the Western Front, in which one side prevailed only to soon suffer a vigorous counterattack and lose what it had gained, the captured high ground of the Messines-Wytschaete ridge remained in British hands.

The victory was as heavenly manna to the government of Britain's prime minister David Lloyd George. He ordered Haig to next take Passchendaele and thereby seize control of the high ground south and east of Ypres, a Belgian city in West Flanders. Also called the Third Battle of Ypres, the Battle of Passchendaele stretched from July 31 to November 10, 1917, and did not repeat the success of Messines. One major hindrance was the impact of the French army mutinies, which left Haig and the British on their own. In addition, Haig was slow to organize the main assault, and the delay between the advances achieved at the Battle of Messines and the Battle of Passchendaele blunted the effectiveness of the British assault.

And there was yet more British blundering. Although the assault began with the biggest preparatory artillery barrage of the entire war—65,000 artillery shells lobbed from 3,091 guns—the fire fell mostly on the ground over which the British troops were to advance. The heavily cratered earth was pounded by the heaviest rains the region had seen in three decades, the no-man's-land becoming an all-but-impassable swamp. Fatally slowed down, the attackers became targets for German defensive fire that had been well prepared during the lull between the Messines and Passchendaele operations. Stuck in the mud, British soldiers were cut down by machine guns from the trenches and strafing fire from German aircraft. As if this weren't enough, the Germans unleashed a newly developed chemical weapon, mustard gas, a caustic aerosol that caused severe burns on contact with skin, eyes, and the lining of the lungs (figure 19).

Figure 19. Doughboys had their first experience with chemical warfare in the Great War. The US Army had its own chemical units and made liberal offensive use of "poison gas" against the Germans. NATIONAL ARCHIVES AND RECORDS ADMINISTRATION

The assault was a testament to a combination of bad luck and inept command, but it was also a testament to the incredible grit of British soldier. The infantry took Passchendaele Ridge as well as Passchendaele village by November 6. The gain of five miles cost 300,000 British dead and wounded, plus 8,528 French casualties. German losses were also high, at 260,000, but Haig fell under heavy criticism from the British public and many politicians. As he was about to launch the attack at Cambrai,

France, about fifty miles south of the Belgian battleground, Haig could do no more than hope for the best.

General J. H. G. Byng's Third Army was the instrument of attack, and for the first time in the war, large numbers of tanks—some two hundred—formed part of the advance. They had been delivered to the front by the US engineers, and, despite many breakdowns and other failures, the new weapons punched a five-mile-wide breach into the so-called Hindenburg Line, the principal German entrenchments. General Byng sent in a combination of cavalry—yes, cavalry was still a mainstay of the British Army—and infantry. The Germans had been stunned, dismayed, and demoralized by the ease with which the tanks had rolled over and through their trenches. Now, however, as the British were just beginning to exploit the breach, those same vehicles, which had seemed so fearsome, began breaking down in large numbers. German reinforcements rushed in to plug the gap, which the British cavalry and infantry, were simply unable to re-breach.

Greatly discouraged, on December 3, Haig ordered a partial withdrawal. The assault had cost each side some forty-five thousand casualties, killed, wounded, or taken prisoner. By comparison, the number of Americans killed or captured was slight—seventeen—but the action did occasion a letter of praise to General Pershing from no less than General Haig.

Dear General Pershing:

GENERAL HEADQUARTERS BRITISH ARMIES IN FRANCE,

December 6, 1917.

I have much pleasure in forwarding herewith for your information a copy of a report submitted to me by General Byng, Commanding the British Third Army, on the gallant conduct of the companies of the American 11th Engineers (Railway), in and near Gouzeaucourt on November 30.

I desire to express to you my thanks and that of the British forces engaged for the prompt and valuable assistance rendered, and I trust that you will be good enough to convey to Colonel Hoffman and his gallant men how much we all appreciate his and their prompt and soldierly readiness to assist in what, for a time, was a difficult situation. I much regret the losses suffered by these companies.[2]

General Byng reported:

1. *Two and one-half companies of the American 11th Engineers (Railway) . . . having an effective strength of 8 officers and 365 O. R., were employed by me, during the recent operations, on broad-gauge [railroad] construction.*

2. *At 7 a.m., on November 30, 4 officers and 280 men of this regiment were employed at the GOUZEAUCOURT yard in railway construction.*

3. *At 7:15 a.m., the hostile barrage came down onto GOUZEAU-COURT. About 7:30 a.m., Major Burbank, who was in command, ordered a general retirement. This was effected in the face of artillery and machine-gun fire at the cost of a number of casualties.*

    A certain number of men who had taken refuge in dugouts, were cut off by the German infantry. Some of these managed to effect their escape and at once joined up with British units and fought with them throughout the day.

    About 7 a.m., FINS, where the remainder of the men were, began to be heavily shelled. The order was given for the men still remaining in the camp (about 85) to scatter in the fields.

4. *The whole party was then assembled under their officers and fell in. Arms and 200 rounds of ammunition were served out to each man. By noon, 7 officers and 265 men were present for duty.*

5. *The O. C. Regiment reported to the Headquarters 20th Division, at SOREL offering the services of his detachment for duty wherever most required, and asked for orders. He was ordered to assemble his force as a reserve.*

    At 3 p.m., the party was employed in digging trenches close behind our line. By 6 p.m., these trenches were finished to a depth of 4 feet.

6. *I desire to draw attention to the initiative shown by Colonel Hoff-man, and to express my thanks to the 11th Engineers (Railway) for the assistance they rendered to this army at a critical period in the day's operations.*[3]

Colonel G. M. Hoffman sent his own report to General Pershing on December 8, 1917. He pointed out that the men of the 11th Engineers were "unarmed and the attack (a complete surprise) was accompanied by heavy shell and machine-gun fire both from enemy troops and numerous low-flying aeroplanes." Although casualties were over 10 percent, "the retirement was effected in an orderly manner and with coolness which has received praise from British officers present."[4]

The 11th Engineers were the unlikely recipients of America's baptism of fire on the Western Front. Although they were not a combat unit, they operated trains and repaired track almost continuously under enemy artillery fire. They also delivered ammunition, under machine-gun fire, to an artillery battery located within five hundred yards of the German outpost fortifications. At one point, on November 30, during a major German counterattack, the enemy advance swept past one of the American crews, the members of which managed to conceal themselves rather than surrender—which would have been the "sensible" thing to do, vastly outnumbered as they were.

SOMME DEFENSIVE
The Battle of the Somme (map 3) spanned July 1 to November 18, 1916, before the United States entered what was then the European War. The operation had been conceived by the French and British as a massive offensive to draw off German manpower from the Verdun sector, where the French were being slaughtered in defense of the complex of fortresses and fortifications in and around the ancient city of Verdun. Beyond relieving pressure on Verdun, Joseph "Papa" Joffre, at the time the general in chief of the French army, insisted that France had to go on the offensive. Its honor, its very soul, depended on it. The British commander in charge, Douglas Haig, was not optimistic about the outcome of the great operation, but he felt obliged to serve his ally. In the end, after more than

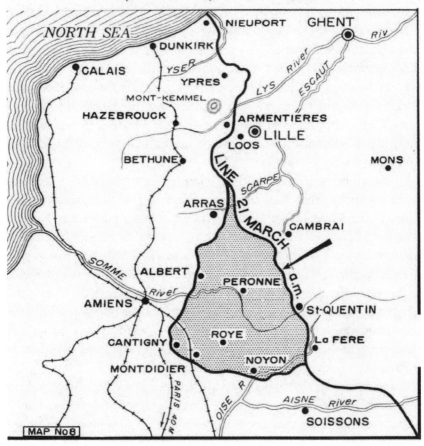

Map 3. Somme Defensive. US ARMY CENTER FOR MILITARY HISTORY

five months of continuous combat, Haig managed to claw out an advance of some six miles into German-held French territory. The cost had been 420,000 Britons killed or wounded (70,000 men per mile gained). French losses were had been just under 200,000. The Germans suffered a catastrophic 650,000 casualties. Much as the French had refused to yield ground at Verdun, the Germans held onto French territory along the Somme beyond all rationality.

The consensus of historians is that the Somme, an orgy of devastation, had ended inconclusively. Kaiser Wilhelm II was appalled by the losses, both at the Somme and Verdun. He might have contemplated earnestly seeking a negotiated peace—the very "peace without victory" that Woodrow Wilson, still pursuing a policy of neutrality, urged upon the belligerents. But the likely collapse of Russia and the insistence of his top commanders kept the kaiser going. The following year, czarist Russia disintegrated in revolution and, during October and November 1917, the Austro-German victory over Italy at the Battle of Caporetto gave Germany numerical superiority on the Western Front—at least until the newly arrived and arriving Americans were ready to be committed to battle.

The German emperor and the German high command were at an inflection point. They had a narrow window to push the reeling Anglo-French forces over before the Americans became a presence to be reckoned with. Even as its manpower reservoir dwindled, even as its economy, drained by war and choked by a British naval blockade, was bringing its people to the brink of starvation, the German army needed to mount a decisive offensive that would break the Allies before the Americans arrived in force. Erich Ludendorff, by this time the ruling generalissimo of Germany, was prepared to combine newly massed artillery tactics with new patterns of infantry attack, whereby troops sought to infiltrate the weak points in the Allied lines, in a decisive offensive.

On March 21, 1918, the offensive began against the hard-won British positions along the Somme. A titanic artillery barrage was loosed, after which no fewer than sixty-two German divisions probed, breached, and smashed the British line, achieving a spectacular penetration along a fifty-mile-wide front. Ludendorff targeted Amiens, the communications hub on the Somme that marked the contact point between the British right flank and the French left. Seize and hold Amiens, and the Germans could split the French and British armies. As commanders on both sides well knew, the strategy of divide and conquer had stood the test of time like no other.

Field Marshal Haig was not a charismatic commander. Indeed, many of his men resented what they believed was his prodigal, even psychopathic, willingness to spend their lives. Yet, down to the captains and the privates, the British realized the cost of defeat, and the BEF rallied to the defense of Amiens. Within days, before the end of March, Ludendorff's all-out offensive was bogging down. Not everyone on the British side appreciated this fact at the time. For the Germans had won a significant tactical victory, having advanced forty miles in eight days—on a Western Front where progress was characteristically measured in yards or meters. Along the way, the Germans had taken seventy thousand prisoners and inflicted some two hundred thousand other Allied casualties, killed or wounded. Nevertheless, the German offensive ended as a strategic failure. Despite their casualties, the Allied armies remained intact and in contact with one another.

At this point, General Pershing and his still embryonic army could offer no strategic assistance and precious little tactical help. Pershing did make one compromise, however. Although General Henri-Philippe Pétain, soon to replace Robert Nivelle as commander in chief of the French army, agreed with Pershing on the wisdom of fielding all American divisions under American command in an independent American I Corps, Pershing, on March 25, offered him any AEF division that could be of immediate service, even if this meant postponing the creation of I Corps. To his credit, Pétain resisted yielding to panic. Instead of feeding an American division willy-nilly into the meat grinder, he proposed using the American troops to relieve French divisions that were posted in quiet sectors, so that these seasoned French divisions would be freed up for action against the Germans on the Somme. Pershing agreed. At the same time, Field Marshal Haig asked the American general for the use of any available heavy artillery or engineer units. Pershing responded that he did not yet have heavy artillery, but he dispatched three engineer regiments north, to the BEF sector.

Pershing's more flexible attitude toward cooperation with the Allies was one positive result of the German offensive. Earlier, the mere prospect of such offensives—following the Italian defeat at Caporetto in November 1917—had moved the British and French leaders to create with the United States the Supreme War Council to coordinate actions and strategy across the Western Front. Thus, when the Ludendorff offensive smashed into the Somme line, all three Allies agreed to appoint one commander to coordinate the Somme Defensive. The man chosen was French general Ferdinand Foch. At first, his assignment was to coordinate forces around the Amiens salient. This evolved into coordinating all Allied land forces, including the Americans. His brief fell short of full command authority, but Foch was an extraordinarily forceful and charismatic leader. He quickly won the respect—and compliance—of General Pershing.

As at Cambrai, US Army participation in the Somme Defensive was mainly restricted to engineers. When the Ludendorff offensive smashed through the British lines near Peronne on March 21, 1918, it was the US Army 6th Engineers Regiment that hurriedly built bridges to move the British Fifth Army. Haig, however, also drew on Companies B and D of the Sixth Engineers to help occupy the old French trenches, which were dubbed the Armies Defense Line. The assembled force, which included British troops plus the two engineer companies, was generally referred to as "Carey's Force," after Major-General George Glas Sandeman Carey, the Briton who commanded the Amiens Defense Line.

In addition to the 6th Engineers, elements of the US 12th and 14th Engineers Regiments as well as the 17th, 22nd, 28th, and 148th US Army Aero Squadrons also participated in combat activities. The action, however, was on a small scale and is most thoroughly documented for Companies B and D of 6th Engineers.

The 6th Engineers had arrived in France on December 20, 1917, having embarked from the United States on December 4. On February 10, 1918, Companies B and D, along with regimental headquarters troops, boarded trains for Peronne, to conduct heavy bridge construction. The work was interrupted on March 20 by the initial attacks of the German offensive. The engineers' first order of business was to mine the bridges they had just built in order to deprive the enemy of their use. During this work, on March 22, Peronne was under heavy artillery bombardment, forcing the engineers to pull back to Chaulnes.

Here, another major task faced them. A detail of three engineer officers and twenty-three soldiers set about preparing the mammoth British Fifth Army engineer dump for destruction—again, to prevent

German capture of useful materials. The rest of Companies B and D, some 15 officers and 530 men, were put to work building hasty defenses near Demuin, after which, on March 27, the engineers hopped trucks for a distribution depot near Warfusee-Abancourt east of the town of Villers-Bretonneux. Here they were issued British Enfield rifles and sent to a frontline trench as ordinary infantry. This may be the first use of US troops as ordinary infantry riflemen in Europe. From March 27 to April 3, the engineers held the portion of trench they had been assigned. It was especially hazardous duty, since the trenches they occupied were unfinished and shallow, having been little more than traced in the earth. The engineers-turned-riflemen turned engineers again long enough to complete the excavation of the trenches—work that was done under continuous machine-gun and rifle fire. Added to this, for the first four days, was intense artillery bombardment (figure 20).

On March 29, following one especially heavy artillery barrage, the Germans charged the sector and were successfully repulsed. A relief party

Figure 20. American sector under artillery bombardment—location and date unknown. WIKIMEDIA

was dispatched to rescue the engineers but was almost entirely wiped out before it reached them. It was not until April 3 that the detachment was relieved and allowed to rest for two days near Amiens before being sent, on April 6, to begin laying plank roads and building heavy bridges in front of the city. The idea was to facilitate moving heavy artillery to the rear in the event of more attacks.

●

The participation of the US engineers both at Cambrai and in the Somme Defensive is typically ignored in accounts of the AEF or is described as action that was "minor" and "ad hoc." It was, in fact, hard labor under frontline fire—with some intervals served as trench-fighting riflemen. At the very least, Cambrai and the Somme Defensive demonstrated a willingness and ability to fight in sectors that were subjected to heavy and determined German assault. Little noticed, the experience in the waning days of 1917 and early spring of 1918 boded well for the battle-readiness of the US Army, which would be prepared to fight on a strategic level well before the 1919 deadline General Pershing had set.

CHAPTER 7

Lys

April 9–27, 1918

ALTHOUGH THE GERMAN OFFENSIVE ON THE SOMME WAS CHECKED strategically, the tactical advances the enemy made in March and April prompted British and French commanders once again to pressure Pershing to release AEF troops—any troops who were even remotely ready to be sent into a trench. The new Supreme War Council prepared a document designated Joint Note No. 18, which assigned priority of British sea transport to shipping American infantry regiments at the expense of other divisional elements—artillery, cavalry, engineers, support troops, and so on. The British went even further, asking that transportation be limited to riflemen and machine-gun crews, not even complete infantry units, for all of April through July. General Pershing folded his arms. He insisted that all American divisions be shipped intact, as complete operational units, with all proper divisional components.

As the Germans continued to press their offensive, the Allies argued in separate negotiations conducted in London, Washington, and France, and often at cross-purposes. Through it all, Pershing retreated only slightly. In April, in conference with Lord Alfred Milner, the new British war minister, he agreed to a modification of the earlier six-division plan whereby British vessels would transport six complete American divisions to train with Marshal Haig's armies. Now Pershing accepted a change that allowed all the infantrymen—riflemen and machine gunners—to be transported first (map 4).

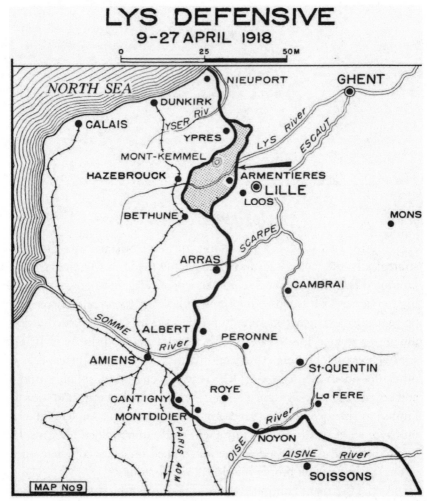

Map 4. Lys Defensive Operations. US ARMY CENTER FOR MILITARY HISTORY

As for Ludendorff's offensive on the Somme, it had bogged down by April 5, but by this time the Germans had succeeded in pushing a forty-mile-wide salient into the Allied lines. Marshal Ferdinand Foch, the newly appointed head of the Supreme War Council, shifted French reserves to check the German advance at Montdidier. This timely shift was critical in rendering the offensive a strategic failure despite its significant, forty-mile-wide tactical success.

●

Neither the Allies nor Erich Ludendorff seem to have appreciated the extent to which the German offensive had fallen short of its strategic objective, which had been to achieve a permanent breakthrough that would separate the British line from the French line. The Allies were alarmed by the German advance and were, accordingly, angered by what they regarded as Pershing's destructive obstinacy. As for Ludendorff, he was sufficiently pleased with the results of the costly offensive to double down on it. His obsessive focus was now to inflict as much loss on the British and French as possible before the Americans could enter the war in force. He therefore launched what was code-named the Georgette Offensive against British positions at the Lys River, which formed part of the Franco-Belgian border.

The offensive had significant strategic stakes in that it directly threatened the English Channel ports, which were the operational lifeline between Britain and France. The impact of the German first-wave attacks was devastating. A Portuguese division fighting under British control in the sector was all but entirely wiped out. This was terrible in itself, but it also opened a gap that immediately threatened the British flank. Key to defending an entrenched position is protecting the flanks of the army. If an enemy can get around the flank—outflank the defender—he can bring to bear the full force of an attack against the defender's side and rear, places where massed defensive firepower is not available. The enemy might even be able to envelope the defenders and "roll them up," depriving them of room to maneuver, creating chaos, and causing heavy losses.

Indeed, on April 9, the situation quickly turned critical. After three hours, during the initial attack, the German Sixth Army broke through the gap in the British line in Flanders on a twelve-mile front along the Lys River, south of Ypres. The enemy reached open country *behind* the British rear lines. The defense began collapsing at several points, and it was looking as if the BEF in this sector would in fact be enveloped, rolled up, and perhaps destroyed.

As it turned out, by April 12, there was good news and bad news for the BEF. It had managed a more-or-less orderly withdrawal—orderly in that the force, though diminished, remained intact and under command. That was the good news. The bad news was that the BEF had been forced far back from its initial position. The troops were being pushed inexorably toward the English Channel. Once they reached that point, they would have nowhere to go and would therefore be defeated en masse—either wiped out or compelled to surrender.

Sharing in the fate of the BEF were three US Army units, which had been attached to Haig's forces in this operation. They were the US 1st Gas Regiment (30th Engineers Regiment), the 28th Pursuit Squadron of the US Army Air Service, and the 16th Engineers Regiment. The Americans were therefore numbered among the troops to whom Sir Douglas Haig's "Special Order of the Day," issued on April 11, applied. It is among a small handful of truly memorable field orders issued by any commanding officer in World War I. That it was authored by Haig, an officer hardly known for his command presence or battlefield eloquence, let alone his rapport with troops, makes it the more extraordinary. The document would be known as the "backs to the wall" order:

> *To all ranks of the British Army in France and Flanders.*
>
> *Three weeks ago today the enemy began his terrific attacks against us on a 50-mile front. His objects are to separate us from the French, to take the Channel ports, and destroy the British Army.*
>
> *In spite of throwing already 106 Divisions into the battle and enduring the most reckless sacrifice of human life, he has as yet made little progress towards his goals.*
>
> *We owe this to the determined fighting and self-sacrifice of our troops. Words fail me to express the admiration which I feel for the splendid resistance offered by all ranks of our Army under the most trying circumstances.*
>
> *Many amongst us now are tired. To those I would say that Victory will belong to the side which holds out the longest. The French Army is moving rapidly and in great force to our support.*
>
> *There is no other course open to us but to fight it out. Every position must be held to the last man: there must be no retirement. With*

our backs to the wall and believing in the justice of our cause each one of us must fight on to the end. The safety of our homes and the Freedom of mankind alike depend upon the conduct of each one of us at this critical moment.

(Signed) D. Haig F. M.
Commander-in-Chief
British Armies in France[1]

In essence, Marshal Haig was ordering his soldiers to stand, fight, and die. It was hardly an appealing prospect, but, surprisingly, the order succeeded in inspiring the defenders. They stood their ground, and they began to push back, too, so that, by April 29, Ludendorff finally broke off what was his second grand offensive.

The American engineer troops, who had been attached to the British chiefly to build or rebuild rail lines, were hurriedly "armed and equipped with British rifles and bayonets." Reinforcements—additional engineers—were requested, "sent up unarmed by the American Expeditionary Force, and on arrival . . . equipped with [British] rifles, bayonets. scabbards. and slings." The 16th Regiment of railway engineers began laying railroad track on April 9 and completed eighteen miles by the end of the German offensive. The 30th Engineers (Gas and Flame[thrower]) had "participated in front line offensive actions against the enemy for the entire month along the Lys sector" on March 21 and 28. Companies A and B of the 30th Engineers "continued operations with British Expeditionary Forces as stated in March report. Each company was divided into four platoons and each platoon was attached to one of the [BEF] Special Companies." In concert with those companies, the Americans "were actively engaged in gas attacks against the enemy, using projectors, Stokes mortars, and cylinders."[2] This is a revealing example of how the Allies used chemical warfare at this late stage of the war. When "poison gas" was first used on a large scale in 1915, it was deployed using pipeline or hose that was laid into no-man's-land and fed by cylinders. Gas was released against the enemy trenches through these pipelines or hoses. Later, the Allies used Livens projectors, mortar-like weapons that lobbed not gas shells but drums filled with chemical agents. Both of these modes of deploying chemical weapons were handled by engineers. Artillerymen were responsible for firing chemical-filled artillery shells.

The American engineers were withdrawn from the front lines on April 22.

•

Part of B Flight of the US Army Air Service 28th Aero Squadron, which had been attached to the 18th Squadron of the Royal Flying Corps (RFC), was transferred to the RFC 40th Squadron for duty at Lys. American pilots served variously in combat on the Lys front, mainly flying De Havilland 9 "day-bombers" against German artillery positions. Even though powered heavier-than-air flight was "invented" in the United States by the Wright brothers in 1903, American aviation quickly fell behind that of the European countries. In no field was the slow progress of American flight more evident than in the military application of aircraft. Hence, as British reports at Lys put it, the Americans attached to RFC squadrons were still in the process of "receiving . . . their initiation in modern [aerial] warfare" when they pitched in to fly missions with the overtaxed British air service. The Americans' missions were "long-distance day bombing and reconnaissance missions over the lines of the [German] First and Fifth Armies" (figure 21).[3]

•

While the Battle of Lys was under way, an AEF combat division fought its first engagement, although the action was a strictly local operation. During late April, Major General Clarence Edwards's 26th (Yankee) Division was assigned to a quiet sector near St. Mihiel in the Meuse department of the Grand-Este, northeastern France. The quiet was shattered on April 20 when the division came under heavy German artillery fire, which preceded an attack by a German regiment intent on capturing the village of Seicheprey.

The German attackers, 2,800 regulars spearheaded by 600 elite shock troops, pinned down the 26th with the artillery barrage and then launched an infantry assault that overran two US companies. The Ger-

Figure 21. American pilots had a great deal to learn from their French and British instructors. NATIONAL ARCHIVES AND RECORDS ADMINISTRATION

mans occupied the trench line in front of Seicheprey. Edwards ordered a counterattack, which, however, was delayed in getting under way—a problem entirely due to the Americans' lack of experience and, quite possibly, some hesitancy under fire. By the time the counterattack began its advance, the Germans had pulled back. The enemy had lost 160 killed but also took more than 100 American prisoners and inflicted some 669 other casualties, killed and wounded.

●

General Pershing was mortified by the poor showing of the 26th Division, and mortification was one state of being the general found intolerable. He was reportedly furious. The bad news from Seicheprey could not have come at a worse time, when Pershing was fighting the battle over "amalgamation"—absorption of US troops into British and French forces—versus maintaining the independence of the US Army in coherent command units. The Seicheprey fiasco bolstered the Europeans' argument that the Americans were not ready to fight on their own. Specifically, both French and British officers questioned the ability of US commanders, who were unaccustomed to leading anything larger than a regiment, to handle divisions, let alone corps and armies.

In May, a summit of Allied and US leaders—minus President Wilson—was convened at Abbeville, France. Led by the irascible French premier George Clemenceau, the Allied contingent now very pointedly raised the issue of amalgamation—and did not let go of it over the full course of the two-day conference. Everyone present pressed General Pershing to relent and agree to transport only American infantry units—riflemen—while leaving other divisional elements behind—at least through the summer of 1918.

At one point in the conference, an exasperated Marshal Foch demanded of Pershing: "You are willing to risk our being driven back to the Loire?"

If Foch thought it was a rhetorical question, he was mistaken.

"Yes," Pershing replied without hesitation. "I am willing to take the risk. Moreover, the time may come when the American Army will have to stand the brunt of this war, and it is not wise to fritter away our resources in this manner."[4]

Pershing countered Foch by suggesting that the Allies were becoming panicky over the German offensive and overestimating its impact. He implied that this overestimation might be a cynical ploy to bully him into bowing to amalgamation. He insisted that he would not be bullied.

After two bitter days of debate and accusation, Pershing proposed to continue his agreement with Lord Milner—to give infantry units initial priority of transport to France—through the rest of May and all of June. As for when transportation of complete American divisions would begin, it was agreed to table further discussion until the approach of July. By the so-called Abbeville Agreement, it was resolved that British transport vessels would carry 130,000 American infantry troops in May 1918 and another 150,000 in June. American vessels would be used for the shipping of artillery, engineer, and the other support and service troops necessary to build in France an independent US army.

Fortunately for General Pershing and the AEF, the first American combat engagement of the Aisne Campaign (May 27–June 6, 1918), the Battle of Cantigny, would prove far more satisfactory than the humbling at Seicheprey.

CHAPTER 8

Aisne

May 27–June 6, 1918, including the Battle of Cantigny

THE THIRD BATTLE OF THE AISNE WAS PART OF THE SPRING Offensive—or *Kaiserschlacht* ("kaiser's battle")—that Erich Ludendorff had begun in March. Although Ludendorff shared power as Germany's top military leader with Paul von Hindenburg, he was by 1918 Germany's de facto generalissimo. Despite the nation having been brought to the edge of extremity by the war, Ludendorff managed to channel massive resources into a series of all-out offensives that began in the spring of 1918 and continued up to the Armistice of November 11 in that year. The third of his offensives targeted the Chemin des Dames, a ridge running between the valleys of the rivers Aisne and Ailette. Its charming name—"The Ladies' Path"—belied the fact that this ridge was the focus of three brutal Great War battles: the First Battle of the Aisne (September 13–28, 1914), the Second Battle of the Aisne (April 16–May 9 and October 24–26, 1917), and the Third (May 27–June 6, 1918; see map 5). This repetition, battles fought and refought, was emblematic of the entire war on the Western Front: bloody desolation with remarkably little change in the course of the struggle.

For Ludendorff, the objective of the Third Battle was to once and for all capture the ridge, which commanded high ground and also provided passage between the river valleys and therefore a route for a major breakthrough, one that would put German forces within striking distance of Paris. The battle opened with a massive and stunning surprise attack, which Ludendorff code-named *Blücher-Yorck*, after two Prussian generals who had been victorious against Napoleon. This opening conflagration spanned May 27 to June 4.

The Germans began that first morning early with an initial artillery bombardment. Such an "artillery preparation"—as it was called—was standard procedure for softening up an objective before the infantry was released to attack it. In the case of the May 27 attack, however, the Germans adapted the so-called rolling barrage that French general Robert Nivelle had introduced and used much earlier in the war, in the Battle of Champagne (September 25–November 6, 1915). Instead of shelling the enemy and *then* following up with an infantry attack, the rolling barrage moved ahead of the infantry advance. It required very accurate and disciplined fire to keep from shelling one's own advancing troops, but the great advantage of the rolling barrage is that the defenders had little to warn them of a coming attack. Moreover, because the artillery and the infantry operated simultaneously, the defender had no opportunity to recover from the barrage before he was overwhelmed by the attacking infantry.

In Ludendorff's version of the rolling barrage, the artillery fire was both more intense and more closely coordinated with the infantry advance. The shells fell very directly in front of the attacking infantry-men, so that the relationship between the artillery fire and the advancing infantry was so intimate, as it were, that the tactic earned the name *Feuerwalze*—"fire waltz." It was a diabolical choreography between infantry and artillery. Four thousand artillery pieces were employed on May 27, their object not being out-and-out destruction so much as forcing the defenders to cower in trenches and bunkers. Theoretically, this would allow the attackers to outflank and envelop the defenders with relative impunity.

The *Feuerwalze* hit the British especially hard. The Aisne area was under the overall direction of French Sixth Army commander, General Denis Auguste Duchêne, but it was four divisions of the British IX Corps, under Lieutenant-General Sir Alexander Hamilton-Gordon, that held the Chemin des Dames Ridge. Hamilton-Gordon was effectively subordinate to Duchêne, who, having regained the ridge in the Second

Battle of the Aisne, did not want to risk losing it in the Third. Accordingly, he ordered Hamilton-Gordon to pack his forces tightly into the front trenches. This was intended to strengthen resistance to an infantry attack. French commander in chief Henri Philippe Pétain had issued explicit orders forbidding just such a tight troop disposition, however. Unlike Duchêne, he understood that artillery would be as much a part of any attack as infantry, and he knew that troops massed together in trenches have no room for maneuver or retreat. In ignoring Pétain's order, Duchêne transformed the British under his command from soldiers into artillery targets. The horrific *Feuerwalze* therefore did more direct damage than the Germans could have hoped for.

Ludendorff was an adherent of so-called Hutier tactics, named after German general Oskar von Hutier, who had used them at the very outset of the Spring Offensive in March 1918. The leading characteristic of these tactics was to enable mass infiltration of the enemy lines by employing extreme violence, beginning with the *Feuerwalze* and following up with anything else calculated to increase the enemy's confusion and panic. Chemical warfare—"poison gas"—was perfect for making this mayhem. Accordingly, a poison gas barrage was laid on following the *Feuerwalze*, and as soon as the gas had lifted, German storm troopers—elite shock troops—commenced their infantry assault.

The combined effect of the barrage, the gas, and the first wave of shock troops enabled the Germans to tear a twenty-five-mile gap in the Allied lines. Within just six hours, the Germans had plowed through eight divisions along a line between Reims and Soissons. The Anglo-French position on this portion of the Western Front was pushed back to the Vesle River.

By May 30, a German victory in this Third Battle of the Aisne seemed assured. Some fifty thousand Allied soldiers were now prisoners of war, and eight hundred French and British artillery pieces were in enemy hands. All that remained to complete the triumph—and quite possibly win the war—was advancing into Paris itself. After four more days of fighting, on June 3, the German armies were just thirty-five miles outside of the French capital.

What happened next, however, was what always happened to Ludendorff's massive, all-out offensives: the onset of exhaustion and logistical breakdown. The Germans had advanced far and fast, which meant that their supply lines were stretched thin. Food and ammunition ran short. Success, great as it was, had cost many casualties, losses that could not be made up out of the inadequate military reserves of 1918. Muscle and will faded and failed while numbers dwindled.

Now it was the Germans' turn to suffer counterattacks, and on June 6 the advance ground to a halt on the Marne. Once again, Paris had been reprieved. True, the Allies were no closer to winning the war than they had been before the Third Battle of the Aisne, but it was also true that they had managed not to lose it.

●

The Americans contributed one division, the 1st Division, to the Third Battle of the Aisne. The unit had arrived in the area in mid-April in response to the Lys offensive (chapter 7). Marshal Pétain assigned the division to a sector near Montdidier, south of the principal site of the Somme Defensive (chapter 6) and along the line on which the German advance toward Amiens had been arrested.

The 1st Division's new commanding officer, Major General Robert L. Bullard (figure 22), was one of Pershing's favorites. The AEF commander admired what he always admired in his best officers: the combination of extreme aggressiveness and extreme competence. Bullard was anxious to be employed in an offensive capacity, and he appealed to his French corps commander to assign him an offensive mission. In the end, it took the intercession of Pétain himself to bring about the assignment. Bullard and his troops were to attack and seize the village of Cantigny, not far from Montdidier and held by the Germans. Its greatest value was its position, perched atop high ground that formed the very tip of the German salient—the farthest enemy penetration on the Somme front. Bullard knew that the Germans would defend this possession fiercely.

Bullard chose the 28th Infantry Regiment to make the attack (figure 23). By the scale of the Great War, it was by no means a vast

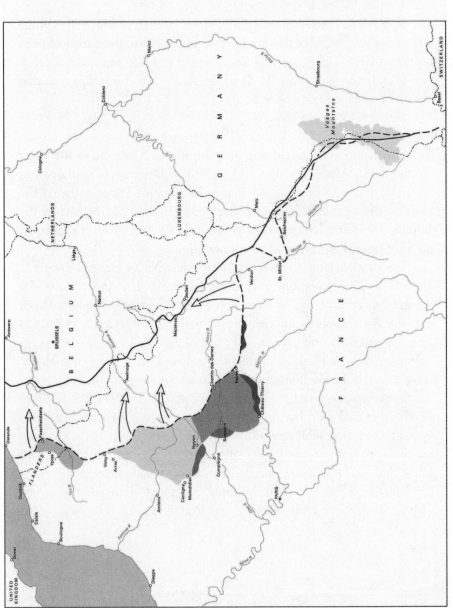

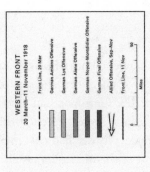

WESTERN FRONT
20 March–11 November 1918

Front Line, 20 Mar

German Amiens Offensive

German Lys Offensive

German Aisne Offensive

German Noyon-Montdidier Offensive

German Final Offensive

Allied Offensive, Sep–Nov

Front Line, 11 Nov

0   Miles   50

Figure 22. Robert Lee Bullard commanded the 1st Infantry Division at Cantigny. Later, he commanded III Corps and then the US Second Army.
WIKIMEDIA

objective. The salient was small. Nevertheless, if the AEF could prove itself—and redeem itself after Seicheprey (chapter 7)—confidence among the French and British allies would be significantly increased. Bullard wanted to leave nothing to chance. He prepared and rehearsed the operation thoroughly, keenly aware that the French had already twice taken and twice lost Cantigny.

Figure 23. Doughboys go over the top at the Battle of Cantigny. NATIONAL ARCHIVES AND RECORDS ADMINISTRATION

At 5:45 on the morning of May 28, the Americans unleashed a preparatory artillery barrage. At 6:45, Colonel Hanson Ely ordered his men over the top—out of their trenches. A total of 3,564 men were committed to the attack. The initial artillery barrage had been largely a counter-battery operation that targeted German artillery positions. Bullard had arranged for a rolling barrage to follow in sync with the infantry advance. It was a high-stakes test of the Americans' training. Their task was to advance at a precise rate of one hundred meters every two minutes, which was the rate of advance of the rolling barrage just ahead of them. Fail to keep up with the barrage, and its effect would be wasted; the advancing troops would be vulnerable to defensive fire. Overtake it, and American soldiers would fall to friendly fire.

Supported admirably by American and French artillery as well as by French tanks and aircraft, the 28th—augmented by two companies of the 18th Infantry (three machine-gun companies and a company of engineers)—wrested Cantigny from the grasp of the German Eighteenth

Figure 24. US gunners-in-training load a 240-mm. trench mortar. The instructor, at left, looks on. NATIONAL ARCHIVES AND RECORDS ADMINISTRATION

Army. Thanks in no small part to close cooperation with the French— who provided air cover as well 368 heavy artillery pieces, trench mortars (figure 24), flamethrowers, and the soldiers to man them all—the attack went very quickly. The Schneider tanks of the French 5th Tank battalion handily neutralized deadly German machine-gun nests, and the Americans took the village in about a half hour. Afterward, the 28th advanced beyond the village proper to take up a defensive position about a half kilometer beyond Cantigny.[1]

●

If taking Cantigny had been relatively easy, holding it was another matter altogether. The 28th Regiment repelled no fewer than six German counterattacks over the next three days. By this time, the French had moved their artillery assets to oppose the German offensive elsewhere, so the Americans had to rely on their own field guns. Fortunately, the army artillerists proved quite skilled, and their defensive counterfire was effective at dispersing some of the counterattacks and discouraging the formation of others.

As it was, the German counterattacks were poorly coordinated with their own artillery. This made the enemy infantrymen ripe targets for Ely's defenders. Nevertheless, the 28th absorbed three full days of counterattacks and nearly continuous artillery shelling before the regiment was relieved by soldiers of the 18th Regiment.

The AEF succeeded in reducing the German salient at Cantigny, which expanded its own modest front by about a mile. To be sure, within the context of the massive Third Battle of the Aisne, the Battle of Cantigny was a minor affair that ended in a minor victory. American forces had suffered 1,603 casualties, including more than 300 killed. This was out of total Allied losses in the Third Battle of the Aisne of 127,000 killed, wounded, or captured. Yet Cantigny persuaded the French—if not quite yet the British—that American *divisions*, complete military units under US command, could be relied on to help resist the German effort to take Paris. The victory was a prelude to two much larger American military achievements, beginning with Belleau Wood (June 1–26, 1918; chapter 9).

CHAPTER 9

Belleau Wood

June 1–26, 1918

By June 1918, it was almost impossible to imagine any place in or near the Western Front that had not been beaten into mud and desolation by nearly four years of boots, bombs, and shells. Yet no more than thirty miles east of Paris, there was such a place. It was the Bois de Belleau, Belleau Wood, an ancient hunting preserve owned by a wealthy Parisian sportsman whose château lay just within the woods. In extent, this oasis within the chaos of war was little more than a mile north to south, and at its widest, east to west, perhaps a thousand yards across—in all, about half the size of New York City's Central Park, though it was no means a park, but, rather, a thicket of woods rising above a shaggy blanket of under-growth. On its perimeter were glistening fields of chest-high winter wheat.

By the time the US Marines arrived in the vicinity of the Wood at the end of May 1918, the oasis had become what USMC colonel Alber-tus W. Catlin described as a "dark threat . . . as full of menace as a tiger's foot, dangerous as a live wire, poisonous with gas, bristling with machine guns, alive with snipers."[1] The Germans had discovered it, and they found its dark tangle the perfect place for a complex of machine-gun nests to support a breakthrough to Paris.

If Belleau Wood was an obscure place, the US Marines were an obscure fraction of the AEF. A single brigade, the Fourth, of about ten thousand marines was attached to the US Army's 2nd Division in this sector. Indeed, as General Pershing and other top US Army officers viewed the action in and near this scrap of land, the Battle of Belleau Wood was a small affair, worth little notice amid the much larger action of the Aisne-Marne Defensive (chapter 12), of which it was officially classified as a mere episode. To both the French and the American public, however, the very name "Belleau Wood" assumed the symbolic importance of a latter-day Thermopylae, the battle, fought in 480 BCE, in which a small number of Spartans held off the vast armies of King Xerxes I of Persia. The US Marine Corps emerged from the Belleau Wood cloaked in the mantle of warriorhood and heroism that they would wear into World War II and that they wear to this day.

Although the Battle of Belleau Wood is properly associated most closely with the marines, the marines in fact not only operated as part of the army's 2nd Division (map 6) but were also commanded by Brigadier

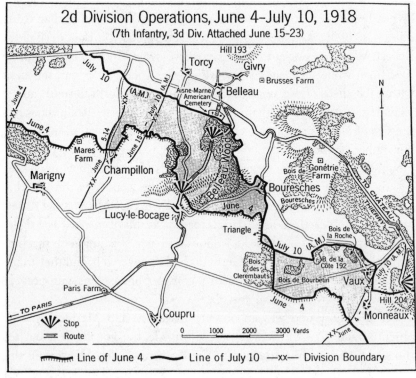

Map 6. US 2nd Division Operations in and around Belleau Wood. WIKIMEDIA

General James G. Harbord, an army officer who had relieved 4th Brigade's marine commander, Brigadier General Charles A. Doyen, after he fell seriously ill. Moreover, two complete army divisions ultimately fought in actions associated with this battle, as did elements of the French Sixth Army and the British IX Corps.

●

The third of Erich Ludendorff's all-out offensives may have failed strategically, but it did bring a devastating tactical victory at Chemin des Dames, sending some fifty German divisions storming toward the Marne River line, which defended Paris. French troops were scattered under the overwhelming attack (see chapter 8). In an effort to stem the tide bearing down on the French capital, the US 2nd Division, which General Pershing had assigned to French command, was put aboard *camions* (canvas-canopied French trucks ubiquitous on the Western Front) for transport east toward Meaux and the farm country between the large villages of Château-Thierry and Soissons. Their orders were to augment the French forces fiercely engaged in the sector and to create an unbreakable wall between the advancing enemy and Paris.

The troops of the division lumbered along at the rate of a few kilometers an hour for most of May 31. Many a doughboy would remember—for the rest of his life and with sincere loathing—the endless, tedious, bone-shaking trips on *camions*. A large number of the AEF soldiers and marines did not arrive until June 1—and, when they did, they were immediately engaged in a hot defense. The 4th Marine Brigade was positioned on the 2nd Division's left flank, and the 3rd (Army) Brigade on the right. The marines confronted the German divisions along an arc that ran northward from Triangle Farm (the endpoint of the 3rd Brigade's left flank) to the right flank of the French 167th Division, which was just north of Marigny. From June 1 through June 5, various units of the 2nd Division fought the German onslaught, defeating attacks mainly with rifle fire, which was highly unusual in a war dominated by artillery and machine guns.

The Germans made repeated attempts to capture the marine position at Les Mares Farm. These attacks were beaten back by the 55th Company

(Captain John Blanchfield commanding), 2nd Battalion (under Lieutenant Colonel Frederick M. "Fritz" Wise), 5th Marine Regiment. This successful stand against the German onslaught is what specifically evoked comparisons between the marines' actions and those of the Spartans. Les Mares Farm became the equivalent of Thermopylae; for this French farm was just thirty miles from Paris, and the struggle for it was the closest the Germans had come to the French capital since August 1914. Here, during the first five days of this fierce yet relatively small-scale battle, is where Germany came as near to winning the Great War as it had in nearly four years. Few doubt that, had the German forces broken through the marines here and the rest of the 2nd Division in this sector, the way to Paris would have been clear. Even fewer doubt that the fall of Paris would have taken the French out of the war. That, in turn, would have prompted the BEF to withdraw back across the Channel. As for the Americans, they were, in June 1918, in no position to fight Germany on their own. The AEF would have had to return to the United States. Never at any time in 1918 was total Allied collapse a greater possibility. What Winston Churchill would say in 1940 of the role the victorious RAF (Royal Air Force) played in the Battle of Britain might well have been said some two decades earlier about the marines in June 1918: "Never in the field of human conflict was so much owed by so many to so few."

●

The triumph of the marines at this early stage of the action around Belleau Wood was followed by some two weeks of continual combat. Even as Wise's battalion was holding fast, the exhausted French troops in front of the 2nd Division's line were falling back through the American lines. Most marched through in silence, but one Frenchman, a major of chasseurs, bumped up against marine captain Lloyd Williams's second in command, a Captain Corbin. In breathless, heavily accented English, the French major reported that his lines had been overrun, and he instructed Corbin to withdraw *his* line. By way of resisting the order, Corbin pretended not to understand. The exasperated major took a pad from inside his coat and wrote out in plain English an order to retreat. Corbin passed the paper on to Captain Williams. He glanced at the order and spat out to Corbin, "Retreat, hell! We just got here."[2]

For at least two days, no French troops stood between the Germans and the Americans—and the Americans nevertheless more than held their own. French general Joseph Degoutte, whose troops had been melting away, now ordered his own 167th Division—which had been relatively unscathed in battle—to join the US 2nd Division in a counteroffensive against the Germans who were in the vicinity of Belleau Wood. The 4th Marine Brigade attacked on June 6. The action was led by Major Julius S. Turrill's 1st Battalion, 5th Marine Regiment, with the objective of capturing high ground designated Hill 142. Turrill was supported by the 3rd Battalion, 5th Marine Regiment under Major Benjamin Berry. The objective Berry was to take and hold in this supporting attack was Belleau Wood proper. The assault on the German-held Wood was also augmented by Major Berton Sibley's 3rd Battalion, 6th Marine Regiment, which flanked Berry on the southeast. Finally, the 2nd Battalion of the 6th Marines, under Lieutenant Colonel Thomas Holcomb, was assigned to cover Sibley's right flank and to capture the village of Bouresches, which was on the southeastern periphery of Belleau Wood. The idea was to envelope the Germans holed up in the cover of the Wood.

Here, at last, the inexperience of the marines showed itself. French intelligence was reporting that Belleau Wood did not harbor any Germans. The marine commanders did not believe this to be true, but they assumed, based on the report, that Belleau Wood must be only lightly held. Instead of confirming this assumption with reconnaissance, they went ahead with the attack—and because they assumed that Belleau Wood was only lightly held, if at all, they did not order a preparatory artillery barrage. The result was that Turrill's two marine companies, the 49th (Captain George W. Hamilton) and the 67th (First Lieutenant Orlando Crowther), which began their offensive at 3:45 in the morning, were instantly ambushed by heavy machine-gun fire *and* artillery. This pinned them down in Belleau Wood (map 7), in the dark and without any detailed map.

Realizing that his men were effectively sitting ducks, Hamilton ordered them to continue to advance, arguing that it was better to be a moving target than a stationary one. They were decimated by machine-gun fire from no fewer than thirty-six German nests, but the survivors nevertheless got through to the other end of Belleau Wood and advanced into the village of Torcy, where occupying Germans finally cut them down. In the meantime, the 67th Company advanced into a deep ravine just outside of Belleau Wood—and took heavy fire. Yet by seven in the morning, survivors from the 49th and 67th companies, with support from platoons of the 17th and 66th companies, threw up a hasty defensive line on Hill 142. The 3rd Battalion, 5th Marines, rushed to support them on their right flank.

At this point, Colonel Albertus Catlin, commanding the 6th Regiment, was given command of the afternoon's attack. Lieutenant Colonel Logan Feland was assigned to lead the left flank of the line, which was held by the 3rd Battalion, 5th Marines. Two companies (96th and 79th) of the 2nd Battalion, 6th Marines, were specifically designated to proceed with the capture of Bouresches.

But Belleau Wood itself remained an elusive objective. It was so rugged and so overgrown that it was virtually impossible to know where the enemy was within it. The Germans enjoyed complete cover and concealment for machine guns and riflemen. Yet, with the marines in position at the periphery of the Wood, the commanders decided that the attack had to be launched.

It became a bloodbath. Machine-gun fire poured out from the woods, targeting both marine battalions. Hardest hit was the 3rd Battalion, 5th Marines, which had to traverse the treeless, level, thoroughly exposed wheat field on the edge of Belleau Wood. The 3rd Battalion, 6th Marines, attacking the southern end of the Wood, also encountered fire from numerous machine-gun nests. Most of this battalion got farther than the marines who had approached from the wheat field—but only barely. Instead of being cut down in the open, amid the golden sheaves, they were hit almost immediately upon entering Belleau Wood.

While Belleau Wood was being contested, the 96th and 79th companies of the 2nd Battalion, 6th Marines were rapidly advancing

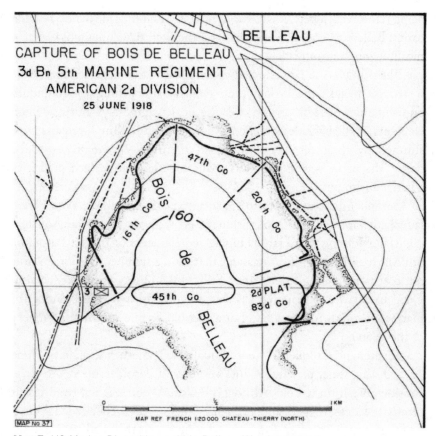

Map 7. US Marine Dispositions within Belleau Wood. WIKIMEDIA

against Bouresches. Of approximately three hundred men, just twenty unwounded survivors, under Second Lieutenant Clifton B. Cates, entered the village, fought the German defenders, and held onto Bouresches until reinforcements arrived.

June 6 ended as the bloodiest day in USMC history up to that time. More men fell in combat on that single day than in the 143 years of Marine history that had preceded it.

•

At the end of June 6, the 5th Marines still held Hill 142, which was one of the three objectives of the attack. Bouresches, the second objective, was being reinforced, albeit slowly. Right now, it was in marine hands, but just barely. Belleau Wood, however, was still the exclusive domain of German machine gunners and riflemen.

The 4th Marine Brigade had already lost many marines in the June 6 struggle to take the Wood. Their tenacity and willingness to endure punishment would be proved over the next twenty days, during which elements of the brigade launched five more assaults. The Germans were stunned by their ferocity and cursed them as *Teufelhunden*—"devil dogs." The name was intended as a slur, but the marines accepted it as a badge of honor.

Several minor attempts to make inroads into Belleau Wood were launched—and failed—through June 9. At 4:30 on the morning of June 10, Major Johnny "the Hard" Hughes led elements of the 1st Battalion, 6th Marines, in a significant assault that took a number of German lives but cost more among the marines. Still, Hill 142 was firmly clenched in Devil Dog jaws, and Bouresches was occupied by a growing number of marines. The 6th Marines had but a toehold on the southern periphery of the Wood.

Lieutenant Colonel Wise personally led another assault on June 11 and, this time, penetrated the woods to a considerable depth—too considerable, it turned out. Although Belleau Wood was not large, it was utterly trackless, rugged, and, even after shelling, densely tangled. Wise's men became disoriented and soon gave up much they had gained—but not everything. The marine toehold in its objective had been enlarged. Encouraged, Wise mounted a second assault at six that same evening. The gain could be measured in yards, before it was arrested. But it held.

●

By this point, the German defenders were wearing down. The great influenza pandemic of 1918 broke out in January and did not end until December 1920, after claiming twenty million to fifty million lives and sickening a half billon people. By June and July 1918, the pandemic was sweeping the trenches of the Western Front. It hit everyone hard, but because the Allies—and especially the Americans—were fresh, healthy, and well-fed, the flu was less devastating among their ranks than among those of the Germans. The enemy had been in the woods for many days. Hunger, exposure, and, now, disease were taking their devastating toll.

As for the 4th Marine Brigade, it had been moving and fighting since May 31. Action had been virtually continuous for nearly three weeks. Rations were still available, but the last hot meal the marines had enjoyed was days earlier, and it was their only full meal in some twenty days. Even the marine commanders began to admit that the brigade was approaching the end of combat endurance and needed, at the very least, a breather.

An army relief column arrived in the form of the 7th Infantry Regiment of 3rd US Division. The soldiers took up and held what the marines had gained, and the 4th Marine Brigade retired, regrouped, and rested. The unit returned to the fray on June 23 with an attack launched at seven that evening. Led by the new commander, Major Maurice Shearer, the 3rd Battalion, 5th Marines at last made a significant incursion into Belleau Wood. Two days later, on June 25, Shearer led an advance from the opposite—northern—end of the objective. The remaining battered, reduced, ailing, and generally weakened German defenders were killed or captured. Shearer dispatched a laconic but triumphal message to headquarters: "Woods now U.S. Marine Corps entirely."[3]

●

The cost to the 4th Marine Brigade was some 4,600 officers and men killed or wounded. This represented more than half the entire marine force committed to combat at the time. General Pershing was nevertheless loath to elevate the marines' achievement too highly. He believed that comparisons between the US Marine Corps and the US Army—which vastly outnumbered it, especially on the Western Front—were not only invidious but destructive to the morale of both the public and the army. The French, however, saw only that *American* warriors had shown themselves capable of virtually superhuman prowess in the defense of Paris and of France. On June 30, 1918, Brigadier General James G. Harbord, the only US Army general ever assigned to command a marine brigade, cast a blind eye on Pershing's sentiments and proudly published an order issued by French Sixth Army commander General Joseph Degoutte:

In view of the brilliant conduct of the 4th Brigade of the 2d U.S. Division, which in a spirited fight took Bouresches and the important strong point of Bois de Belleau, stubbornly defended by a large enemy force, the General commanding the VIth [French] Army orders that henceforth, in all official papers, the Bois de Belleau shall be named "Bois de la Brigade de Marine."[4]

Later, Harbord would write, "The effect [of the marine action at Belleau Wood] on the French has been many times out of all proportion to the size of our brigade or the front on which it has operated. . . . They say a Marine can't venture down the boulevards of Paris without risk of being kissed by some casual passerby or some *boulevardière*. Frenchmen say that the stand of the Marine Brigade in its far-reaching effects marks one of the great crises of history, and there is no doubt they feel it." Harbord then cast the cool protocol of military communication to the winds by adding *three* exclamation points to his statement of awed admiration for the marines under his command: "What shall I say of the gallantry with which these marines have fought!!! I cannot write of their splendid gallantry without tears coming to my eyes. There has never been anything better in the world."[5]

The final tally of 2nd Division casualties—both US Marine and US Army—in action between June 1 and July 10 was 217 officers and 9,560 enlisted personnel killed, wounded, captured, or missing. The 4th Marine Brigade alone lost 126 officers and 5,057 men killed or wounded. No one knows how many Germans became casualties, but their losses were certainly higher (figure 25).

Were Belleau Woods and environs worth the cost to the AEF? General Tasker Bliss, US Army Chief of Staff, remarked to Pershing that he believed the battle had "stopped the German drive and very possibly saved Paris." In remarks written in 1936, General Robert L. Bullard, who commanded the newly created Second US Army, concluded, "The marines didn't 'win the war' here, but they saved the Allies from defeat. Had they arrived a few hours later I think that would have been the beginning of the end."[6]

Figure 25. This photograph, which may have been staged for propaganda purposes, shows American soldiers "at close grips with the Hun," assaulting a bunker.
LIBRARY OF CONGRESS

Other military figures, years after the war, dismissed Belleau Wood as something of a "prestige" objective rather than a strategic one. General Matthew Ridgway angrily opined that Belleau Wood should be added to the tragic gallery of "prize examples of men's lives being thrown away against objectives not worth the cost." He called it "a monument, for all time, to the inflexibility of military thinking in that period."[7]

The strategic thinking in the spring and summer of 1918 was that Belleau Wood, a kind of natural fortress, was just too dangerous to leave in enemy control. Almost without doubt, the initial defense of the Belleau Wood sector saved Paris. Whether the offensive afterward launched against Belleau Wood proper was so urgently needed is doubtful. Yet the final taking of Belleau Wood was of extraordinary psychological value to the Allies. It inspired America, unleashing a torrent of enlistments—especially in the USMC. It inspirited the battered, war-weary French nation and its military at precisely the moment that such an injection of renewed hope and enthusiasm was most needed.

Chapter 10

Montdidier-Noyon
and Champagne-Marne

June 9–13, 1918, and July 15–18, 1918,
including the Battle of Chateau-Thierry

WHILE THE US 2ND DIVISION WAS INVOLVED IN AND AROUND BELLEAU Wood (chapter 9), the US 1st Division was on the move. The first complete unit to arrive in France, it was, by the end of April, attached to the VI Corps of the French First Army and was moved to an area north of Paris. On April 27, 1918, command of a sector west of Montdidier, just behind the French front lines, was assigned to the 1st Division. On June 2, the 1st Division was ordered to take over from French troops even more of this front, so that the French soldiers could be released for frontline service. On June 3, elements of the division moved their line forward to improve the US position north of American-held Cantigny.

Once in position, it became apparent to 1st Division G-2—Intelligence—that something ominous was taking shape on the division's new front. An intelligence summary reporting on June 3–4 was issued on June 4:

I. Infantry:

The enemy's infantry appears to be working very hard consolidating his position. Groups of enemy observed in front of Point 2508 evidently working [trench-digging, wire-laying] parties, as they were protected by covering detachments.

Intermittent machine-gun fire during the night on our front lines in the region of CANTIGNY, Bois de CANTIGNY and GRIVESNES.

Machine guns have been located at points 26.18, 22.33, 15.55, 28.09 and vicinity of 26.25.[1]

The June 4 summary went on to report, "Our artillery apparently hit an enemy ammunition dump at 31[.]22 at 21:05 h [9:05 pm]. Several fires in MONTDIDIER during the night." American troops also noted the sudden appearance of new enemy observation posts. "Searchlights were active in the region of MONTDIDIER. The enemy threw up an unusual number of green rockets [the usual signal for commencement of an artillery barrage] and no barrage followed." The German infantry was reported as "quiet," but the artillery as "quiet but regulating" [readying aim and range], and enemy aircraft were reported as "active"—a sure sign of reconnaissance preparatory to an attack.[2]

Major General Robert Lee Bullard, the 1st Division commanding officer, responded proactively to the intelligence reports by ordering raids to obtain prisoners for interrogation. An Operations Memorandum signed by Bullard's chief of staff was issued to the division's 2nd Brigade on June 4:

The army has directed a heavy [artillery] fire of interdiction and harassing fire throughout the night until further orders.

The corps directs that the divisions profit by their fire by making raids tonight (June 4/5) or tomorrow night for the purpose of obtaining prisoners. . . . It desires prisoners from the front between CANTIGNY and BELLE ASSISE [Farm].[3]

In response to the order, the brigade adjutant, Major J. R. Brewer, issued a more urgent order that day to the commanding officer of the 26th Infantry Division: "For prompt action, tonight if possible, it is of the utmost importance that a prisoner be taken tonight from the front of the 26th Inf."[4]

During the Great War, prisoners were often obtained for interrogation through trench raids. These were extremely hazardous missions carried out at night by small teams. After blackening their faces with burnt cork, the members of the raiding party stealthily made their way through the barbed wire and other obstacles that littered the no-man's-land separating their trenches from those of the enemy. Typically, the distance between the opposing frontline trenches was a few hundred yards.

Although the raiders were armed with rifles, bayonets, and hand grenades, the weapon of choice was the US M1918 "Knuckle Duster" trench knife. Fearsome, brutal, and stealthy, it was also imperfect. It featured a triangular stiletto blade, which was designed to resist breaking—yet often broke. The pommel at the end of the grip and knuckle guard was intended to be used as a weapon for fracturing an enemy's skull, and some troops accordingly referred to the feature as a "skull crusher." But this application proved impractical, and, in the end, the trench knife was nothing more or less than a stabbing weapon.

The raiding party would creep up on the sentries guarding a small, preferably isolated, portion of an enemy frontline trench. The raiders would identify their target by looking for the glow of a cigarette or listening for the low hum of conversation. The sentries were not candidates for capture but were marked for as quiet a death as possible, lest they sound the alarm. Once the sentries were disposed of, the raiders tossed grenades into the trench dugouts where troops slept. In the resulting chaos, they would snatch a prisoner or two and beat a hasty retreat to their own trenches. At this point, the greatest risk was falling victim to friendly fire. To prevent such an outcome, the sentries guarding one's own trenches were informed of the raid beforehand, and a system of passwords or sign-and-countersign was used, so that the returning raiders could identify themselves. The system, however, did not allow for sentries who failed to receive word of the evening's mission or who were simply nervous and trigger happy.

As the raiding party did its work, new intelligence emerged on June 5:

The enemy's infantry continues vigorously his work of consolidating his positions. A small enemy patrol was seen early this morning in front of our positions in the Bois de FONTAINE. It was driven away by our rifle fire. There was intermittent machine-gun fire on our front line during the night. . . .

Attention is invited to the following facts. During the last few days the enemy has shown great activity in [artillery] fire for adjustment on both our trenches and artillery.[5]

In other words, enemy artillerists were clearly identifying their targets and adjusting their heavy guns accordingly.

Interrogation of prisoners (presumably taken in raids) and deserters—numerous Germans, hungry and dispirited, came over to the Allied lines—"confirmed the rumors of an impending attack in the region of MONTDIDIER," a bulletin reported. "It is reasonable that this attack will extend to a part of our [the US] front. The arrival of the staff of the [German] XXVI Reserve Corps in the region of TAHURE on our front seems to confirm this hypothesis."[6]

●

The anticipated attack did indeed come, on June 9, when Erich Ludendorff followed up on the Aisne Offensive, which had bogged down (chapter 8), with a relatively small-scale advance against the Montdidier-Noyon sector. The 21st German Division attacked French positions along a twenty-three-mile front that ran from Montdidier to the Oise River. Thanks to a combination of American intelligence and their own, the French were not taken by surprise. Although the Germans penetrated some nine miles into the French lines between Montdidier and Noyon, the French counterattack was swift and effective. The fighting went on until June 12, leaving the Germans with almost nothing to show for their heavy losses.

It was on the first day of the German attack, June 9, that the US 1st Division became involved, falling under very heavy artillery bombardment from "midnight until 4 a.m." The shelling was directed against the American "front lines and rear areas with high explosive and gas shells"—the gas being chlorine-arsenic and bromine-arsenic.[7]

●

Between March 21 and June 13, 1918, Erich Ludendorff hurled four major offensives against the Allies, hoping that they would have a decisive effect *before* the Americans could be deployed in fully significant numbers. The result of these operations was paradoxical. Each German offensive ended with a tactical victory in that the Germans gained ground and thereby erased any gains the Allies had made in repelling the Germans since the autumn of 1914. Yet, strategically, these gains—real though they were—delivered no lasting benefit to the Germans. Nowhere along the Western Front had Ludendorff managed to create a decisive advantage. Worse, each offensive cost the German army dearly. During this period, the German forces suffered more than six hundred thousand killed, wounded, captured, and missing. While this was two hundred thousand fewer casualties than the combined French and British armies had incurred, the Germans, by the late spring of 1918, had no way of replacing their losses, whereas the Allies now had access to growing numbers of American troops.

By June, thanks to the new arrivals, the balance of manpower on the Western Front was nearing parity. By July, it would tip in favor of the Allies, whose side of the scales would continue to weigh heavier and heavier as autumn neared. Without doubt, the Ludendorff offensives were acts of desperation, but the German generalissimo was correct in concluding that Germany's only chance for victory was to achieve a decisive breakthrough before Americans became too plentiful on the Western Front. As offensive after offensive failed, however, and as German losses mounted, German morale, both in the trenches and on the home front, declined precipitously. The absence of a decision in the land battle cut yet more deeply into German morale as the Royal Navy's blockade continued to strangle and starve both the military and the homeland. Suffering in the multifarious forms of continual combat, hunger, fatigue, privation, and influenza was the collective wound at which relentless Allied propaganda was squarely aimed. British and French aircraft made frequent sorties over both the German trenches and the German cities, dropping leaflets that exhorted mutiny and rebellion. It was an effort both to destabilize the government and to force the German leaders to come to the table and commence negotiations.

The propaganda offensive only added to Ludendorff's desperation. Rejecting the very notion of negotiation, he drew up two more offensives for July. With the Americans still understrength, he saw these as Germany's last chance for victory.

The first of the July offensives was intended to capture Reims, which would make it easier to keep supplying the German salient that bulged southwestward from just outside of Reims to Château-Thierry and then north to Soissons, northeast to Montdidier, just east of US-held Cantigny, and then, finally, northeast to Vimy. As long as this quite large salient remained in German hands, the Allies would be obliged to spend their reserves in attempting to reduce it. Ludendorff was determined that the salient would not be reduced, and, once he was content that it had been made secure, it was his intention to launch an even larger offensive. This one would not be directed against the French, but against the British, in Flanders.

The first of the planned July offensives stepped off on July 15, with a double-pronged assault on either side of Reims. The attack did not fall upon the Allies as the surprise Ludendorff had intended it to be. Not only had plans leaked out of Berlin, but Allied observation aircraft had detected unusual and massive troop movements as well as the rapid shifting of German units behind the enemy front. Ferdinand Foch, as supreme Allied commander, acted quickly to draw up all available reserves. Philippe Pétain, the French commander in chief, arrayed his soldiers for something that had been lacking in French tactics for most of the war: effective defense in depth. This type of troop disposition was intended to provide quick and certain rotation in and out of the front lines, helping to ensure that reasonably fresh troops would make continuous contact with the enemy. Moreover, defense in depth allowed the defender not merely to arrest but to exploit any considerable penetrations by the enemy, who would be swallowed up by the defenders much as antibodies engulf bacteria that assault and infect a body.

Thanks to able intelligence and highly competent force management by both Foch and Pétain, the German advance east of Reims fell very short of its objective. Nevertheless, the western prong of the attack did succeed in advancing across the Marne near Chateau-Thierry.

●

After the Battle of Belleau Wood and associated action in its vicinity (June 1–26, 1918; chapter 9), the 6th Brigade of the newly arrived US 3rd Division was thinly strung out across a seven-mile front from Château-Thierry to Varennes. The sector was relatively quiet until 12:10 on the morning of July 15, when German artillery opened up with a preparatory barrage. At 3:50 in the morning, the static artillery barrage gave way to a rolling barrage in front of the 10th Division's attack around the west end of Reims. The Germans broke through the French defensive lines and began crossing the Marne in pontoon boats. As the enemy came across the river, the assault was directed dead against the 6th Brigade.

The US 30th, 38th, and 28th Infantry Regiments all engaged the offensive fiercely. The 38th covered a bend on the Marne River between Mezy and Sauvigny. The French division positioned just east of the US 38th Infantry in this bend of the river collapsed almost instantly under the assault, retiring a full five miles south of its own starting point before it was able to re-form into some semblance of order. The sudden withdrawal, which had been made without warning to the Americans, left the right flank of the 38th entirely exposed to the German attack. One unlucky company, Company F, which was positioned opposite the village of Varennes, was struck on both flanks as well as its front. Incredibly, Company F withstood this enveloping onslaught—as did the rest of the 38th Infantry (figure 26). It was an achievement that would earn the regiment the honorific sobriquet "Rock of the Marne." To this day, the parent unit of the US 38th Infantry, the 3rd Division, retains "Rock of the Marne" as its motto.

The aptly named commanding officer of the 38th Infantry, Colonel Ulysses Grant McAlexander, wrote about the performance of his unit in a memorable after-action report dated July 31, 1918:

5. The Action: The action began at midnight July 14/15, 1918, with a bombardment of guns of various caliber, reported to consist of eighty-

Figure 26. Men of the 2nd Battalion, 38th Infantry, 3rd Division with French refugees on the road outside of Montmirail, France, June 1, 1918. The refugees had fled during the German Champagne-Marne offensive. NATIONAL ARCHIVES AND RECORDS ADMINISTRATION

four (84) batteries. The firing was rapid until 1:55 a. m., when it became moderate and remained so all over the area occupied by this regiment, with one exception, up to the movement of starting the rolling barrage along the railroad line at about 3:45 a.m.

Immediately preceding the rolling barrage there was apparently a concentration of artillery fire on the railroad line. The Germans pushed forward their preparations for crossing the MARNE under cover of smoke, tear and sneezing gas near the river, and lethal gas farther south. The French batteries of artillery in the subsector east of me are reported to have withdrawn at about 1 a.m., July 15, 1918, and the French infantry withdrew at about 4 a.m., after probable severe loss. This withdrawal exposed my right flank to hostile attack on a front of over four (4) kilometers. Attempts to cross the MARNE at three (3) places in my subsector were made: one in front of Co. E *and another in front of Co. H were repulsed by rifle and Chauchat [a French-made machine gun] fire and hand grenades. The third place was in front of Co. G, made by the [German] 6th Grenadiers. This was successful after the complete extermination of the platoon of that company on the river bank. A second platoon of Co. G on the north side of the railroad embankment was likewise exterminated after desperate hand-to-hand fighting. The third platoon of this company advanced over the railroad and engaged the enemy in similar manner and drove them off, which permitted the fourth platoon to first counterattack, then to resist a flank attack coming from the southwest of MEZY. The do-or-die spirit of this battalion prevented any Germans from entering our lines except as prisoners, of whom there were over 400 from this one point. It was here that by aid of Co. H the 6th Grenadiers were destroyed.*

On the right flank of the front line battalion, Company F occupied trenches specially constructed to meet any possible contingency of retirement by the troops of the sector adjoining me on the east. Here this company fought throughout the day of the 15th and repeatedly repulsed and counterattacked the 5th Grenadiers until they, too, were driven, defeated and all but destroyed back towards JAULGONNE. That regiment did not again appear in action.

The battalion was withdrawn by order of higher authority to the aqueduct line on the night of July 15, after having sustained an action on its front and both flanks for over 14 hours. As far as known, not an officer or man abandoned his duty during those trying hours. The annals of our army do not record a more heroic action.

Companies B and D, during the 15th/16th, protected the rear and right flank of the 2d Battalion in a series of attacks that made possible the holding of the valley behind them.

To the 3d Battalion fell as hard a lot as can be imposed upon soldiers, that of having to remain constantly exposed under fire with no opportunity to return it. My praise for these battalions must, in fairness, be equally divided.

It is of interest to note that at the time the shelling first started, practically every company, except those in the front line, had working details of from seventy-five to one hundred men under supervision of the engineers engaged in digging trenches. In a great many instances these details were over half a kilometer from their respective positions, especially in the support battalions. In spite of the heavy bombardment, the officers in charge kept perfect control of their men, held them under cover, separated and organized their own men, and reported them back to their companies and positions when the barrage lifted.

The action of July 16 consisted principally in repulsing repeated attacks by the enemy from the northeast and east along the ridge east of the SURMELIN and as far south as CONNIGIS. During the afternoon the pressure became so great that a change of front along the Surmelin was required under a severe fire. On the night of the 16th, superior authority ordered the occupation of the woods line.

6. Result: This regiment fought the German 10th and 36th Divisions to a standstill and captured prisoners from each of their six attack regiments.

7. Commendations: I wish to record my praise and appreciation of the heroic manner in which every officer and man of the regiment clung with unflinching tenacity to his position until he was ordered to leave it. Of the attached units, I wish to commend especially the machine gun companies of the 9th Battalion. I wish further to acknowledge with extreme gratitude the assistance given me by Major General J. T. Dickman and Brig. Gen. Charles Crawford during the heat of the battle that raged with my regiment as its center.

The work of the Allied artillery was beyond praise; but I am under a debt of especial gratitude to the American artillery of our division.

The personnel of the Y.M.C.A. aided in the care of the wounded in a splendidly unselfish manner and while under a severe fire [figure 27].

Recommendations of officers and men for special awards are forwarded separately.[8]

Figure 27. YMCA women serve hot chocolate to doughboys in France. NATIONAL
ARCHIVES AND RECORDS ADMINISTRATION

•

Indeed, the 38th Infantry proved to be more than a "rock." Although a large portion of the entire regiment was outflanked on three sides, it managed to repulse the attack. This blunted the German advance so completely that the offensive sputtered and stalled. Seizing this as an opportunity, at 4:45 on the morning of July 18, a combination of French forces, including some African colonial units, and the US 3rd Division forces between Fontenoy and Château-Thierry mounted a counterattack.

It was the very last thing the Germans expected, and the element of surprise had been wisely preserved by the Allies' daring choice of launching the counterattack *without* the usual preparatory artillery barrage. Once the attack got under way, however, it was led by a very tightly synchronized rolling barrage that advanced before the infantry. For that matter, fought across a twenty-five-mile-wide front, the counteroffensive came as something of a welcome surprise to the Allies themselves. Remarkably, it was the first counteroffensive the French had attempted in more than a year. In the counteroffensive, US forces fought mainly around Soissons and Château-Thierry, in collaboration with French forces, but at one point the American units, in their zeal, moved far ahead of the French and fought, in effect, *behind* enemy lines.

Remarkable though the counteroffensive was, Pershing, when he came to write his final report on the operations of AEF during the Great War, did not choose to highlight the American role in it. Instead, he chose to lavish a rare display of superlative praise on the stand of the 38th Infantry: "A single regiment of the 3d Division wrote one of the most brilliant pages in the annals of military history in preventing the crossing at certain points on its front, while on either side the Germans, who had gained a footing, pressed forward."[9] Pershing appreciated aggression, but, even more, he admired do-or-die endurance, which, to him, was the mark of a supremely disciplined military force.

•

The major AEF units involved in the Champagne-Marne action were the 3rd, 26th, 28th, and 42nd Divisions, the 369th Infantry, and supporting elements. In all, some eighty-five thousand US soldiers fought in this action. It was, therefore, a much larger action than the Battle of Belleau Wood, no matter how heroic that had been. What it proved was not only the heroism and courage of the individual American soldier, but the ability of American officers to command units larger than the regiment, an issue that had earlier been in doubt. Pershing would use this proof to maintain independence of command, even when American units were nominally attached to French corps or armies. Moreover, the symbolic value of an *American* regiment, the 38th Infantry, successfully withstanding a major German offensive (map 8) that had sent a larger French unit running was far beyond easy calculation.

The performance of the 38th Infantry and the 3rd Division to which it belonged surely lifted Allied hopes. Perhaps even more important, it served to dash the hopes of both the German military and the German

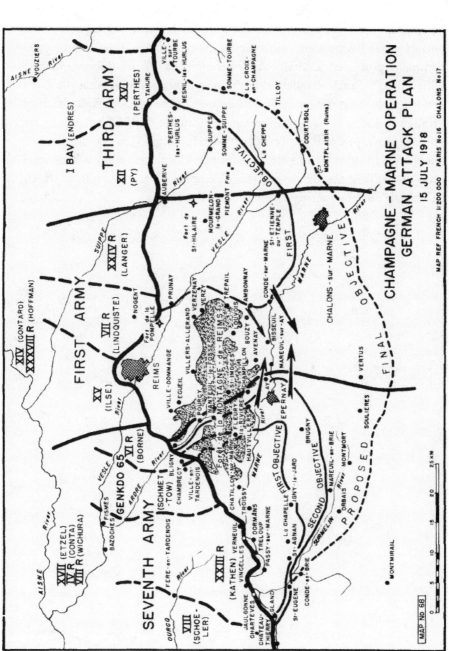

Map 8. German Attack Plan for the Champagne-Marne Offensive. US ARMY CENTER FOR MILITARY HISTORY

people. For the Champagne-Marne Offensive did not merely stall and die; it suffered a sharp counterattack, during which the warrior zeal of the newly arrived Americans was abundantly in evidence. The German government promoted Ludendorff's operations as *Friedensturmen*—"peace offensives." The name reflected the government's sense of what the German people most earnestly wanted now—not the quick and easy victory Kaiser Wilhelm II had promised in the summer of 1914 but, after four bloody years, peace. That this fifth *Friedensturm* failed to bring peace not only forced Ludendorff to abandon his plans for a second July offensive— this one against the BEF—but was an emotional body blow from which Germany and the Germans would not fully recover.

CHAPTER 11

Aisne-Marne

July 18–August 6, 1918

ERICH LUDENDORFF'S FOURTH OFFENSIVE ON THE WESTERN FRONT—
the Champagne-Marne drive of July 15–18, which was stemmed by
Franco-American forces (chapter 10)—failed to disrupt French planning for an offensive to be launched against the German Marne salient.
This menacing bulge westward into the French line was anchored on
its southeast end near Reims and on its northwest base near Soissons.
French army chief Pétain distributed orders on July 12 for an attack by
five French armies to be made on July 18. The Tenth, Sixth, Ninth, Fifth,
and Fourth Armies were positioned around the salient from left to right.
The lead element of the attack was to be the five divisions of the French
Tenth Army's XX Corps, which, as configured at the time, included the
US 1st and 2nd Divisions.

●

General Pershing had fought vigorously against anything resembling
the haphazard absorption of American troops into the French or British
armies. Faced with what seemed the imminent collapse of the exhausted
and depleted French and British armies, the American general relented
to the extent of allowing full divisions, under US command organic to
the divisions, to be attached to French corps. He remained concerned
that even this degree of subordination to a foreign army would obscure
the achievement of American arms and would be met with outrage

on the American home front, especially by the mothers and fathers of American doughboys.

In the case of the Aisne-Marne campaign, however, Pershing needn't have worried. Early in the morning of July 18, when the American 1st and 2nd Divisions (in company with a French Moroccan division) went over the top behind a heavy rolling barrage, they were not consigned to obscurity, but placed in the very vanguard of the first full-scale French offensive in more than a year. (The impromptu counteroffensive against Ludendorff's stalled fourth offensive was strictly localized and conducted on a relatively small scale as an attack of opportunity [chapter 10].) In company with the Moroccans, these two American divisions would be responsible for delivering the first—and principal—blow against the German position at the northwest base of the Marne salient, near Soissons. Pershing could have asked for no placement more prominent than this.

•

The overall plan for the offensive assigned two of the French armies to attack on July 18 toward the village of Braine on the Vesle River, which flows through Reims and feeds into the Aisne River from the southeast. The objective was deep within the middle portion of the German salient. To the north of this objective, the French Tenth Army was assigned to attack between the Aisne and the Ourcq Rivers. In the south, the French Sixth Army would launch its attack between the Ourcq and the Marne. Together, the attacks were intended to isolate the salient, cutting off all lines of communication. Thus isolated, it would be rendered more vulnerable to strike by the French Fifth and Ninth Armies, which were to strike the salient on its eastern flank. Those forces, however, had to finish dealing with the German Champagne-Marne offensive (chapter 10) before they could be redirected to offensive operations against the Marne salient.

The final objective of the French offensive was the total reduction of the Marne salient. By this point in the Great War on the Western Front, while Ludendorff had hopes of achieving a war-winning breakthrough to Paris and while General Pershing contemplated building an American army capable of launching from its own sector an independent offensive directly into the heart of Germany, French commanders—including even the relentlessly aggressive Ferdinand Foch—were thinking in terms that may strike a modern reader of history as better suited to a geometry teacher than to a military commander. Acceptable progress, even for the most ambitious offensive operations, was defined as "straightening" the front—that is, eliminating the salients that bulged into the French lines and "reducing" them to more-or-less straight lines. Some modern critics of Allied World War I strategy condemn this approach as pointlessly obsessive, arguing that the Allies would have been better off targeting specific areas for major, all-out breakthrough attempts. As those in command saw it, however, a salient represented the threat of an attack with the potential of outflanking the defenders and even being able to get around them and attack from the rear. At the same time and conversely, an enemy salient also represented an opportunity to *make* a flanking or enveloping attack, hitting the nose and sides of the bulge and then pinching the salient off at its base, thereby isolating the forces within. It was rather like catching the enemy army in its own bag and then, before the enemy could withdraw, tying off the end that was open to the enemy's territory.

Using the cover of the thick forest of Villers-Cotterêts, French Tenth Army assault troops stealthily organized themselves three days before the attack. These troops spearheaded a general attack against the western flank of the Marne salient by twenty-three French divisions and the 1st and 2nd US Divisions, which had been assigned to the French XX Corps. Administratively, both divisions were part of Major General Robert Lee Bullard's III Corps. In response to General Foch's urgent request, however, Pershing had detached them and dispatched them to the Aisne-Marne sector as operationally part of the French XX Corps, but it was his intention that Bullard assume direct tactical command. As it happened, the troops arrived in the assembly area at the front well before Bullard arrived, and they were therefore immediately turned over to the French commander. When Bullard finally arrived, he, too, was attached to the XX Corps—as its *assistant* commander. It was an accommodation he and Pershing agreed to in the interest of moving a critical operation rapidly forward.

Three additional American divisions were also rushed to the sector to take part in the first days of the offensive. The US 4th Division contributed one infantry brigade each to two corps of the French Sixth Army. The US 26th Division was assigned to hold the east flank of the French Sixth Army, and the 3rd US Division was attached to the French Ninth Army (figure 28).

●

The Franco-American attack stepped off on July 18. The secrecy of the preparations had been preserved not only by forest cover but by the decision to forego the customary artillery preparation, which softened up enemy defenses but at the cost of warning the enemy that an attack was imminent. By foregoing the initial pounding, the Franco-American commanders preserved the element of total operational surprise. Moreover, the offensive had been so thoroughly prepared that many of the initial assault units had been pre-positioned in their attack stations on the night of July 17. This greatly increased the pace of the assault and further leveraged the element of surprise.

Figure 28. Doughboys fighting during the Aisne-Marne campaign. NATIONAL ARCHIVES AND RECORDS ADMINISTRATION

To make up for the absence of a preliminary barrage, French artillery provided a short but very intense rolling barrage to accompany the initial advance. In addition, more than 550 Schneider tanks were used to support the infantry on an ongoing basis as they attacked the German trenches. Using tanks in this way would become customary French practice. Because the French Schneider CA tanks had a top speed of about five miles per hour, they were not capable of moving much faster than the pace of an infantry advance. This prompted French commanders to use them not as a separate arm but as a means of supporting the infantry. Only later in 1918, under the command of Lieutenant Colonel George S. Patton Jr., would tanks begin to come into their own as armored vehicles that could be used in advance of infantry movement—or even separately from infantry operations.

While the initial assault came off without a hitch, the cover of darkness, compounded by a heavy downpour of rain and extremely muddy roads, slowed the movement of the main body of American troops to the front. As H-hour approached, it began to look as if the AEF would be late. Not so, however. Despite the inclement weather, the 1st and 2nd Divisions, which were to participate in the opening operations, somehow managed to arrive in the proverbial nick of time. Indeed, the 2nd Division infantry debarked from their *camions* and marched rapidly to their jump-off point barely in time to move immediately into action. They had arrived quite literally within minutes of H-hour.

The two divisions were part of the spearhead of the French XX Corps attack. The assault was launched at dawn—4:45 a.m.—and was aimed at capturing and holding the high ground south of Soissons. In the process of executing the mission, the troops severed rail lines communicating with the main German body to the east, thereby beginning the isolation of the Marne salient. Acting in concert with the Moroccan 1st Division, the American 1st and 2nd Divisions attacked across an unbroken three-division front. The 1st Division (Major General Charles Summerall commanding) was positioned on the northern flank, Major General James Harbord's 2nd Division took the southern flank, and the Moroccans were placed in the center, between the American units. By eight o'clock on the morning of July 18, the two American divisions had advanced a spectacular three miles or more and had achieved their objectives for the day. It was a most auspicious beginning.

●

On July 19, XX Corps—and the American 1st and 2nd Divisions, with the Moroccan 1st—resumed their attack. By this time, however, the Germans were ready for them. All through the night, the German defenders had been extensively reinforced with machine guns and field artillery. The rapid progress of the first day of the assault now seemed something out of a dream as shells exploded and machine-gun rounds forced the attackers to hug the ground. The Americans continued their advance, but it was now against a brutal headwind of fire. The fighting on this second day of the offensive was hard and costly—so costly that General Harbord requested the relief of his 2nd Division, which was duly replaced by a French unit. It certainly had earned a rest. During two days of combat, the 2nd had advanced more than eight miles. Its troops captured three thousand German prisoners, along with sixty-six field guns. Casualties, however, were heavy, at nearly four thousand killed, wounded, or missing.

While 2nd Division recuperated, Summerall's 1st Division remained in action and on the line for three more days of tough fighting, during which its men interdicted the road between Soissons and Château-Thierry and tore up the railroad between Villers and Cotterêts. This accomplished, the division then hunkered down to defend the high ground overlooking Soissons. During what was for this division a full five-day battle, the 1st captured 3,800 prisoners and seventy guns from the *seven* German divisions that had been thrown against it. Outnumbered as the American division was, the victory was an extraordinary achievement. But it had not come cheaply. Seven thousand of its number became casualties, including some one thousand killed. Among the officers in the field, the casualty rate was a devastating 73 percent.

The American divisions were not unique in the heavy cost they had incurred. The entire French XX Corps was depleted in the attack. Nevertheless, the losses had purchased an important operational triumph. Not only did the XX Corps action take a heavy toll on the Germans but it forced German high command to shift men to the defense of the salient, which meant that the Ludendorff offensive east of Château-Thierry had to be aborted and all remaining German footholds on the Paris side of the Marne withdrawn and relinquished. Finally—and most important— the 1st and 2nd Divisions had been so thorough in their destruction of roads and railroads that the German supply line through Soissons was entirely choked off. With the salient now untenable, the Germans began a withdrawal from it.

●

South of the French Tenth Army's front, the French Sixth Army also launched its attack on July 18. With the French force that day was Major General George H. Cameron's US 4th Division, which attacked in support of the Sixth Army's II and VII Corps. For the next two days, from July 18 to July 20, the 4th Division advanced some four miles in two different sectors—units of the division supporting two different French corps.

Yet more remarkable, the US. I Corps, under Major General Hunter Liggett, conducted a fighting advance up the center of the Marne salient *for four weeks*, part of the time in company with the US 26th Division and the French 167th Division. Together, these formations advanced beyond Belleau Wood, progressing ten miles during July 18–25.

And then I Corps kept going. Over the next three weeks, it continued to roll up gains against dogged German defenders (figure 29). From July 25 to August 3, I Corps advanced in concert with the US 42nd Division. From August 3 to August 12, it hooked up with the 4th Division and crossed first the Ourcq River and then the Vesle. This advance totaled fifteen miles—all of it gained in virtually continuous combat. On August 12, higher headquarters ordered I Corps to withdraw to the rear-echelon Toul sector and prepare for the next offensive, which would be on the Somme (chapter 12).

●

What does a beaten army look like? The effect of the Aisne-Marne offensive on the German Seventh Army is apparent from a dispatch

Figure 29. American snipers of the 166th Infantry (formerly 4th Infantry, Ohio National Guard) "pick off Germans" on the outer edge of Villers sur Fre, France, July 30, 1918. WIKIMEDIA

sent to the Operations Section of the German Supreme Headquarters on July 24, 1918:

> *TO: Supreme Headquarters, Operations Section*
>
> *The Seventh Army reports that the following divisions are no longer fit for offensive action and must be replaced in the very near future . . . a total of 18 divisions. . . .*
>
> *If the battle is to be fought to a finish in the combat zone south of the AISNE and VESLE, then it is necessary to bring up fresh forces of all arms, including army artillery.*
>
> *Exact numbers cannot yet be given. They cannot be foreseen. But the expenditure of forces mentioned above will serve as a general indication.*

There is no doubt about it that the enemy will continue the battle. He has sufficient forces available for this purpose.

Under these circumstances this headquarters does not believe it to be expedient for us to fight the battle to a finish south of the VESLE. Considerable portions of the army and the service of supply are being destroyed and used up, thereby more and more reducing the forces available for attacks from our side.

Therefore this headquarters recommends that the Ninth, Seventh and First Armies be gradually withdrawn behind the AISNE and VESLE.

In the bend south of the AISNE and VESLE there are at present 27 divisions on the front. The AISNE and VESLE front requires 14 divisions in the front line.

This headquarters will explore whether any purpose is served in maintaining an advance position forward of the AISNE and VESLE.[1]

●

The AEF also fought in the portion of the Aisne-Marne offensive conducted east of Château-Thierry. Here, on this segment of the Marne line, the US Third Division had been vigorously active since early June. When the Aisne-Marne operation was preparing to step off in mid-July, the 3rd Division was called on to keep the German forces occupied and pinned down while the French Sixth and Tenth Armies advanced into position. While the French attacks developed, the 3rd maintained this supporting and blocking role until July 20, when the division was attached to the French XXXVIII Corps, with which it crossed the Marne and spearheaded operations to clear the northern bank. As the Germans withdrew from their positions here, elements of the division gave relentless chase, distressing the Germans with their dogged determination.

In motion and heavily engaged for days, the 3rd Division continued to fight forward until it was relieved by the 32nd Division on July 29. The 32nd picked up right where the 3rd had left off. It continued the Franco-American advance all the way to the Vesle River. At this point, on August 1, General Bullard and his III Corps arrived and finally took from the French XXXVIII Corps full tactical control of the 32nd, 28th, and 3rd Divisions. This put the US I and III Corps together, independent of French command, on the front lines. For a short time, both Europe and America had a preview of what an independent American army would look like in the Great War.

•

The Aisne-Marne Campaign concluded on August 6, having brought to an end the threat of a German breakthrough into Paris. This alone was a major achievement, but the offensive also paid three even more significant dividends. First, it returned to Allied control several key rail lines. No longer would Allied forces be exclusively at the mercy of slow-moving *camions* traversing roads that were often more rutted mud than level highway. Second, the combination of the defeat of Ludendorff's fourth offensive (chapter 10), followed immediately by a small counterthrust and the great Aisne-Marne offensive, dashed Ludendorff's hopes and plans for a fifth offensive—this one planned against the BEF in Flanders.

Finally—and perhaps most significantly—the Aisne-Marne operation wrested the war's initiative out of German hands for the first time since the autumn of 1914. This was a spectacular reversal of fortune, and the Germans would never recover the momentum they had lost.

The AEF had played a significant role in the offensive. Strictly by the numbers, it was not the starring role, yet it had been a star turn. The American army acquitted itself courageously, boldly, and with high degree of professional competence. It had shown a selfless willingness to suffer casualties, and it had produced results. Moreover, the AEF proved itself to be a most reliable ally. From the German point of view, surely Erich Ludendorff must have recognized that the window through which he had hoped to snatch victory—before the American army could make a significant contribution to the contest on the Western Front—had now slammed shut. Even without huge numbers yet deployed, the American army had revealed itself as a formidable opponent.

On this portion of the Western Front, the successful conclusion of the Aisne-Marne campaign positioned Franco-American forces to continue to apply steady pressure against the Germans. From the middle of August to the middle of September, the US III Corps accompanied French forces in an advance *east* of the River Vesle. The Marne salient had thus been thoroughly reduced.

The US 32nd Division remained active in the sector. From August 28 to September 1, under the command of Major General William G. Haan, the division attacked German positions north of Soissons, taking and occupying the important town of Juvigny. From here, elements of the division penetrated two and a half miles into German lines. Early in September, the US 28th and 77th Divisions took up the action, advancing and attacking to the north, stopping just short of the Aisne River on September 16.

In all, eight AEF divisions—the 1st, 2nd, 3rd, 4th, 26th, 28th, 32nd, and 42nd—fought in the Aisne-Marne offensive and, in some cases, fought conspicuously as spearheads of the attack. Some 270,000 American soldiers took part, with more than twelve thousand of them becoming casualties.

●

While the Aisne-Marne offensive was still being fought, in an Allied conference on July 24, Ferdinand Foch presented his program for the rest of 1918. Its goal was the reduction of the three principal German salients: the Marne salient, an objective well on its way to realization; the Amiens salient (figure 30); and the St. Mihiel salient. Achieving these objectives was intended to prepare for a final, general Allied offensive toward the end of the year. Foch believed that the war could be ended in total victory by late 1918 or early 1919. Eliminating the salients would allow free communication and movement behind the French front, which would give the Allies a great advantage in mounting the culminating operation.

General Pershing took the opportunity to ask Foch to assign the reduction of the St. Mihiel salient to the AEF. That Foch enthusiastically agreed to the assignment signified his heightened confidence in the American soldier and in American military leadership. Pershing now pressed his case for the creation of a fully independent American army. Earlier in the month, on July 4, he had named Lieutenant Colonel Hugh A. Drum as the projected First US Army chief of staff. As such,

Figure 30. American soldiers get acquainted with their French brothers-in-arms near Amiens. WIKIMEDIA

Drum was ordered to begin establishing army headquarters. With this process in motion, Pershing met twice more with Foch, on July 10 and 21. On July 22, Foch announced his agreement to the organization of the First US Army, as well as to the creation of two exclusively American sectors: a "temporary" combat sector in the area of Château-Thierry, where I Corps and III Corps were already active and would serve as the foundation on which the new army could be rapidly built up; and a quiet sector east of this, extending from Nomeny (east of the Moselle River) to a point north of St. Mihiel, the agreed-upon theater of operations for the First US Army.

Foch formally issued an announcement of the organization of the First US Army on July 24, with the formation to become effective on August 10. General Pershing was named as its commanding officer, and its headquarters was established at La Ferté-sous-Jouarre, west of Château-Thierry. Fifteen months had passed since the US Congress had declared war on Germany, and now the United States had an American army in France.

CHAPTER 12

Somme Offensive

August 8–November 11, 1918

THE SO-CALLED RACE TO THE SEA WAS A SERIES OF DESPERATE RECIP-
rocal flanking maneuvers the Allies and Germans executed between September 17 and October 19, 1914, in an effort to position for an enveloping
attack that each hoped would prove decisive. In the end, the maneuvers
proved futile, each adversary always aiming to get around the northern
flank of the other. All that was achieved was the anchoring of the north-
erly end of the Western Front on the North Sea coast of Belgium. This
left neither side any place to go and thus catalyzed the stalemate that soon
congealed the Western Front into four years of mutual slaughter in highly
static trench warfare. As a result, while historians and the combatants
themselves distinguish numerous named battles, offensives, and counter-
offensives between 1914 and November 11, 1918, World War I on the
Western Front in a very real sense was one continuous battle or campaign.
Perhaps the more appropriate phrase would be *continuous combat*.

Thus, what many official histories, including that of the US Army,
call the "Somme Offensive" may be more accurately called by the more
colorful alternative name of "Hundred Days Offensive," which more
accurately describes the closing period of World War I. Whichever name
we use, the Hundred Days Offensive or the Somme Offensive may be
discussed as large-scale fighting along the Western Front from August 8,
1918, to the Armistice of November 11, or as the following series of often
overlapping engagements: the Battle of Amiens (August 8–12, 1918, also

called Third Battle of Picardy), Second Battle of the Somme (August 21–September 2, 1918), Battle of Mont Saint-Quentin (August 31–September 3, 1918), Battle of Savy-Dallon (September 10, 1918), Battle of Vauxaillon (September 14, 1918), Meuse-Argonne Offensive (September 26–November 11, 1918; chapter 16), Battle of Saint-Quentin Canal (September 29–October 10, 1918), Fifth Battle of Ypres (September 28–October 2, 1918), and the Battle of Cambrai (October 8–10, 1918). Some histories of World War I distinguish even more battles; however, all of them describe portions of the same continuous combat that made up the war's last hundred days.

However we anatomize it, the Somme Offensive or the Hundred Days Offensive focused on northern France and Belgium, and its overall result was to force the Germans—who had been fighting the Western Front war on French and Belgian territory since August 1914—into an eastward withdrawal. The war ended before the bulk of German forces had been pushed out of French territory, but they were clearly on their way, the offensive having sent them into retreat behind what the Allies called the Hindenburg Line (figure 31) and the Germans called the *Siegfriedstellung*—the "Siegfried emplacement."

Figure 31. "American soldiers on the way to the Hindenburg Line" during the Meuse-Argonne offensive, the largest battle the US Army fought to that time.
COLLIER'S MAGAZINE PHOTOGRAPH, NATIONAL ARCHIVES AND RECORDS ADMINISTRATION

An incredibly formidable complex of concrete fortifications, dugouts, tunnels, and trenches, the Hindenburg Line extended ninety miles from the Aisne River just east of Soissons north to Saint-Quentin and on to Arras. It was the westernmost of three major German defensive works, which were built as positions from which to make effective fighting withdrawals when necessary. Once the Germans had withdrawn beyond the Hindenburg Line, however, the Armistice became inevitable—yet that did not mean the bloodshed was diminished. As the Americans and their Allies would discover, the Great War was fought at full intensity right up to the eleventh hour of the eleventh day of the eleventh month of 1918.

Of the major "Hundred Days" battles, American soldiers fought at Amiens, the Second Battle of the Somme, Meuse-Argonne (chapter 16), Saint-Quentin Canal, and the Fifth Battle of Ypres. The major US-involved actions are discussed here.

●

One of the most useful overviews of American participation in the Somme Offensive was published in "The Army Flag and its Streamers" by the US Army Center of History in 1964 and updated in 2015. The summary is worth quoting at length:

> On 8 August the British began limited operations with the objective of flattening the Amiens salient. This attack marked the beginning of the great Somme Offensive, which continued until hostilities ceased on 11 November. The British Fourth Army, including the American 33d and 80th Divisions, struck the northwestern edge of the salient in coordination with a thrust by the French First Army from the southwest. No artillery barrage preceded the attack to forewarn the enemy. Some 600 tanks spearheaded the British assault, which jumped off during the thick fog. The completely surprised Germans quickly gave up 16,000 prisoners as their positions were overrun. Ludendorff himself characterized 8 August as the "Black Day of the German Army." The Germans were forced to fall back to the old 1915 line, where they reorganized strong defenses-in-depth. Haig then shifted his attack farther north to the vicinity of Arras on 21 August, forcing the Ger-

mans to withdraw toward the Hindenburg Line. By the end of the month they had evacuated the whole of the Amiens salient.

The drive to breach the main Hindenburg Line began at the end of September. The American II Corps (27th and 30th Divisions), forming part of the British Fourth Army, attacked the German defenses along the line of the Cambrai–Saint-Quentin Canal, capturing heavily fortified Bony and Bellicourt on the 29th. By 5 October the offensive had broken through the Hindenburg Line, and the Allied forces advanced through open country to the Oise-Somme Canal (19 October). During this phase of the operations the 27th and 30th Divisions alternated in the line. When the American II Corps was relieved on 21 October, it had served 26 days in the line and suffered 11,500 casualties.

The British advance in the Somme region continued until the Armistice, constituting the northern arm of Foch's great pincers movement on the Germans' vital lateral rail communications system. The key junction at Aulnoye, southwest of Maubeuge, was reached on 5 November. A total of about 54,000 Americans participated in the Somme Campaign.[1]

●

The collapse of the fourth of Erich Ludendorff's offensives (chapter 10) demoralized the German army and the German people even as it reinvigorated the Allies. Nevertheless, the strategically failed offensive had inflicted more casualties on the Allies than on the Germans. Not that the numbers told the whole story. The impact of losses is both a matter of quality and quantity, and the German units that had absorbed the heaviest losses were made up of the very best soldiers in the German army. They were the shock troops or "storm troopers": soldiers trained in complex Hutier assault tactics and other highly effective methods of attack. Much as genuine food items were now being replaced by unpalatable and non-nourishing *ersatz* rations throughout Germany, thanks to the relentless Royal Navy blockade, so the cream of the German military was being diminished by combat and diluted by replacements drawn from among rear-echelon troops, reservists, home guard, overage men, wounded veterans who had been invalided out of the service, and even former German POWs liberated from Russian prison camps, typically in pitiable condition. By the late summer of 1918, the German army had become decreasingly capable of mounting anything resembling an offensive.

During the closing hours of the fourth Ludendorff offensive, General Sir Douglas Haig began planning a major counterattack east of Amiens using the British Fourth Army, which had recently been reorganized and reinforced. In all, ten British, five Australian, four Canadian, twelve French, and a single US division would be involved in the battle, which was intended to keep the critical Amiens-Paris railroad open and available to Allied transport while reducing the Amiens salient, a massive German strongpoint, which had been created during Operation Michael, the Ludendorff offensive of March 1918.

By August 8, when the Battle of Amiens commenced, Haig had assembled some 440,000 men and had done so while preserving remarkable secrecy. Among these soldiers were those of the US 33rd Division, which was attached to the British army instead of the French. In support of the Amiens operation, the British brought more than 2,000 guns, 500 tanks, and 800 planes. The French contributed an additional 1,100 aircraft. The assemblage of manpower and equipment added up to a massively superior force hurled against just 10 regular German divisions and 4 reserve divisions with no more than 365 aircraft among them.

The Battle of Amiens battle opened at 4:20 on the morning of August 8 with an unusually massive rolling barrage that would, before it was complete, fire some 450,000 shells on the five German divisions directly facing the Allied front. In the first wave, eight British, Australian, and Canadian divisions advanced and attacked. By midmorning, an early fog had lifted to reveal utter catastrophe throughout the German front lines. Entire divisions had been wiped out in the onslaught, leaving a gaping wound through which the Canadian and Australian forces advanced as much as eight miles along a very broad front. They surged toward and through the German artillery line, accepting the surrender of more than fifteen thousand German troops. This, even more than the loss of life and materiel, is what struck horror in the heart of Erich Ludendorff. Famously, he pronounced August 8, 1918 to be the *Schwarzer Tag des deutschen Heeres* ("black day of the German army"). It was not a label denoting the army's military defeat, and it was not an assessment of the first day of battle as a turning point in the war. Rather, it was Ludendorff's fearful acknowledgment of the sudden collapse of the army's discipline and morale.

The opening day of the Battle of Amiens was not a total success for the Allies, however. In III Corps area, the British 58th Division suffered heavy losses and could not advance. This left the Australian 3rd Division exposed on its flank and vulnerable to severe enfilading German fire from machine guns and artillery positioned on Chipilly Spru, a high-ground ridge jutting into a slow horseshoe bend north of the Somme. To neutralize this deadly fire, the US 131st Infantry (of the US 33rd Division), which was attached to the British 58th Division, was ordered to attack and take the ridge. Plans were hastily drawn up for a night march to the line of departure for the attack. To ensure that the men would reach their starting positions in time, the regiment was obliged to make the last four miles at double-time. At 5:30 on the morning of August 9, the 131st attacked. With support from elements of the Australian 4th Division, which was on the opposite bank of the Somme, the Americans captured both Chipilly Spru and took all of the German positions supporting it. Its mission accomplished, the American regiment was transferred to the operational control of the Australian 4th Division, which it joined in an attack on Etinehem on August 13. The 131st remained "in the line"—in active combat—until August 19.

●

The Anglo-Australian advance continued during August 9—though not at the explosive pace of August 8—and the fighting at that time widened to encompass Montdidier, a location at which the French took up the offensive. The attrition among the British tanks—five hundred had been instrumental in the first day's triumph—was remarkably heavy, revealing the machines' essential lack of durability and reliability. After just four days of combat, the five hundred had been reduced to six tanks still functioning. Nevertheless, on August 10, it became apparent that the Germans were beginning to withdraw from the Amiens salient, which they had won in March at great cost in Operation Michael. Even with most of its armor rendered inoperative, the British managed to drive thirteen miles into the German positions by August 13, the day after the Battle of Amiens ended.

●

The results of the Battle of Amiens were most auspicious for the opening of the Somme Offensive. As the British war correspondent Philip Gibbs observed, thanks to the victory at Amiens, the enemy was put "on the defensive" and the initiative on the Western Front had been firmly taken into Allied hands. Such was the *strategic* impact of the battle. As Gibbs further noted, however, "the change has been greater in the minds of men than in the taking of territory. On our side the army seems to be buoyed up with the enormous hope of getting on with this business quickly," whereas the Germans seem "no longer [to harbor] even a dim hope of victory on this Western Front. All they hope for now is to defend themselves long enough to gain peace by negotiation."[2] There was truth in this assessment, as even Ludendorff had spoken of the German army's "black day"; however, the bloodletting was far from finished.

By August 27, when journalist Gibbs wrote his report on the Amiens battle, the Allies had captured almost fifty thousand prisoners and five hundred guns in an ongoing offensive in which operations were now virtually continuous—although historians set August 21 as the beginning of the next major battle of the offensive, the Second Battle of the Somme.

The Allies went into the new action in high spirits, dismissing the twenty-two thousand casualties suffered on August 8 alone as rather light—which, by grim World War I standards, they were. The innovative weapons of combat did not fare so well, however. As mentioned, five hundred tanks were down to six after only four days in action. As for the large number of Allied aircraft on the front, fully a quarter of them had been lost in the opening assault on August 8.

The general attack, as the Second Battle of the Somme, resumed along a thirty-five-mile front on August 21 with what some histories denominate separately as the Second Battle of Bapaume, named for a village to the north of the Somme River. German High Command ordered officers to give up no territory but to fight for every inch. Ludendorff hoped to restore discipline to his army while depriving the enemy of any further momentum. The German view from the ground, however, was increasingly hopeless. And with good reason. The Second Battle of Bapaume quickly blossomed into a major advance against the German Second Army, which began to fall back across the entire thirty-five-mile front, extending from a point south of Douai to La Fère, which was south of Saint-Quentin. On August 22, the important town of Albert was captured. Four days later, the British First Army broadened the attack by an additional 7.5 miles, and this phase of the Second Battle of the Somme is sometimes called the Second Battle of Arras.

Bapaume fell to the British on August 29, and the Australian Corps crossed the Somme under cover of darkness on the night of August 31. In the Battle of Mont Saint-Quentin (August 31–September 3, 1918) and the Battle of Péronne (September 3–4, 1918), the Australians broke through the German lines, making a spectacular advance that British Fourth Army commanding officer General Henry Rawlinson called the greatest military achievement of the war.

•

On September 2, Canadian forces penetrated the defensive line the Germans called the Wotan Stellung and the British referred to as the Drocourt-Queant Switch, east of the Hindenburg Line proper. On the same day, the Australians took Mont Saint-Quentin. The combination of these two gains drove the Germans more deeply behind the Hindenburg Line, although they withdrew very much in fighting order, conducting a fierce rear-guard action that made extensive and deadly use of their machine-gun units.

Despite the ongoing cost, the Allied penetration of the Hindenburg Line was indeed a reason for celebration. An interlocking, six-thousand-to eight-thousand-yard-deep, multilayered complex of entanglements, fortifications, elaborate trenchworks, and bunkers, it was the strongest defensive line on the Western Front. The strongpoints placed at strategic intervals along the Hindenburg Line created interlocking fields of fire, which were extremely efficient in their lethality. Impressive though it was, the line was as yet incomplete when the Allies attacked. A layer called the forward battle zone (and sometimes called the outpost zone) and a second layer, the main battle zone, were supposed to be complemented by two easterly lines: a support zone and a reserve zone. Neither of these had been built when the breaching of the line began. Nevertheless, the portion of the Hindenburg Line in the British sector was replete with pillboxes and dugouts as well as a veritable maze of trenches and multiple belts of barbed wire. Moreover, the retreating Germans had concentrated themselves in a portion of the defensive complex that was positioned behind the Saint-Quentin Canal, which presented a formidable obstacle in itself. It was a ship canal, in effect a monster moat, water-filled (of course), thirty-five feet wide, with banks rising from between fifty and a hundred feet at a steep fifty-degree angle. Only at a single point south of the village of Bellicourt did the canal pass through a tunnel, which made this crossing a land bridge by which the canal could be traversed. Recognizing this as a vulnerable point, the Germans sited their main defensive position directly in front of the subterranean canal and heavily augmented its defenses.

In planning his attack against the Hindenburg Line at this point, Australian general John Monash determined that his corps needed fresh troops to take the canal and breach the Hindenburg Line at this point. Accordingly, the US II Corps, consisting of the 27th and 30th Divisions (minus their artillery and support elements), was placed under the operational control of Monash and the Australian Corps. In planning the assault, the Australian general assumed that the Hindenburg Line's forward battle position would already be under Allied control, leaving only the main battle layer to be taken. He therefore determined to position the US 27th and 30th Divisions in the vacated forward battle position to use as a line of departure for an attack on September 29 against the main battle support positions, to which (Monash believed) all the Germans had retreated. The no-man's-land between the forward and main battle zones was about four hundred yards. The Monash plan called for the Australian 3rd and 5th Divisions to pass through the Americans even as they were pressing their attack on the main battle zone. Having passed through, the Australians were to advance some four thousand yards beyond the main battle zone to take the incomplete and only partially fortified reserve line. In this way, the American-Australian attack would penetrate through the entire Hindenburg Line—all three zones—in this area in a single mighty stroke.

It seemed like a feasible notion, but it went wrong from the start.

In the northern portion of the US sector, which was held by the US 27th Division, the British III Corps had spent a full futile week trying to take the forward battle line, but failed before it was relieved on September 25. Even though the frontmost line was still occupied by German troops, Monash was loath to change his plan, and he therefore ordered the US 27th Division not merely to advance to a position that had been made ready for it, but to attack and seize its own line of departure—the very objective that the British III Corps had failed to achieve in an entire week's fighting! The order specified that this operation was to be carried out on September 27, two days before the main attack was scheduled to step off.

No objection was forthcoming from the American 27th Division, which covered a front that was four thousand yards wide and that was defended by three German strongpoints: Quennemont farm, Guillemont farm, and the Knoll. The American commanders decided to mount their attack using all three battalions of the division's 106th Infantry Regiment. The assault, supported by a dozen tanks and companies K and M of the 105th Infantry, stepped off at 5:30 on the morning of September 27.

The 106th went into the attack with some two thousand riflemen in twelve rifle companies. At this point, however, the regiment was critically short of officers. A smoke screen was deployed to cover the advance of small assault parties, which also took advantage of a heavy morning mist. Despite this, the German defenders poured on a heavy fire, forcing the attack back to its starting line with heavy casualties. Seventeen of the eighteen officers committed to the attack were killed or wounded, and on the next morning, September 28, the entire 106th regiment could muster no more than nine officers and 252 men.

The US 27th Division subsequently reported 1,537 casualties, virtually all of them from the 106th Regiment. But as of the end of day on

September 28, nobody knew how many 106th Regiment doughboys were still holding their positions in the German trenches or were taking cover somewhere in no-man's-land. The commanders decided to roll the dice and go forward with the main attack, as planned, on September 29, using as the line of departure the rear trenches of the forward line that was held by the US 30th Division. This line, however, was a thousand yards in front of the position held by the 27th Division. The plan—in truth, it was more of a hope—was that the 27th, coming up from behind, would steal that thousand yards at H minus 1 (one hour before H-Hour, the appointed time of the attack), catch up to the 30th Division, and then attack abreast with it, on its right, at H-Hour.

"Stealing" a thousand yards exposed to enemy fire was a very long shot at best—and its chances for success were further diminished by a step taken to avoid making those missing soldiers of the 106th Infantry victims of friendly fire. Instead of laying down the rolling barrage directly in front of the 27th Division's advance, it was decided to register (aim) it a thousand yards *behind* the German defenders, who were still dug in from Quennemont farm to the Knoll. In short, the barrage would offer the attackers no protection—and probably cause minimal casualties among the Germans.

As scheduled, the attack commenced at 5:50 on the morning of September 29. British artillery laid down an intense barrage of some 427,000 rounds—every one of which fell *behind* the enemy. In consequence, the defenders were very much alive and well and capable of manning their machine guns, which cut down the men of the US 27th Division as they advanced. The attack was composed of two battalions of the division's 107th Infantry on the left and two battalions of the 108th Infantry on the right, each with an additional battalion in support. The 107th also had support from a 350-man provisional battalion, which was all that was left of the ill-fated 106th Regiment. Behind these attackers was the 105th Infantry, serving as the division reserve.

On the far right of the attack, small-unit teams of the 108th Infantry were able to take portions of the Hindenburg Line south of Bony. They were later reinforced by troops of the Australian 3rd Division. In the center and left, the small-unit assault elements were rapidly joined by all the support elements—and a good thing, too, since the fighting in this area was intense, especially around the Knoll.

It was midday before elements of the 10th Australian Brigade of the Australian 3rd Division joined in the attack, but by the end of the day on September 29, the entire German forward position was in Allied hands. This, however, put the attackers still two miles out from their assigned objective, which was the main battle zone. So far, the 107th Infantry had lost 337 men killed and suffered an additional 658 wounded. This gave the regiment a record no unit wants: the highest single-day total loss of any US regiment in World War I. As for the 108th Infantry, its losses were nearly as heavy, and they included every single officer in the assault companies. For the period between September 21 and October 2, the 27th Division incurred 4,642 casualties.

In the 30th Division sector, the attack went forward as scheduled. The 119th and 120th Infantry, four battalions arrayed abreast from north to south, launched their attack at 5:50 a.m. from the German forward battle zone and advanced through mist and heavy smoke. By 7:30, the 119th had passed through the main battle position of the Hindenburg Line, only to suffer heavy casualties from attacks on its left flank, which had been exposed when it overran and left the 27th Division far behind. As for the 120th Infantry, it reached Bellicourt, behind the main battle zone of the Hindenburg Line, immediately atop the Saint-Quentin Tunnel. From here, the regiment pushed on to the German support zone at Nauroy by 11:00 in the morning.

The American regiments had breached the Hindenburg Line—but at a heartbreakingly high cost. Losses to the 30th Division for September 29–October 2, were 505 killed in action or died of wounds and 1,989 wounded. In the meantime, south of the American divisions, the soldiers of the British 46th Division crossed the canal and, by nightfall, had overrun the main and support positions on their front. Together with the portion breached by the Americans, the Hindenburg Line had been penetrated through on a six-mile front.

On September 30, the attack continued, minus the battered and depleted 27th and 30th US divisions, which were withdrawn from the line—at least mostly. For doughboys of the 27th and 30th who happened to be intermingled with Australian units that were still in combat, relief would not come for several more days. The US II Corps was given a few days' rest and then sent back into the line to relieve the Australian Corps.

•

By the beginning of October, with the Hindenburg Line breached, it was abundantly clear that the German army had lost the ability to resist a sustained Allied offensive. It was also apparent that the US Army, now over a million strong in France and growing, was capable of turning the tide of battle, even when it represented a relatively small portion of the Allied force in any one sector.

For the Allies, this was good news. And yet the German army was still very much a functioning army. It may have been dispirited, but it was still a disciplined force and a lethal one. It offered a credible and vigorous defense when attacked, and while it now seemed incapable of launching a major offensive, it still could mount vigorous counterattacks, at least locally.

The US 117th Infantry learned this the hard way when, on the morning of October 7, it was conducting a "line-straightening attack," seeking to flatten a salient in preparation for a new general attack planned for October 8. The regiment advanced boldly, progressed several hundred yards, and then withered under intense machine gun and rifle fire. Thus battered and bloody, it joined in the major British Fourth Army attack on October 8 as part of the US 30th Division. The Americans advanced a full ten miles to the Selle River during three days of combat. The division suffered some 2,600 casualties, a thousand from 117th Infantry alone.

The US 30th Division rested at the Selle River line, where it was joined on its right flank by the 27th Division. On October 17, the two divisions crossed the Selle and, over the three days that followed, fought through toward the Sambre Canal. The two divisions continued as part of the Somme Offensive until late October. On the night of October 19–20, the 30th Division was relieved. On October 21, the 27th Division was also relieved. This ended the US Army participation in the Somme Offensive, which continued with British, British Empire, and French forces until the Armistice of November 11, 1918.

CHAPTER 13

Oise-Aisne

August 18–November 11, 1918

THE CONCLUDING PHASE OF THE AISNE-MARNE OPERATIONS (CHAPTER 11) brought the Allies to the Vesle River, which flows into the Aisne. This was very near the eastern base of what had been the Germans' Marne salient. At this point, General Jean Degoutte, commanding the French Sixth Army, was ordered to consolidate his positions on the south bank of the Vesle and to establish bridgeheads preparatory to crossing the river as part of a general advance by all French armies on this front. Thus, between August 4 and August 8, 1918, the Vesle River front was stabilized. Except for a few small isolated areas, the enemy was in possession of the northern bank of the Vesle.

On August 8, Philippe Pétain issued "Instructions for the Generals Commanding the French Group of Armies of the Reserve and the French Group of Armies of the Center":

> *I. The battle now in progress between the OISE and the SOMME does not permit us to execute at present the powerful stroke which appears necessary to throw the enemy back from the heights north of the VESLE and force him to withdraw north of the AISNE. That result can, however, be obtained by a different maneuver.*
>
> *Consequently, the French Fifth, Sixth, and Tenth Armies will at once organize strongly the positions south of the VESLE. . . .*

The bridgeheads secured north of the VESLE will be preserved, widened, and reinforced, not by increasing the forces occupying them, but by carefully coordinating the infantry and artillery fires and by suitable field works.

Furthermore the outposts will maintain contact with the enemy and make every effort to take prisoners.

II. This attitude of waiting will not prevent intensive study and preparation for a decisive blow which we may be called upon to deliver at any moment in order to drive the enemy back north of the AISNE.

The attack would be made by the Sixth Army. Its first objective would be the plateau between the VESLE and the AISNE.[1]

The order went on to instruct the armies to hold what isolated ground had already been gained north of the Vesle, and to make extensive preparations for renewing the general advance. At this point, in August, the American units in the sector were III Corps, commanded by Major General Robert Lee Bullard, and including the 28th Division, 32nd Division, and the 77th Division. On September 15, 1918, the 370th Infantry Regiment arrived in the Aisne-Vesle sector. A so-called colored regiment in the racially segregated US Army of the period, the 370th was nominally part of the 93rd Infantry Division, an organization, however, that existed mainly on paper for administrative purposes. The 370th was entirely at the disposal of the French (figure 32).

As written, Pétain's instructions implied a status of waiting and inaction. Indeed, the Allied advance was effectively stalled on the Vesle line from the first week in August to early September; however, there was sharp, sometimes intense, fighting during the period between the Aisne-Marne and the Oise-Aisne operations. The Americans held about six kilometers of frontage from St. Thibaut to Fismes and were in numerous bitter fights to hold what General Degoutte called "bridgeheads" at Bazoches, Chateau du Diable, and Fismes-Fismette. For the Americans, the Oise-Aisne operations were a kind of interim or transitional mission between Aisne-Marne (chapter 11) and St. Mihiel

Figure 32. "Some of the colored men of the 369th (15th N.Y.) who won the Croix de Guerre for gallantry in action. Left to right. Front row: Pvt. Ed Williams, Herbert Taylor, Pvt. Leon Fraitor, Pvt. Ralph Hawkins. Back Row: Sgt. H. D. Prinas, Sgt. Dan Storms, Pvt. Joe Williams, Pvt. Alfred Hanley, and Cpl. T. W. Taylor." Black soldiers served in segregated units under white officers (above company level). At first, most "colored" units were relegated to labor assignments, but, in combat, they often compiled exemplary records of high performance and heroism. RECORDS OF THE WAR DEPARTMENT GENERAL SPECIAL STAFFS

(chapter 15). Most of the combat involved fighting to hold on to gains that had already been made.

The kind of fighting related to the so-called bridgeheads rarely gets into histories of World War I, but the US III Corps commanding officer, Major General Bullard, left a vivid picture of what it was like to serve on the Vesle front. He noted that much of the sector was mostly quiet except "up in our front lines," where "contact with the enemy was close and dangerous":

The conditions there were never easy. The narrow stream of the Vesle was the general line of separation of my front line and the enemy. I do not know who put it there—whether the French did it long ago or the Germans in their last retreat—but the river was full of concealed barbed wire. It was as much as a man's life was worth to attempt to cross, whether by swimming or wading. From one end to the other of my front line this was the condition, and I confidently expected, and so it turned out in the end, that no crossing of this stream would ever be made except upon a general advance.[2]

The points General Degoutte had designated along the Vesle as bridge-heads, Bullard noted, were all within range of German-held high ground, namely "the river bluffs and hills just to the north [of the American position on the south bank of the river]. Advance at any point on my front seemed hopeless from these so-called bridgeheads. Yet the French general was constantly insisting upon [my ordering] raids [to be made] from these small points with a view to enlarging his 'bridgeheads.'"

These small operations seemed to me to offer no chance worth the risk and the loss of life. On my right and left were French corps that apparently took quite the same view. In Fismette, the portion of the village of Fismes [Fismes itself was on the south bank] on the north side of the Vesle, I had a single company of infantry, 150 men, of the 28th (Pennsylvania) Division. One day I was ordered to make a raid with this company. It was carried out with great determination, but the bluffs of the river to the east, north, and northwest were lined with enemy machine guns, and the company, thus covered on three sides by the enemy's fire, had no success. It was driven back into its cellars in Fismette. This company could be rein-forced and fed at night only across a broken bridge, now not even a foot bridge. This crossing was swept from two directions by enemy machine-gun fire, and men crossed, whether by day or night, only at intervals, and then only a man at a time. In short, men could not count on getting across.

It was evident that whenever the enemy desired he could wipe out the company on the north bank of the Vesle. After its failure in the raid ordered by General Degoutte, I ordered that company withdrawn to the south bank of the Vesle man by man at night. My chief-of-staff, who was very much in favour of the French general's idea of "bridge-heads," knew of the order which I was going to give. When I returned from Fismes late in the afternoon, I found the French general at my corps headquarters and learned that my chief-of-staff had informed him of my order to withdraw the company. The French army commander ordered me at once to replace it. This was done.

Three or four days after this, without my being able to reinforce it or save it, completely at the mercy of the enemy, this company was wiped out by an enemy attack. Then I noticed that the French communiqué of the day reported that my IIIrd Corps had repulsed an enemy attack. When the French army commander appeared at my corps headquarters he offered me as consolation for his error this French communiqué. It was at least acknowledgment of the responsibility for the mistake.[3]

Bullard decidedly did *not* feel consoled "for the loss of the company, or for the only accident of my military career." Accordingly, he wrote to General Pershing on August 28 to inform him of what had happened:

My Dear General:

I am informed that to-day's German communiqué (which I have not seen) states that the Germans captured at Fismette yesterday 250 Americans. A part of my command until yesterday occupied Fismette.

I had there some 190 officers and men altogether, infantry. If you will look upon the map you will see the position of Fismes, a large village on the south bank of the Vesle. Just opposite Fismes on the north bank is the small village of Fismette. Opposite Fismes the village of Fismette, and no more, was occupied by us. Ten days ago, after a German attack upon Fismette which almost succeeded, I saw that Fismette could not be held by us against any real attempt by the Germans to take it and that to attempt to continue to hold it would, on account of the lay of the surrounding terrain, involve the sure sacrifice of its garrison, to which help could not be sent except by driblets at night. I therefore decided and began to withdraw the garrison of Fismette some 300 metres back across the Vesle River into Fismes. Before this was finished, the French general commanding the Sixth Army, to which I belong, arrived at my headquarters and, learning of my orders for withdrawal from Fismette, himself, in person, directed me to continue to hold Fismette and how to hold it. My orders were changed in his presence and his orders were obeyed. Yesterday morning the Germans made a strong attack upon Fismette from two directions, taking the village and killing or capturing almost all of our men who were in it.[4]

Some time later, Bullard noted, he saw General Pershing himself. "He was much irritated and asked me with vehemence: 'Why did you not disobey the order given by General Degoutte?'" Bullard wrote that he did not answer General Pershing's question because "it was not necessary to answer. The General had spoken in the vehemence of his irritation."[5]

For American forces to be attached to and under the orders of a foreign ally was often very difficult. General Pershing had agreed to the assignment of III Corps to the French Sixth Army. Accordingly, the orders of its general had to be obeyed. Sometimes this put American field commanders like Bullard in what seemed to be impossible situations. As for what the soldiers themselves felt, the doughboys of the 28th Division (who were principally recruits and draftees from Pennsylvania) were moved to christen their portion of the Vesle front "Death Valley," not just because of the foolish orders that had gotten some of them killed or captured, but because any attempt to move by daylight in any part of the area close to the river invited German fire—and not just rifle fire and machine-gun fire. The Germans, well dug in on the north bank of the Vesle, used field artillery to snipe at doughboys careless enough to move standing up or in groups. Shelling with chemical munitions, mainly mustard gas, was also frequent. Bullard later remarked, "I have rarely, if ever, seen troops under more trying conditions . . . they were on the spot and they stayed there."[6]

•

What finally broke the deadlock on the Vesle was an attack by the French Tenth Army north of Soissons in late August. Although it was understrength and still struggling to recover from fierce combat in the Aisne-Marne offensive (chapter 11), the US 32nd Division took part in this attack. On August 30, elements of the division captured the village of Juvigny, which received coverage in the British and British Empire press. A New Zealand paper, *The Mercury*, printed dispatches issued through London:

> *The Americans capture of Juvigny (five miles north of Soissons) was a remarkable exploit. The town lay on the further slope of the hill. Two parties crawled among shell-pits over the crest, and got near the town before they were observed. They rushed the town, in which there were a thousand Germans. Fighting and a fierce bayonet attack resulted in 350 [German] prisoners being taken, and all the rest of the Germans were killed or wounded.*
>
> *FRENCH GENERAL'S ADMIRATION.*
> *LONDON, September 2.*
>   *A despatch from the American Army in France said:—The Americans have again cracked the German defence north of Soissons, making the new American position secure near Terny Sorny. The Americans are at the apex of the Allied forces on that part of the front. The French general, [Charles] Mangin, the commanding officer [of the French Tenth Army], has expressed to the American commander his admiration for the American units' work, admitting his surprise that troops comparatively new should conduct themselves with such dash, and brilliancy.*[7]

Gaining Juvigny gave the Allies high ground that was key to breaking through the Vesle front early in September. The 32nd Division was ordered east on September 9 to become part of the newly created independent US First Army. This left the US III Corps in this sector with the 28th and 77th Divisions. Operating under the control of the French Sixth Army east of Soissons, the III Corps covered the Vesle River from Braine to Courlandon. After the Franco-American breakthrough across the Vesle, the Germans withdrew north into the valley of the Aisne. The III Corps divisions took part in pursuing the withdrawing German units and carried out several successful local actions, but did not achieve a decisive breach of the German line before the corps and its divisions were also relieved and sent to join the US First Army. The 28th Division left the sector during September 7–8, and the 77th during September 14–16.

After the departure of the US 77th Division, only the "colored" regiment, the 370th Infantry, remained in the sector, assigned to French command, until the November 11 Armistice. Although the regiment was often relegated to labor duty, it did see combat with the French. The III Corps did not participate in the Oise-Aisne operations after September 16, but shifted entirely to St. Mihiel (chapter 15) and Meuse-Argonne (chapter 16). The Oise-Aisne sector continued to be active until the Armistice on November 11, by which time the French armies in this area had reached the Belgian border. Some eighty-five thousand US troops had participated in the Oise-Aisne operations. [8]

CHAPTER 14

Ypres-Lys

August 19–November 11, 1918

DURING THE SPRING AND EARLY SUMMER OF 1918, ERICH LUDENDORFF had thrown five offensives against the Western Front. Four were in France: the Somme Offensive (March 21–April 4), the Aisne Offensive (May 27–June 4), the Montdidier-Noyon Offensive (June 8–12), and the abortive fifth offensive, the Champagne-Marne (July 15–17). One offensive, the Lys (April 9–29), chronologically the second of the five, was in Flanders, the borderlands of northern France and Belgium. This area, through which the Lys River flows, is a wet, flat plain conducive to combat. It was the scene of horrific battle for the BEF from early in the war. The very worst of the fighting was concentrated toward the north of the area, around the town of Ypres and, just to the northeast, Passchendaele, with no fewer than five battles between October–November 1914 and September–October 1918 bearing the name of Ypres.

By the spring of 1918, the portion of the Western Front extending from the English Channel south through Ypres and thence across the Lys River to the vicinity of Arras, was manned by the Belgian, British, and French armies. Allied offensive operations in the last "Hundred Days" of the Great War were known as "Ypres-Lys," and beginning on August 19, as part of Ferdinand Foch's final "Grand Offensive," the Belgians, the British Second Army and the French Sixth Army, with elements of the US II Corps (27th and 30th Divisions) attached, were tasked with reducing the Lys salient, anchored in Ypres and Passchendaele at its northern end and extending down to the villages of Festubert and La Bassee just below its southern end. The Lys River cut through the middle of the salient, roughly from the northeast to southwest. The US 27th and 30th Divisions were involved in the Ypres-Lys operation from August 19 to September 4. In mid-October 1918, the US 37th and 91st Divisions were put under the command of what was called the French Army of Belgium, which was part of the Groupe d'Armées des Flandres, under the command of King Albert of Belgium. These two divisions operated in Ypres-Lys (map 9) from October 28 to the Armistice on November 11, 1918.

Thus, US army involvement in this portion of the Western Front came in two phases. The first phase, from August 19 to September 4, saw the reduction of the Lys salient. The second, from late October to the Armistice, was a general assault eastward toward and beyond the Scheldt (Escaut) River.

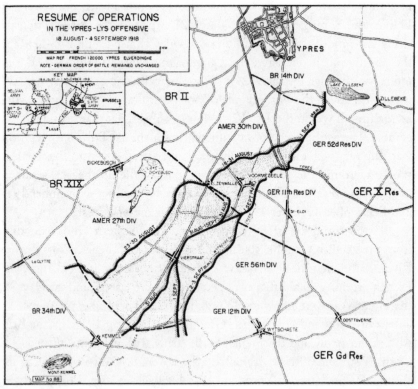

Map 9. Operations at Ypres-Lys. US ARMY CENTER FOR MILITARY HISTORY

●

Operations against the Lys salient took place from August 19 to September 5 and involved mainly the British II Corps and XIX Corps of the British Second Army, the US 30th Division, under Major General Edward M. Lewis, and the US 27th Division, under Major General John F. O'Ryan. Both divisions were stationed along the Lys salient just south of Ypres.

On September 11, Major General G. W. Read, II Corps commander, summarized the "recent operations of II Corps":

2. The 30th Division went into the line as a division with British artillery in the CANAL sector on the British Second Army front on August 16.

3. The 27th Division went into the line as a division with British artillery in the DICKEBUSCH sector on the British Second Army front on August 22.

4. The II Corps Headquarters with British corps troops was prepared to take over the sector occupied by these two divisions on August 30, when on that date orders were received from British G. H. Q. [General Headquarters] withdrawing the [U.S. II] corps from British Second Army front and sending them to G. H. Q. reserve, the corps headquarters and the 27th Division to Third Army area and the 30th Division to First Army area. Under present instructions, the corps is held in G. H. Q. reserve in readiness for use as the situation may demand and is at present in training.

5. On September 1. the enemy on the Second Army front started a retirement [withdrawal from the Lys salient] in which he was closely pressed by our troops. The whole of the 27th and a part of the 30th Division became involved and took part in the attacks on his rear guard in which they took all the objectives allotted to them. Upon the completion of this operation they were withdrawn as above described. A more detailed report of their part in this operation will be submitted later.

6. For the present they are engaged in no operations, but as they are in reserve in readiness for immediate action, the daily situation and operation reports will be continued, stating the fact if there be no change.[1]

What is indirectly apparent from General Read's report is that the French and British attacks on the Lys salient very quickly prompted the Germans to withdraw from it. The American divisions, therefore, took no active role in reducing the salient. The laconic tone of Read's summary suggests little action, which, however, is highly misleading. The two American divisions were, in fact, very active—not in reducing the salient, but in "pressing" the enemy as it withdrew from the salient. The objective was no longer merely to gain territory, but to kill the enemy army, and that meant pursuing it.

From August 21 to August 30, the 27th Division was in action at Dickebusch Lake; from August 9 to September 2, elements of the division were engaged at the village of Voormezeele, with many elements of the 30th Division joining in the action there from August 31 to September 2. Doughboys of the 30th Division fought at Lankhof Farm from August 31 to September 2, and the 27th Division pursued withdrawing German troops from Mont-Kemmel to Vierstraat Ridge from August 31 to September 2. The 30th Division was successful in taking all of its objectives. The 27th had a more difficult time in its pursuit of the retreating Germans, who proved very effective in fighting rearguard actions. The 27th Infantry's operation (as a later report characterized it) consisted "of attacks and counterattacks, under organized artillery and other fire support, finally resulting in the assault, capture and consolidation of VIERSTRAAT Ridge, a position of great tactical importance."[2]

The 30th Division accomplished all aspects of the mission assigned to it, capturing an important lock on the Ypres Canal, Lankhof Farm, and the village of Voormezeele. In addition, as the division commanding officer reported in a document submitted on October 5, 1918, during the operations of August 31–September 2, 1918, "this division took from the enemy a strip of ground comprising approximately one square mile. Sixteen prisoners (O. R.) were captured, one of whom was severely wounded and evacuated to hospital. Two machine guns and one *granatenwer-fer* were captured, and a small amount of ammunition and stores."[3] The "granatenwerfer" was a weapon originally designed—remarkably enough—by an Austrian priest for use by the Austro-Hungarian army. It was adapted by the German army as a grenade thrower, firing small grenades, each with a fourteen-ounce charge of high explosive, to a maximum range of 330 yards at the rate of four or five grenades per minute.[4]

The 30th Division report continues:

(a) It is estimated that enemy losses in killed were between ninety and one hundred: many dead bodies were actually seen. Enemy wounded is estimated at about two hundred.

(b) Our Losses: In the two days on which actual fighting took place, August 31, and September 1, our losses were: Officers killed 2, wounded 2. [Enlisted men] killed 35, wounded 126.[5]

The 27th and 30th Divisions continued their operations. On September 3, the commanding officer of the German 8th Infantry Division filed an assessment of American tactics:

The rearguard battles of the past 3 days have shown that the withdrawal of our line confronted the American troops with a task to which they were by no means equal. Presumably, the initial employment of the American 27th Div. at the front was to accustom it to quiet position warfare. Our Ploegsteert movement forced the division immediately into mobile warfare. This fighting demonstrated that the inexperienced troops do not yet know how to utilize the terrain in movement, work their way forward during an attack, or choose the correct formation in the event the enemy opens artillery fire. The infantry and artillery reports agree that the enemy has suffered heavy losses in his advance, in his assembly movements, and in his numerous attacks, which were executed over-hastily and on the spur of the moment without or with only slight artillery support. The enemy artillery is weak, cautious, and unsteady. . . . Cooperation between the infantry and artillery is not yet discernible at this time.

I express my full appreciation to the rear guards and the entire artillery for their achievements of the past 3 days. Good observation, quick firing on identified movements, proper conduct on the part of the rearguards, and steady machine-gun and rifle fire when the enemy attacked repelled the enemy with costly casualties at whatever point he pushed forward. The superiority of our infantry is clearly obvious.

I expect that every one will do his utmost in his place to inflict the heaviest possible damage on the Americans, whose state of mind is generally known, and to obliterate once and for all with withering fire their desire to renew the attack in case they should venture to advance against our Ploegsteert position.[6]

The deprecating and patronizing tone of the German report seems poorly suited to the commander of a combatant force in the act of fleeing from the position it had been assigned to hold and defend. On the next day, September 4, the tone changed, as the American pursuit during September 1–2—now aided by British artillery—became more effective. One German 8th Infantry Division report begins, "After violent artillery fire which opened suddenly without warning the enemy attacked entire division at 6:30 a.m." Another report from the same day continues:

By employing heavy smoke screening after short violent artillery preparation. the enemy has succeeded in penetrating the sector of the 11th Res. Div. and in occupying the Nachtigallhoehe [Rossignol Hill]. Counterattack to recapture the hill has been ordered. Enemy success was due primarily to the heavy smoke screening. which blinded our artillery and machine guns as well as masked the enemy assembly preparation and attack.

The same procedure will be expected in the event the enemy continues his attack against our sector. If smoke screening of a sector is recognized. the artillery will deliver waves of annihilation fire. All front machine guns will fire into the smoke screen. The enemy himself will be blinded if he penetrates the screen. He will not know the location of our machine-gun nests. His attack is bound to fail. if all machine guns and rifles fire in definite directions previously determined by the rearguard and combat battalion companies. In case of smoke screening. sweeping fire will be laid particularly on the roads. The shell-crater area will greatly impede the advance of the attacker in the smoke. The roads enable him to advance rapidly without losing direction. Furthermore. tanks can be moved forward on the roads under the protection of smoke.

If the enemy screens his own position or approach routes with smoke. we will fire similarly into the smoke screen with a greater number of batteries. since screening indicates the assembly of reserves or even tanks under some circumstances.[7]

Yet another German report from September 4 states: "The 8th Inf. Div. can be proud of its fine success in its first encounter with the Americans in so completely using up one American brigade in 2 days that it had to be withdrawn from combat because of exhaustion." Reading further into the report, we encounter a section titled "Fighting Qualities," which is an assessment of the condition of the German 8th Infantry Division:

Of late the depletion of forces was fairly high in consequence of the strenuous work in field fortification and the comparatively high number of casualties.

In addition, the number of intestinal cases has increased, some proving to be dysentery. [Others, presumably, were influenza, which was becoming epidemic throughout all of the militaries, but especially among the ill-fed and exhausted Germans.]

For these reasons and on account of its weak combat strength the division can be considered fit for combat only in this sector.[8]

The German reports from September 4, which cover the action from September 1–3, reveal a proud but defeated army. Still, there was more than a grain of truth in the German assessment of the performance of the 27th Division. While the combat-hardened 30th Division had captured all objectives assigned to it and then some, the 27th Division was inexperienced and new to combat. Its men paid a penalty for having been thrown into an active sector instead of being transitioned into combat via experience in a "quiet sector." Elements of the 53rd Infantry Brigade of the 27th Division advanced successfully during August 31 and September 1, even against stiff resistance on that day. But when the advance was continued on the night of September 1, a heavy German counterattack forced the brigade back after it had advanced only 820 yards. The entire 27th Division was relieved during the night of September 2–3, sent to the British Third Army area near Doullens, and assigned as part of the general headquarters reserve. During its action in the Ypres-Lys offensive, the callow 27th suffered 1,336 casualties, including 185 killed.

●

Both the 27th and 30th Divisions were withdrawn from the Ypres-Lys operation before the Fifth Battle of Ypres began on September 28. That battle was therefore fought entirely by the Groupe d'Armées des Flandres—consisting of twelve Belgian divisions, ten British divisions of the Second Army, and six French divisions of the Sixth Army under the command of King Albert I of Belgium, with the French General Jean Degoutte as chief of staff. The British achieved surprise by attacking without advance artillery preparation across a 4.5-mile front while the Belgians made a simultaneous attack to converge with the British. The combine Allied attacks cut through the German frontline trenches quickly. Having been reduced to just five divisions here, the Germans were outnumbered nearly six to one.

The British-Belgian forces advanced some six miles, recapturing much of what had been abandoned by the British in earlier Ypres battles. The Groupe d'Armées des Flandres continued to advance until October 2, when the force outran its supply lines and also found itself confronted by the arrival of German reinforcements. To compound the predicament, heavy downpours of rain began, which turned all roadways into soup and completely cut off supplies to the Allies. Belgian and British aircraft were pressed into service to drop emergency rations by parachute—the first time this had been done on any significant scale in the Great War.

Although the advance had bogged down, the Fifth Battle of Ypres was unquestionably a significant Allied victory. For the cost of about nine thousand casualties among the British and Belgians, the Allies had captured some ten thousand Germans (the number of Germans killed and wounded is unknown) and had advanced eighteen miles. This put the Groupe d'Armées des Flandres in position to continue the offensive through Flanders with the Battle of Courtrai (October 14–19). In the course of this engagement, the Groupe d'Armées, led by King Albert, mounted an attack along its entire front as the Germans withdrew from the portion of the sector south of the Lys. By October 20, the cities of Ostend and Bruges had been recaptured from the Germans, and the Allied left flank was now at the neutral Netherlands frontier. The war in Belgium was nearly finished.

At this time, Marshal Ferdinand Foch requested that General Pershing send another two US divisions into the sector for attachment to the Groupe d'Armées des Flandres. Pershing chose the 37th and 91st. Their mission was to bolster a final drive across the Scheldt (Escaut) River, which runs from France northeast across western Belgium and the southwestern Netherlands. The new Allied offensive was to cross the Scheldt southwest of Ghent. The operation began on October 31 and continued through to the Armistice of November 11.

●

The 37th Division arrived in the Hooglede area in Flanders on October 18 and joined the XXX Corps of the French Sixth Army. During the night of October 29–30, the 37th relieved the French 132nd Division along the Courtrai-Ghent railroad. On the morning of October 31, at 5:30, supported by a rolling barrage courtesy of the French artillery, the American division attacked toward the east. Through heavy German machine-gun and artillery fire, the Americans managed to move two and a half miles toward the Scheldt. They dug in for the night before resuming the advance on November 1. At this point, the Germans had begun a withdrawal, and the 37th managed a five-mile advance in a day's march. In the course of the advance, the division captured the villages of Cruyshauten and Eyne. The 37th was now on the west bank of the Scheldt River.

On the next day, November 2, the doughboys of the American division used felled trees found near the river to improvise a hasty bridge across the narrow waterway, and, under heavy fire, they forced a crossing during November 2–4. After, the entire unit had crossed and moved out about a half mile east of the river, the division was confronted by a German counterattack, which it repulsed. Having fought for five days and suffering 1,500 casualties, the 37th was relieved by the French 12th Division on the night of November 3–4.

The 37th Division was transported to the Thielt area for rest and preparation to resume the battle. On November 8, the division received orders to support the French XXXIV Corps and moved out, relieving both the French 11th and 12th Divisions on November 10 along the Scheldt north of its previous crossing of that river. A French attempt to cross at this point had been repulsed on November 9, but the 37th succeeded in making the crossing on November 10. It took and held the far bank as the Germans withdrew. That evening, the division resumed its advance. The end of the war at 11 o'clock in the morning of the next day, November 11, found the 37th Division two and a half miles east of the Scheldt.

●

The other US Army division Pershing sent at the request of Foch, the 91st, was battle-hardened by punishing service at St. Mihiel (chapter 15). Arriving in the Ypres-St. Jean area on October 16, this division relieved the French 164th Division and joined the French VII Corps in its advance and attack toward the Scheldt River. Joining the general assault at 5:30 on the morning of October 31, the 91st immediately captured Spitaals Bosschen, woods near the point of departure. The slow progress of a French division on its right exposed the 91st to heavy fire on that flank, but the Germans withdrew on November 1, opening up the way before the US division, which made a five-mile advance to the outskirts of the Scheldt River town of Audenarde. The German occupiers of Audenarde offered fierce resistance, and fighting lasted three days before the 91st won possession of the river town on November 3. Just as the 91st was preparing to cross the Scheldt in continuation of its eastward advance, the French 41st Division relieved it.

The 91st was given a brief rest before joining the French XXX Corps on November 10, a day spent in pursuit of withdrawing Germans. From early morning until 11 o'clock on November 11, the 91st continued to advance, all but unopposed. During its brief time in Belgium, the division lost 969 men, killed or wounded.

From August 19 to November 11, some 108,000 American soldiers participated in the Ypres-Lys Campaign. American casualties in this sector for this period totaled 2,043 killed and wounded.[9]

CHAPTER 15

St. Mihiel

September 12–16, 1918

WHEN THE VESLE RIVER FRONT WAS STABILIZED IN EARLY AUGUST (chapter 14), General Pershing, who had succeeded in securing from General Foch authorization to proceed with the creation of an independent US First Army, changed his mind about where that army would be formed. Having obtained Foch's agreement that the new army would be assigned to reduce the St. Mihiel salient (chapter 14), Pershing had planned to organize the force in the Château-Thierry region and then, when it was ready, move it eastward for the St. Mihiel Offensive. The action on the Vesle River front had proceeded more quickly than anticipated, and Pershing now recognized that, if the United States was to play a truly decisive role in the Great War, he had to move more quickly with the mission of the First Army. On August 9, therefore, he won Foch's consent to build up the First Army units not in the relatively rearward sector of Château-Thierry but in the immediate vicinity of the St. Mihiel salient itself.

The American people of 1918 had changed since 1916, when they sent Woodrow Wilson to a second term in the White House because he had "kept us out of war." They were now enthusiastic about America's role in the conflict, and this made it clear to Pershing that the time to fight as an independent military force was now. The continuation of popular support for the war depended on *American* officers leading *American* soldiers to *American* victories. Moreover, the political end President

Wilson wanted to achieve—a seat for the United States at the head of the postwar conference table, a central role for the nation in shaping the future of the world—depended on the American military being unmistakably the author of some of the war's decisive, culminating victories. With Foch's "Grand Offensive" now underway, it was time for American arms to claim a big piece of the fight. And as of late summer 1918, John J. Pershing had more than a million men in France ready to stake their claim in this war.

Up to now, out of urgent necessity, Pershing had yielded in his demand for the absolute independence of the AEF by attaching some regiments, divisions, and even entire corps to the British and French armies. The results—especially in the Aisne-Marne operations (chapter 11) and the Somme Offensive (chapter 12)—had been extraordinarily impressive. But Pershing now keenly felt the pressure of time at his back. He needed to associate the US Army with its own great victory. Besides, as he saw it, reducing the St. Mihiel salient was an ideal assignment. First, the salient was one of the three objectives Foch had identified for the Grand Offensive. Second, it was undeniably of great strategic as well as symbolic importance. Although it was a long-standing German violation of sacred French soil, the Allies had, back in 1915, given up fighting to reclaim it. Now it could be redeemed at last—and by the *American* army. Pershing was also aware that, while St. Mihiel was significant and its reduction a suitably ambitious objective, it was a relatively quiet sector— and had been so since the second year of the war. This made it ideal for an AEF that still consisted mostly of green troops.

Leaving some elements of the US III Corps on the Vesle front, Pershing now shifted other US troops from that sector as well as from the Vosges, from the training areas around Chaumont, and from the British sector. He concentrated these units along the St. Mihiel salient. The initial forces making up the US First Army were three American corps of fourteen divisions and a French colonial corps of three divisions.

On August 30, just as the concentration of American forces was well under way and the First Army taking shape, Ferdinand Foch, freshly promoted to Marshal of France, called on Pershing at his headquarters. The American general had been intensively working with his staff on the plan to accomplish what had been decided in conference with Foch back in July 24: the reduction of the St. Mihiel salient followed by an offensive push against the Germans along the entire front. Now, while Pershing stood among his new army and with plans for the St. Mihiel offensive essentially complete, Marshal Foch stunned him by announcing that he had reconsidered the necessity of the entire St. Mihiel operation. Field Marshal Haig, commander in chief of the BEF, reported his assessment, based on the action on the Vesle front, that the German army had reached a tipping point. Exhausted, hungry, ailing, its best soldiers lying dead on the field, the kaiser's forces were melting away. Haig therefore suggested—and Foch agreed—that the time had come to disrupt the German army by breaking it up and isolating its elements one from another. Foch now wanted to conduct a series of massive converging attacks targeting the enemy's lateral lines of communications. The strategy was as old as the warfare practiced by the Roman Legions: divide and conquer.

Foch's new plan called for British forces to attack southeasterly and the combined Franco-American forces to attack northward from the Meuse-Argonne region. This would bring about a large-scale double envelopment against the entire German army on the Western Front. Achieve this, and the reduction of the St. Mihiel salient would simply be rendered an unnecessary exercise. To carry out the French portion of the plan—essentially an all-out offensive through the heavily forested Meuse-Argonne—Foch needed to divide the US First Army into two segments, which were to be deployed on either side of the Meuse-Argonne, separated by one French army. Moreover, a French general would be assigned to each segment of the dismembered "independent" American army for the purpose of "assisting" the AEF commanders.

Pershing did not debate the new plan on its strategic merits, whatever these may have been. Instead, he rejected it outright as unacceptable to the US Army. Having been promised an independent force under direct American command, Pershing dug in his heels, objected to any division of the US forces, and laid out several counterproposals. Foch rejected each in turn as impractical. With this, tempers flared.

Do you *want* to go into battle? Foch essentially demanded of General Pershing.

"Most assuredly," he replied, "but as an American Army."[1]

With this, the conference ended on a note of highly disturbing discord. With victory in this long and tragic war close at hand, the Allied commanders had reached a bitter impasse. Up to this point, Pershing had been making all the compromises. Although he was determined to maintain the independence and national identity of the American military, he had repeatedly detached regiments, divisions, and even entire corps and entrusted them to French or British command. Now, with a million American young men in France, he intended to field an American army under American command. For political, military, and popular reasons, as well as for the sake of national honor, it was a nonnegotiable issue.

Foch having departed, General Pershing called on the French commander with whom he had the most cordial and sympathetic relationship, General Philippe Pétain. Pétain listened carefully. He was not interested in mollifying Pershing but was truly persuaded by Pershing's arguments in favor of maintaining the independence of American forces. Pétain believed that the wholehearted support and cooperation of the United States depended on the existence of a powerful AEF with its own sector of the front and with independence of command. Pétain therefore suggested to Pershing that the two of them go together to meet with Foch. The American agreed.

The meeting took place on September 2. To Foch, Pétain voiced his support for a new proposal from Pershing. The American general now proposed that the US First Army assume responsibility not just for the St. Mihiel sector but for the entire sector of the front from Pont-à-Mousson through the Meuse valley to the Argonne Forest, a broad front of some ninety miles. Pershing told Foch that he would proceed within two weeks to launch his attack against the St. Mihiel salient, which, he argued, would offer valuable operational advantages to Foch's offensive along the Meuse. Moreover, the St. Mihiel operation would build much needed experience and confidence among the officers and men of the First Army. This would be of inestimable value when the army, having completed the reduction of the St. Mihiel salient, fully joined the French in the Meuse-Argonne operation.

Foch began to yield. He announced that he would accept Pétain and Pershing's proposal with the proviso that the St. Mihiel offensive be strictly limited to the reduction of the salient and would not be followed by the advance behind the salient that had been planned originally. Foch admonished Pershing that, by the end of September, the US First Army would have to turn its attack northward in support of the Meuse-Argonne offensive (chapter 16).

The American commander probably did not smile. No one had ever reported seeing John J. Pershing smile. But he replied to Foch that after the US First Army had wiped out the St. Mihiel salient, it would instantly pivot northward and *still* launch its portion of the offensive against the Meuse-Argonne on the schedule Foch proposed.

With this accord reached, the three men began addressing the details. They emerged with agreement on two discrete American operations supported as necessary by French troops and equipment. First was the elimination of the St. Mihiel salient, an operation to begin on or about September 10. This was to be followed by US First Army participation in the much larger "grand offensive" against the Meuse-Argonne. Starting between September 20 and 25, the new army would attack along the west bank of the Meuse.

Having secured Marshal Foch's approval to proceed with the St. Mihiel offensive (figure 33), General Pershing and his staff began the final planning for an operation against what was a two-hundred-square-mile triangle thrust fourteen miles into the Allied lines between the Moselle and Meuse rivers—a piece of enemy real estate that was the legacy of a German offensive conducted back in September 1914. The boundaries of the St. Mihiel salient were Pont-à-Mousson to the south, the village of St. Mihiel to the west, and the once bitterly contested Verdun area to the north. The lay of the land in this salient was for the most part a rolling plain, but in places it was densely wooded. While the Allies had left this salient alone since 1915, the Germans had been very active landlords. Indeed, they transformed this territory into a vast fortress, thickly sown with bands of barbed wire and planted strategically with formidable

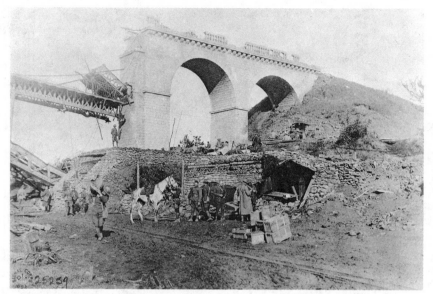

Figure 33. St. Mihiel operation: the headquarters of the US 89th Division is seen below the ruins of a major bridge. NATIONAL ARCHIVES AND RECORDS ADMINISTRATION

artillery positions and many machine-gun emplacements sited to create deadly fields of interlocking fire. Eight German divisions were assigned to the defense of the salient, and an additional five were held in ready reserve.

Pershing's plan was to launch nearly simultaneous attacks against both flanks of the salient. The three-division French II Colonial Corps attached to the US First Army would hit the nose of the salient, while the three divisions of the newly created US V Corps attacked southeasterly toward Vigneulles, one of the villages that was to be liberated. The US V Corps commander, Major General George H. Cameron, was instructed to link up his corps with the three divisions of the US IV Corps, which was assigned to the command of Major General Joseph T. Dickman, an officer who had distinguished himself in the Aisne-Marne offensive (chapter 11). To the right of the V and IV Corps, the I Corps, which consisted of the AEF's most experienced four divisions, was tasked with fighting through to the eastern base of the salient. The timetable was simple. The I and IV Corps were set to begin their attack at 5:00 a.m., the French colonial corps at 6:00, and V Corps at 8:00 (map 10).

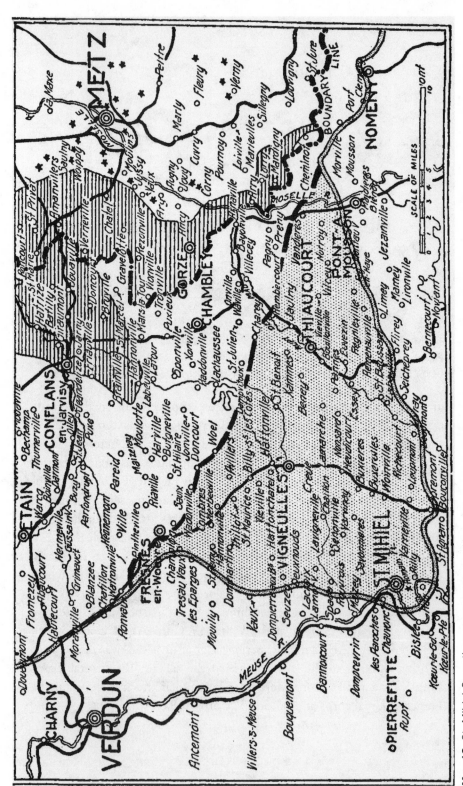

Map 10. St. Mihiel Operations. WIKIMEDIA

●

Pershing had been AEF commander since the spring of 1917, but the St. Mihiel operation was his debut as an army commander. He intended to succeed, and Marshal Foch intended to support him, despite their earlier dispute. Foch and Haig furnished almost all of the artillery, aircraft, and armor to augment infantry operations (figure 34) by the eleven divisions

Figure 34. U.S. artillerymen sight and fire a large howitzer during an "artillery preparation" against German positions preceding an infantry attack. WIKIMEDIA

(seven US, four French) now incorporated into the US First Army for its maiden battle. More than 3,000 artillery pieces were furnished, along with 1,400 planes and 267 tanks. While the equipment was French and British, the pilots were mostly Americans, and one brigade of the tanks was manned by US crews.

Pershing's tactical thinking reflected the newer Western Front ideas, but he was torn over whether to precede the infantry assault with an artillery preparation. In line with the most recent tactical practice, Pershing's original thought was that the benefits of an initial artillery barrage were outweighed by the sacrifice of the element of surprise. As H-hour neared, however, Pershing rethought his original plan and made the decision to launch a four-hour artillery bombardment along the southern flank of the salient and a massive seven-hour barrage along the western flank. Pétain outlined to the American general an elaborate ruse to deceive the German defender into concluding that the first American blow would be delivered to the south, near Belfort. Pershing embraced this scheme, and it proved to be brilliant. As the artillery preparation began at 1:00 o'clock on the morning of September 12, the Germans scrambled to move three entire divisions into the southern sector near Belfort, leaving other areas more thinly defended.

Per the American plan of attack, I and IV Corps infantry, supported by tanks, attacked along a front of twelve miles. The only US tank brigade to see action in World War I fought in the St. Mihiel offensive. It was led by a young officer, who had come to France with the rank of captain and served as General Pershing's adjutant and headquarters commandant. George S. Patton Jr. had been born in Southern California in 1885, but his family hailed from Virginia and had fought for the Confederacy during the Civil War. Patton had never wanted any career other than that of a US Army officer. He graduated from West Point and first served with Pershing during the Punitive Expedition against Pancho Villa in 1916. When the United States declared war on Germany, Patton practically begged Pershing to appoint him to his staff, but, once in France, he grew restless behind a desk and volunteered for a combat assignment with the fledgling US tank corps. A cavalryman by branch assignment, Patton was mesmerized by the possibilities the tank opened up in trench warfare. He completed the full course of tank training and was assigned to create a light-tank training school in France for American soldiers. He designed the curriculum, and then he recruited and trained two entire battalions of tank crews, some of whom he led into battle at St. Mihiel in support of the infantry attack.

Enthusiastically praised by the commanders of the Infantry units he supported, Patton was nevertheless reprimanded by his own superior, Samuel D. Rockenbach, because he had failed to take time off to prepare and send a sufficient number of progress reports. Accordingly, Rockenbach ordered Patton to remain in headquarters henceforth and to direct all of his operations from the rear. As it turned out, Rockenbach's orders failed to stick. After the First Army completed the St. Mihiel operation and joined the Meuse-Argonne Offensive, Patton would lead another tank operation—from the front and in the thick of the action (chapter 16). This time, instead of a reprimand, he would receive a serious wound and the Distinguished Service Cross.

●

Early in the initial attack, IV Corps infantry pivoted on the advance of I Corps to sweep broadly ahead of it over a full five miles. An hour after I and IV Corps got their start, V Corps commenced its attack, at 8:00, and made quick progress. The German response was a vigorous defense but one that was intended less to annihilate the attackers than to buy time to withdraw in good fighting order. The fact was that German high command had already determined to withdraw from the St. Mihiel salient and consolidate forces in this sector's portion of the Hindenburg Line. Division commanders had received the order to withdraw on September 8 but had been dilatory in executing it. Nevertheless, when the American attack came, the Germans were both prepared to withdraw and in a frame of mind to do so. As at the Vesle front (chapter 14), however, the Germans showed themselves to be masters of costly rearguard actions.

As the first day of the St. Mihiel offensive approached the afternoon, the US 1st Division, which had advanced from the south, was well within striking distance of Vigneulles and ten miles from the advancing columns of the 26th Division of the V Corps. This was the situation when Pershing was told that German columns were seen in retreat on roads leading out of Vigneulles, the U.S. objective for the day. Seizing on an opportunity, Pershing ordered the 1st and 26th Divisions, which had fought all day, to continue to press their attacks throughout the night. Pershing resisted the temptation to think of the Germans as a defeated army. He shared with the likes of the Civil War's Ulysses S. Grant the determination to destroy any enemy formation still in the field, whether the enemy was attacking or retreating. Like Grant, Pershing's notion of victory was not the acquisition of territory formerly held by the enemy, but the utter destruction of the enemy. He was determined to kill the opposing army wherever it was, wherever it was headed. He was certainly determined to kill as much of it as he could before it withdrew into the defenses offered by the Hindenburg Line. Pershing's demand that the doughboys keep fighting—and keep dying—right up to the eleventh hour of the eleventh day of the eleventh month would draw criticism from some civilian political contemporaries as well as many later historians. His military colleagues, especially Lieutenant Colonel George S. Patton Jr., offered no such criticism. They saw maximum aggression as the only proper way to create a lasting victory.

●

The 26th Division, which had fought and advanced rapidly throughout the day, did not hesitate to follow General Pershing's order to press on during the night. One of its regiments attacked and took Vigneulles at 2:30 on the morning of September 13. At dawn of that day, a brigade of the 1st Division made contact with the New Englanders of the Boston-based 26th Division. This linkup of two converging American columns within the St. Mihiel salient, together with the taking and occupation of Vigneulles, signaled the successful conclusion of the most important and difficult phase of the entire St. Mihiel operation. By day's end on September 13, in its maiden campaign, the US First Army had taken all of its major objectives (figure 35).

There was still work to do, but within the next three days, the Americans cleared the German army from a salient that had been in enemy hands, unchallenged, for some three years. The new American army

Figure 35. Doughboys advance across a field "somewhere in France," probably in 1918. WIKIMEDIA

suffered about seven thousand casualties, killed, wounded, or missing, but it had inflicted on the German defenders of St. Mihiel more than seventeen thousand casualties—the majority of these prisoners of war. The operation had captured 450 German artillery pieces and a mountain of precious materiel, everything from rations to munitions. That the Germans were on the verge of abandoning the salient when the attack came did not greatly reduce the significance of the victory. The number of troops able to withdraw and fight another day was minus some seventeen thousand, and large stocks of weapons and supplies were either lost or destroyed by the Germans themselves. The enemy was no longer capable of replacing either the soldiers or the materiel. Moreover, the triumph of the American offensive spelled the difference between a voluntary strategic withdrawal and a defeat. It added to the accelerating erosion of German military discipline and morale. It added to the accelerating erosion of the German popular and political will to continue the war.

Operationally, the St. Mihiel offensive liberated the Paris-Nancy railroad for Allied use, providing a major means of transport, supply, reinforcement, and communication from the French rear echelon to the eastern frontier. This would be invaluable to maintaining the breadth, depth, and relentless tempo of Foch's "grand offensive." For Pershing and the US Army, the operation provided much-needed experience, a heightened degree of confidence, and a great deal of prestige among the Allies. For once and for all, the US military earned its place among the Allies as an equal among equals. For President Woodrow Wilson, the military victory would pay a dividend in establishing a new place for America on the world stage.

●

The St. Mihiel Offensive not only gave the doughboys and their officers a degree of combat experience equal to the demands of the Great War in its closing phase but the offensive also ushered the US Army into twentieth-century warfare fought on the largest of scales. Patton had his first experience with armor, the arm with which he would be most closely associated when the Great War did not, after all, turn out to be the war to end all wars and instead, twenty years after the Armistice, was revealed as nothing more or less than the overture to a *second*, even more terrible, world war.

Another arm that rapidly matured during the Great War was military aviation (figure 36). At St. Mihiel, an American officer would lead the largest single concentration of airpower in the Great War. That it should be an American who would take the lead in this manner must have seemed most unlikely at the time. On April 2, 1917, the day President Wilson asked Congress to declare war on Germany, the US military air arm consisted of about two hundred obsolete planes (many of them not even in sufficient repair to be airworthy) and 1,200 officers and men. Of these US Army Air Service personnel, only about sixty were airmen— either pilots, observers, or aerial gunners. The nation in which powered, heavier-than-air flight had been invented in 1903 by the Wright brothers

Figure 36. The US 95th Aero Squadron, which saw extensive action at St. Mihiel and Meuse-Argonne, flew these French Nieuport 28 aircraft. NATIONAL ARCHIVES AND RECORDS ADMINISTRATION

was, in 1917, far behind France, Germany, Britain, and Italy in aircraft technology. When the nation joined the war on April 6, 1917, it neither manufactured nor possessed any aircraft capable of surviving the kind of aerial combat commonplace on the Western Front. Yet there was no shortage of young Americans eager to volunteer as pilots. Even before the US entry into the war, a group of American daredevils joined the French air corps as the Lafayette Escadrille. While their exploits—often more lethal to themselves than to the enemy—were of minimal tactical significance, stories about them thrilled Americans at home (figure 37).

Amid a sudden frenzy for the development of American military aviation, Congress, on July 21, 1917, voted—after less than an hour of debate—$640 million dollars to advance military aviation. It was at the time the largest single appropriation—for any purpose—in the nation's history. The program Congress laid out was fantastically ambitious. American factories were expected to use the money to build 22,625 airplanes and 44,000 engines (the lifespan of an aircraft engine was considerably shorter than that of the airframe) by the end of 1918. As for the US Army Air Service, it was authorized to expand from nearly nothing to 345 combat formations, a force consisting of thousands of men and aircraft.

The magnitude of this collective military-industrial-congressional delusion was apparent by the close of 1917, by which time American factories had rolled out a mere 529 planes, all licensed copies of the already obsolescent—but still serviceable—British-designed De Havilland DH-4. Of greater use to the war effort was the production of a brand-new

R. Lufbery

Sketched at the
Lafayette Escadrille
field near Longpont
as the aviator
was getting into
his "union suit"
preparatory to
flying in a
Chemin-des-Dames
engagement

C. LeRoy Baldridge

Figure 37. An ink-and-wash study of Raoul Lufbery by Cyrus Leroy Baldridge, showing the "aviator getting into his 'union suit' preparatory to flying in a Chemin-des-Dames engagement." A Franco-American air ace, Lufbery served in the French Air Force and the Lafayette Escadrille before US entry into the war and, after US entry, in the US Army Air Service. He was killed in a dogfight near the home airfield of the US 94th Aero Squadron on May 19, 1918. At thirty-three years old, he was a multiple ace, with victories in seventeen engagements. WIKIMEDIA

Figure 38. This airplane was typical of the obsolescent craft American factories produced for the war effort. The photograph was taken on July 25, 1918. NATIONAL ARCHIVES AND RECORDS ADMINISTRATION

type of aircraft engine, which was an original and innovative American design. The "Liberty Engine" was produced in a quantity of 2,390 units by the end of 1917. A year later, by the Armistice of November 11, 1918, American aircraft companies managed to produce 7,000 aircraft (figure 38), of which only 1,200 were deemed worthy of service in Europe—and these almost exclusively used as trainers rather than combat aircraft.

The rate at which pilots and other flying personnel were produced in the United States was far better. As volunteers poured in for US Army flight training, eight army aeronautics schools were established. Those who successfully completed the classroom work were sent to a primary flying field for primary and basic flight training. Cadets who were neither killed nor "washed out" moved on to advanced flight training—sometimes at US Army bases but more often overseas in aviation schools staffed by British, Canadian, French, and Italian pilot-instructors.

The first US flying unit to become operational was the 103rd Aero Squadron on February 18, 1918. It had absorbed personnel from the

Lafayette Escadrille and its British equivalent, the British Flying Corps, both of which were dissolved after US entry into the war. The next month, on March 11, 1918, Lieutenant Paul F. Baer of the 103rd Aero Squadron scored America's first air combat kill of World War I. Somewhat surprisingly, Baer survived the war. Less surprisingly, he became an official "air ace" by accumulating eight confirmed kills.

The US Army Air Service was gradually built up in Europe. Its personnel spent most of 1917 through the late spring of 1918 in quiet sectors, gaining critically needed flying experience. To send an inexperienced pilot into combat was to ensure both his loss and the loss of a valuable aircraft. By July 1918, however, the Air Service (figures 39 and 40) had attained a level of competence equal to that of the other Allied air forces.

Among the volunteers for the Army Air Service was William "Billy" Mitchell, son of a US senator from Wisconsin. After getting a college education, he defied the wishes of his family by enlisting in the 1st Wisconsin Infantry at the outbreak of the Spanish-American War in 1898. He soon discovered a career in the US military and by 1912 earned a highly sought-after assignment to the army's General Staff. He gave this up in 1915, after only three years, to transfer to the aviation section of the Signal Corps, the US Army branch that had charge of the military's aviation program. After attending flight school at Newport News, Virginia, Mitchell earned his wings in 1916 and, later that year, was sent to Europe to observe aerial combat in the Great War. For this reason, Mitchell was already on the continent when the United States entered the war in April 1917. Appointed to the post of air officer of the AEF—in command of all US Army flight operations—he was promoted to lieutenant colonel in June. In May 1918 he became air officer of the US I Corps with the rank of colonel. He became the first US officer of field grade to fly over enemy lines.

Billy Mitchell was a natural aviator who was also well educated in both the art and theory of flight. Unlike many officers who possess passion and technical expertise, he was also a brilliant aerial combat tactician and possessed considerable organizational skills, which included a bold, defiant, and flamboyant flair for leadership. He was given command of a mixed force of Allied pilots—British, French, Canadian, and American— and the whole gamut of military aircraft during the St. Mihiel offensive.

Figure 39. Eddie Rickenbacker was already famous as an American race car driver when he enlisted in the US Army in 1917. He entered the US Army Air Service as an engineering officer, learned to fly in his free time, and earned a slot in the 94th Aero Squadron. With twenty-six confirmed aerial victories, he was a multiple ace and, with three hundred combat hours to his credit, he flew more than any other US pilot in the war. Rickenbacker was awarded the Distinguished Service Cross a record eight times. In 1930, one of these awards was converted to a Medal of Honor. NATIONAL ARCHIVES AND RECORDS ADMINISTRATION

His assignment was to find the most effective ways to use airplanes to support the mission on the ground. He therefore created a series of aerial missions using some 1,400 aircraft in a combination of what today would be called close-air support (then called ground attack), tactical bombing (with battlefield objectives as his targets), and air-to-air combat (dogfighting). This was the largest single concentration of airpower in World War I and a spectacular demonstration of what airpower could do in support of infantry operations. German military commanders took note, and many of the tactics Billy Mitchell pioneered at St. Mihiel and the Meuse-Argonne (chapter 16) found their way into the concept of *Blitzkrieg* the Germans employed in the opening actions of World War II.

Following his success in the St. Mihiel offensive, Mitchell was recognized as one of the leading officers of the Great War. He was promoted to brigadier general and given command of the combined Allies air services for the Meuse-Argonne offensive. Never one to lead from a desk, he personally piloted one of the lead bombers in a formation sent to destroy critical targets behind enemy lines on October 9.

Mitchell's achievements in the closing weeks of the World War I would have earned him a lifetime of military fame and a successful career in the postwar American military—had he not been Billy Mitchell. But he *was* Billy Mitchell, who reveled in the role of military renegade. As assistant chief of the Air Service after the war, he embarked on a no-holds-barred crusade to create a US air force separate and independent from the army—a radical idea at the time. Even more radical, based on his experience commanding Allied air forces during the Great War, he championed the notion of unified command of national military airpower rather than command divided between the army and the navy.

At every turn, he met opposition from the military establishment. When he publicly proclaimed that the airplane made the battleship obsolete, the navy hierarchy was up in arms. He exacerbated the friction in 1921 by leading a squadron of bombers in a demonstration "attack" against the captured German dreadnought *Ostfriesland*. His aircraft sank the ship after 21.5 minutes of bombing. To the credit of naval command, the service quickly embarked on the development of the aircraft carrier as an offensive weapon. Thanks to the impetus Mitchell provided, the US

Figure 40. American soldiers, including those with the US Army Air Service, return to the United States on the RMS *Mauretania*, December 2, 1918. NATIONAL ARCHIVES AND RECORDS ADMINISTRATION

Pacific Fleet entered World War II in possession of the most important strategic naval weapon of the war.

Mitchell (figure 41) continued to campaign for expansion of what was now called the US Army Air Corps and the creation of an independent air force. It did not take long for frustrated superior officers to bring about his demotion to colonel, along with a significantly reduced scope of command authority. Presumably, their hope was that he would resign his commission and walk away quietly. Instead, he accepted his demotion and took his campaign directly to the public, bypassing the chain of command to issue often inflammatory statements to the press. When the US Navy dirigible *Shenandoah* crashed in a thunderstorm on September 3, 1925, Mitchell publicly accused both the Department of War and the Department of the Navy of "incompetency, criminal negligence, and almost treasonable administration of the National Defense."[2] The response fell upon him with terrible swiftness. In highly publicized procedures, he was court martialed for insubordination in December 1925. Found guilty, he was sentenced to five years' suspension from duty without pay. Resigning his

Figure 41. Brigadier General William "Billy" Mitchell was the most important commander of air forces in the Great War. WIKIMEDIA

commission the following year, he was now free to speak out, which he did as a civilian until his death a decade later. Among his visionary predictions was his very early—and much scoffed at—assessment of the grave threat the Japanese navy presented to Pearl Harbor.

●

As early as September 14, 1918, the *New York Times* published "American Official Communique No. 122":

In the St. Mihiel sector we have achieved further successes. The junction of our troops advancing from the south of the sector with those advancing from the west has given us possession of the whole salient to points twelve miles northeast of St. Mihiel, and has resulted in the capture of many prisoners.

Forced back by our steady advance, the enemy is retiring and is destroying large quantities of materiel as he goes. . . .

PERSHING.[3]

The St. Mihiel Offensive had been completed in thirty-six hours (figure 42), after which, true to the promise he had made to Marshal Foch, General Pershing marched the entire US First Army, without rest, sixty miles to the Verdun area to take part in Foch's "grand offensive" against German positions in the Meuse-Argonne. By September 26, on schedule, the army was in position and ready to join the French in the new attack.

Figure 42. American engineers return from the Battle of St. Mihiel. NATIONAL ARCHIVES AND RECORDS ADMINISTRATION

CHAPTER 16

Meuse-Argonne

September 26–November 11, 1918

THE SWIFT COMPLETION OF THE ST. MIHIEL MISSION WAS FOLLOWED BY the movement of the entire US First Army, without rest, sixty miles. The whole army was transported from the eastern edge of what had been a two-hundred-mile-square German stronghold to the area around Verdun (figure 43), the starting position for its involvement in the Meuse-Argonne offensive. The magnitude of this achievement cannot be overstated. During a two-week period, more than 820,000 men, together with tanks, field artillery, and even heavy artillery, were transported over just three miserable roads, always under cover of darkness. While some 600,000 Americans of the First Army entered the Meuse-Argonne sector, 220,000 French and Italian troops were transported out. Of the fifteen American divisions that took over the area, seven had fought in the St. Mihiel operation, three came from the Vesle sector (chapter 14), three from the area of Soissons (chapter 11), one from near Bar-le-Duc, and one from a training area. The complexity of this transfer was managed without any major complication by a young staff officer on Pershing's First Army staff, Colonel George C. Marshall. Proving himself a brilliant logistician in the run-up to the Meuse-Argonne offensive, Marshall would go on to become one of the greatest soldier-diplomats of the twentieth century. During World War II, he served as US Army chief of staff and, after the war, as Harry S. Truman's secretary of state and chief architect of the so-called Marshall Plan for the relief of a devastated

Figure 43. Members of the 101st Field Signal Battalion (formerly 1st Massachusetts Field Signal Battalion) at outdoor church services in the ruins of a church destroyed by shell fire. Verdun, France, 10/18/1918. NATIONAL ARCHIVES AND RECORDS ADMINISTRATION

Europe. Marshall ended his public career as Truman's secretary of defense during one of the most dangerous periods of the Cold War.

The First Army was positioned in an area straddling the Meuse Valley, with the dense Argonne Forest and Aire River Valley on the left. On either side of the Meuse River in the American sector were commanding heights that had to be taken and held. Pershing arrayed his army in three corps abreast, and, at 5:25 on the morning of September 26, after a three-hour artillery bombardment, the infantry commenced its attack in concert with the French Fourth Army on Pershing's left. The enemy here consisted of two German army groups, one under General Max von Gallwitz and the other commanded by the German crown prince, Wilhelm, who had remarked in 1914 at the outbreak of the Great War, "Undoubtedly this is the most stupid, senseless and unnecessary war of modern times. It is a war not wanted by Germany, I can assure you, but it was forced on us, and the fact that we were so effectually prepared to defend ourselves is now being used as an argument to convince the world that we desired conflict."[1] Now both Gallwitz and the crown prince were in the fight of their nation's life.

In the Aisne-Marne offensive (chapter 11), the Allies had encountered poorly prepared German defenses. What confronted Pershing and French Fourth Army commanding officer General Henri Gouraud at the Meuse-Argonne front was very different. Heavily fortified lines were expertly contoured to a rugged and heavily wooded battleground. The First Army's area of operations was fifteen to twenty miles wide, bounded, as mentioned, by the Meuse River (which was too wide and deep to be forded) on the east and by the Argonne Forest and the Aire River on the west. A hogback ridge ran between the river and the forest, southeast and northwest from the villages of Montfaucon, Cunel, and Barricourt. Among the natural obstacles impeding advance to the north were three lines of hills. Moreover, the Argonne was not the only dense woods here. The entire area was dotted with small patches of forest, every one of them a potential German point of covered resistance.

The Germans had had a very long time to study the Meuse-Argonne region (map 11) since 1914, and they had adapted their elaborate fortifications to its rugged terrain. Of greatest advantage to them was the high ground on both flanks of the First Army's advance. This afforded excellent observation as well as ideal positions for artillery to deliver devastating fire on any advance. The way forward had been transformed into a gauntlet with a defensive system consisting of four fortified lines. Multiple barbed-wire entanglements slowed the passage of men past machine-gun nests sited to create interlocking fields of fire. Major strongpoints were augmented by outlying fighting posts of reinforced concrete, which provided defenders with concealment as well as cover. Between four lines of trench, the enemy had developed virtually every natural feature—each patch of trees, each grassy knoll—into a place of covered resistance. All of this was integrated into the Hindenburg Line; the entire system in this sector was some fifteen miles deep. On this line, five German divisions were deployed. Behind the line,

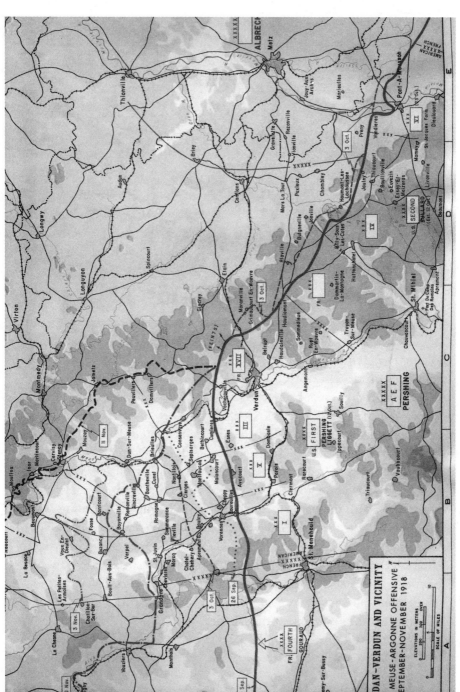

Map 11. Meuse-Argonne Area of Operations. US MILITARY ACADEMY

seven more divisions were held in ready reserve. Marshal Pétain predicted that just to capture Montfaucon, a tiny village of fewer than two hundred residents located on the second of the four lines of defense, would consume the entire autumn.

Buoyed by St. Mihiel, Pershing was far more optimistic. He focused on his army's first assigned objective. It was to attack northward in parallel with the French Fourth Army, and capture the railroad running between Carignan-Sedan-Mézières. This was a principal transport artery for whatever side controlled it. For the Allies, it was a means of supplying a war-ending advance that could run through Luxembourg and Thionville clear through to Metz. Mézières was thirty long miles from the First Army's starting line east of Verdun. Reaching it would mean a fighting advance east of the Argonne Forest. As Pershing planned it, the advance would also outflank the German positions along the Aisne River directly in front of the French units facing them from the west. As the First Army advanced on the rail line, it would catch the Germans between itself and the French Fourth Army, thereby effecting an envelopment.

The attack was planned to put nine US divisions on the line while holding five more divisions in reserve to use for exploitation of whatever gains were made. III Corps, under Robert Lee Bullard, was to attack on the east; Major General George H. Cameron's V Corps targeted the center; and Hunter Liggett's I Corps took on the west. The infantry advance was supported by 2,700 guns, 189 tanks, and 821 aircraft. It was divided into two phases. Phase one called for a penetration to the third German line. It required an advance of some ten miles, during which the First Army would have to clear the enemy out of the Argonne Forest and then link up with the French Fourth Army at Grandpré. When this was accomplished, the second phase would begin. It called for an advance of an additional ten miles to outflank the German positions along the Aisne River, envelop and neutralize these positions, and then make preparations for attacks toward Sedan and Mézières on the Meuse. Ancillary to this main second-phase advance were operations intended to clear the high ground along the east bank of the Meuse.

As the first attacks stepped off on the morning of September 26, they followed a plan calling for two advances on either side of the high ground surrounding Montfaucon. The idea was for the two branches of this advance to link up on the far side of the village *before* the Germans could deploy reinforcements on the heights. The V Corps would make this main attack, taking Montfaucon and then punching through the second German line. V Corps would be protected on its flank by the simultaneous advance of I and III Corps. The artillery attached to these two corps was assigned the mission of providing counterbattery fire to suppress German artillery on the high ground flanking the line of American advance. Pershing's timetable—overly ambitious, in Pétain's estimation—called for capturing Cunel and, to the west of this town, Romagne, by the end of the second day of the offensive.

●

The attack began auspiciously. Through a dense early morning fog, the Americans made their way swiftly over the rough terrain and through successive layers of barbed wire. The sheer weight of American numbers overwhelmed the Germans in the forwardmost positions. However, it must be remembered that a favorite German stratagem in trench warfare was to present a comparatively light defense in the forward positions to draw in the attacker, who could be enveloped by troops defending the middle and rear positions. Pershing had been made keenly aware of this.

On both flanks of the divided advance, progress was rapid. The 4th Division of III Corps, under Major General John Hines, made a four-mile advance and punched through the enemy's second line. Several counter-attacks were mounted against Hines's doughboys, but all were successfully repulsed. On the western flank, Liggett's I Corps also reached all its first-day objectives, lapping up three miles of open ground east of the Argonne Forest. The 77th Division, I Corps, commanded by Major General Robert Alexander, was considerably slower in its advance into the forest proper.

As for V Corps, struggling to advance up the center, things were not going very well. Heavy counterattacks south of Montfaucon checked the initial advance of the corps, but, on September 27, Cameron seemed to get a new purchase on his heavy load. His corps resumed movement toward Montfaucon—the very objective Pétain feared would consume the entire season.

Downpours became torrential during September 27–28, and the advance by all elements again slowed. The First Army kept going ahead, but progress was plodding for the rest of September. Before long, the army's tanks were starting to break down—but not before Lieutenant Colonel George S. Patton Jr. (figure 44) was able to put them to spectacular use. He had proposed a plan for using tanks of the US 1st Tank Brigade to neutralize some of the enemy fortifications, dugouts, and other obstacles in the line of the infantry's advance. His brigade had been ordered to support the 28th and 35th Divisions as they attacked from the west. He intended to give them far more support than they had bargained for.

At about 6 a.m., minutes after the infantry got on the move, Patton pointedly ignored the orders he had received from Brigadier General Samuel D. Rockenbach, commanding officer of the tank brigade, to stay out of the field and direct all action from his command post. Instead,

Figure 44. Colonel George S. Patton Jr. poses in front of a French Renault tank of the US 1st Tank Brigade, 1918. US ARMOR MUSEUM, FORT KNOX, KENTUCKY

Patton walked out into the field to direct operations personally.[2] Armed only with an officer's walking stick and his sidearm, he followed the tank tracks along the Clermont-Neuvilly-Boureuilles-Varennes road until he encountered some of his tanks. No sooner did he make contact than German artillery shells fell upon their position. Machine-gun fire followed, and Patton ordered everyone down. He sent everyone toward the cover of a deep railway cut and waited for the barrage to end. To Patton's distress, more and more infantrymen—in retreat—began diving into the cut. Patton looked ahead and saw some of his tanks stopped in front of a large trench. In an interval between barrages, he hurriedly rallied the infantrymen in the cut and marched them forward to the front trench. As machine-gun fire broke out again, Patton ordered everyone down, then ordered them up to advance to the tanks and lend their muscle to help them get across the trench. The troops obeyed, defying heavy enemy fire and working frantically to tear down the trench walls.

Even as enemy fire, from machine guns and field artillery, reached a new pitch of intensity, Patton refused to get down. Instead, he ordered the infantrymen to hold their ground and continue digging. This time, not everyone obeyed. Some kept digging, while others hightailed it back to the cut. Patton's impulse was to corral them, but he could not take time out to vent his rage. Instead, he seized a shovel and pitched in with digging. When some of the weary, frightened doughboys let up in their labor, Patton urged them on with sharp shovel blows to the helmet.

And still the fire picked up. Men were falling on either side of Patton. He responded by pushing the surviving troops forward, yelling, "To hell with them, they can't hit me!"

At last, with the trench walls reduced, the tanks began rolling over them, and Patton rallied infantrymen behind and among the advancing armor to resume the way forward. He waved his walking stick over his head.

"Let's go get them! Who's with me?"

A hundred or more soldiers ran down the hill with Patton. They dived for cover every fifty feet or so as the machine-gun fire increased. Later, Patton admitted: "I felt a great desire to run, I was trembling with fear when suddenly I thought of my [Confederate Civil War] progenitors and seemed to see them in a cloud over the German lines looking at me. I became calm at once and saying aloud, 'It is time for another Patton to die.' [I] called for volunteers and went forward to what I honestly believed to be certain death. Six men went with me; five were killed."

Patton pressed forward, continuing to wave his walking stick in circles above his head and shouting to the dwindling half dozen still following him, "Let's go, let's go!"

Soon, they were all cut down, except for Patton's own orderly, Private First Class Joseph T. Angelo. He and Patton took cover in a shell hole as the German fire intensified. Impatient, Patton decided to resume his advance.

"We are alone," Angelo told him matter-of-factly.

"Come on anyway," Patton urged.

That is when a machine-gun round tore into his left thigh, exiting near his rectum and creating a hideous through-and-through wound. Patton dragged himself back into the shell hole, where Angelo pulled him in and began bandaging the injury as best he could. As Angelo saw it, there was seemingly nothing to do now but wait for help and probably die waiting.

Though immobilized, Patton saw the situation differently. He ordered Angelo to run back toward the tanks that were now approaching their position and direct their fire against the German machine-gun nests. Angelo understood, and he did as he was told. In short order, the machine-gun fire was silenced.

When Angelo returned to the shell hole, Patton reeled off a list of targets for the tanks and again sent him on his way to relay these orders to the drivers. It was another hour before a medic arrived. Patton asked the man to change his bandage, but insisted that the more critically wounded be helped first. Thus it was yet another hour before Patton was finally put on a stretcher. Even then, he insisted that the medics take him to the 35th Division headquarters so that he could give his report *before* he was carried to Hospital Number 11 for emergency surgery. For Patton, the Great War was over, but he had the satisfaction of having demonstrated the value of armor in supporting infantry attack.

The same rain that was causing the tanks to begin failing was also slowing the forward movement of artillery, and it was generally delaying resupply of the advancing Americans. Yet the very conditions that were impeding the First Army advance in front of Montfaucon were giving the Germans time to get their local reserves up to reinforce the center of their line, south of Cunel and Romagne. When the slogging US battalions finally neared these positions, they were confronted by very heavy machine-gun fire. Once again, the advance bogged down.

But it did not stop. And, slowly but surely, the infantry was able to suppress the machine-gun fire coming from the reinforced German forward positions. Once the Americans began moving into those positions, German artillery brought down fire on what had been the German second line. Then they opened up on the attackers' enfilading fire from the heights of the Meuse and the Argonne Forest. Still, the advance ground on—albeit at greater and greater cost.

●

Of the nine divisions in the initial advance, just three—the 4th, 28th, and 77th—were battle-hardened. The others were newcomers to combat, including the 79th Division, which was tasked with capturing Montfaucon. Its soldiers had been in France a mere seven weeks. In the rugged, often densely forested terrain, amid downpour and heavy fog, the inexperienced troops and their inexperienced officers sometimes faltered. They became disoriented, and coordination of action was lost. The cooperation between artillery and infantry, critical to the momentum of the advance, frequently broke down. Yet, somehow, the First Army managed to advance eight miles into the German lines by the end of September. Despite the inexperience and blundering of some units, the Americans had fought their way through some of the most highly fortified German positions on the Western Front. While progressing eastward, they picked up nine thousand prisoners and huge stocks of materiel, including a hundred artillery pieces.

This was good news, but Pershing recognized the problems and saw that the various units were losing their cohesiveness and intermingling with one another. There was a danger of the First Army becoming the First Mob. He ordered a deliberate suspension of the advance to reorganize.

In their confusion, the Americans were not alone. All across the Western Front, Foch's grand offensive was slowing down as order eroded. Up north, in Flanders, rain and mud retarded advance. Below this, along the Somme, Haig had begun to penetrate the Hindenburg Line—aided by the US 27th and 30th Divisions (chapter 12)—but as October began, the British also called an intermission to strengthen and extend their lines of communications. With everyone pausing during the first few days of October, Pershing rotated three combat-experienced divisions, the 3rd, 32nd, and 1st, into the line and sent the less-experienced 37th, 79th, and 35th to the rear for a rest and some more training.

•

By October 2, the 77th Division had been fighting in the depths of the Argonne Forest for seven days without let up. Then, on that day, it came to a standstill in front of the heavily defended Ravine de Charlevaux. Elements of the division, the 1st and 2d battalions of the 308th Infantry and portions of the 306th Machine Gun Battalion, which had been assigned as an advance unit to probe the way forward, were unaware of the general halt. They kept moving and moved forward into the ravine. While taking heavy German machine-gun fire, they advanced across the floor of the ravine and climbed partway up the slope before establishing a defensive position some three hundred yards long by sixty yards deep, on a steep, rocky, overgrown hillside. Runners were sent to communicate their position to the rear, but this fragile line of communication was quickly severed.

Night descended on the woods. The Americans could hear voices, German voices, on their left. In the dim moonlight that came at intervals when the clouds broke, they could see German soldiers. Totally cut off from the main body of the 77th Division, Major Charles W. Whittlesey, in command of this advance force, deployed his 550 men in a classic defensive square, placing his nine machine guns on the flanks, where they could sweep the valley.

In the meantime, as the interminable night crawled on, the enemy voices grew louder. Then they stopped. And then hand grenades exploded all around the Americans. When the barrage paused, Whittlesey ordered a counterattack, which succeeded in preempting a renewed grenade attack—but seemed to prompt the opening of heavy machine-gun fire.

Whittlesey and his 550-man command were under siege. During the fight, Whittlesey sent out small patrols in hope of finding a weak spot in the surrounding Germans. He also sent out more runners, hoping to reestablish communications with the rear. It was all fruitless; each patrol party sent out—and each runner dispatched—simply further whittled down the number of defenders. As the hours passed, the rations dwindled. An advance patrol traveled light and carried little to eat. As food ran low, the men also missed having overcoats and blankets—something else a patrol did not equip itself with. As for ammunition, that also was disappearing. Nor was there any doctor to treat the wounded. The medic attached to the patrol quickly exhausted his rudimentary first aid supplies and began unwrapping bandages from the dead to reuse on the wounded.

The most urgent need of all was drinking water. As that ran out, individuals made their way to the bottom of the ravine to fill their canteens at the stream. The Germans had already targeted their machine guns at precisely this spot, and they opened fire on the thirsty. Whittlesey issued orders forbidding any more forays to the stream.

On October 4, this "Lost Battalion"—as the press would later dub it—ran up against a new hazard: friendly fire. A rain of American shells came down upon the men. Whittlesey's patrol had been supplied with a few carrier pigeons and had already used all but one. Now Whittlesey took that last pigeon, a bird named Cher Ami—"Dear Friend"—and attached to its foot a message giving the group's position and telling the artillery to cease fire. Astoundingly, where human runners had failed, Cher Ami succeeded, flying safely through the artillery barrage. In a short time, the shelling stopped—and then resumed, now aimed squarely at the German positions.

The Lost Battalion, after a six-day ordeal, seemed on the verge of being saved. Allied aircraft attempted to drop supplies, but each attempt failed, falling too far beyond the American position and straight into enemy hands.

Soon, the Germans began taunting the men in English, trying to goad them into showing themselves. When the taunts failed, they opened up with rifle fire and a machine-gun fusillade. Come the afternoon of October 7, however, the fire abruptly stopped. Whittlesey and the survivors beheld a US Army private with a white flag walking toward them. He called out that he had been captured when he went out to retrieve one of the food parcels that had been air-dropped. He had a message from the German commander. It appealed to Whittlesey, in "the name of humanity," to surrender.

Later, the newspapers would report that Whittlesey scribbled a three-word imperative sentence by way of reply—"Go to hell"—and gave it to the private to bring back to his captors. But the truth was that not only did Whittlesey make no reply but he also refused to send back the messenger, thereby saving him from a POW camp.

After dusk on October 7, the German assault resumed—only to be cut short around 7 p.m. by the arrival of American soldiers. In short order, the position was being held tenuously by First Army doughboys. This allowed Whittlesey and his men to withdraw. Of the 550 men who had become the Lost Battalion, just 194 walked out with their major. A total of 199 had been wounded and 111 killed in 104 hours under fire, without food or medical aid.

●

In a war of vast numbers, stories of individual struggle and heroism were rare and therefore eagerly sought after by the press. The saga of the Lost Battalion became a popular topic of conversation on the home front. It was, in fact, a minor episode in a great offensive, and it occurred mainly during a lull in the American advance, a lull the Germans exploited to reinforce their position with six new divisions, which brought their order of battle up to a total of eleven divisions. The Americans no longer enjoyed so significant a superiority of numbers when, at 5:30 a.m. on October 4, the First Army resumed its general attack.

The mission of the III and V Corps was to capture the heights around Cunel and Romagne, respectively. While this operation was under way, I Corps was tasked with neutralizing the enemy's flanking fire from the Argonne, thereby winning some room to maneuver through the forest. For all three corps, the fighting became especially intense, and progress was slow as a series of frontal attacks were launched in a bid to break through the German lines so that the Americans could position themselves to hit the enemy's exposed flanks.

The III and V Corps made some gains, but the Cunel and Romagne heights remained an elusive prize firmly in German control. On the west, the 1st Division of I Corps racked up three valuable miles, and other I Corps elements took a commanding ridge on the east edge of the Argonne. As fresh American divisions were rotated into line, the Germans continued their own reinforcement efforts. By October 6 they had twenty-seven divisions in the area, although many were understrength.

As the two corps on the east, III and V, pressed their fight for high ground at the very center of the First Army sector, Hunter Liggett's I Corps pulled off a highly effective flanking operation. On October 7, as the 77th Division attacked northward in the Argonne, Liggett sent his 82nd Division westward, directly against the rear of the German positions (figure 45). Surprise was total and devastating. By noon, the Germans began withdrawing from the forest. Within two more days, I Corps was able to report that it had cleared the Argonne of the enemy.

●

As the US divisions of the First Army were engaged in the Meuse-Argonne, other American divisions were attached to French and British units and supported their advances. North of the Meuse-Argonne, Major General George Windle Read's II Corps supported the British advance. During October 2–4, on the western flank of the First Army, the US 2nd Division, attached to the French Fourth Army and now commanded by US Marine Corps major general John A. Lejeune, seized Mont Blanc Ridge, which deprived the Germans of the only natural defensive line south of the Aisne River—and delivered that commanding position to the Allies.

Figure 45. The most celebrated American hero of World War I, Alvin C. York—Sergeant York—was a Tennessee farmer and religious pacifist who received the Medal of Honor (presented in person by General Pershing) for leading an attack on a German machine-gun nest, taking 35 machine guns, killing at least 25 enemy soldiers, and capturing 132 during the Meuse-Argonne Offensive. Marshal Ferdinand Foch personally decorated him with the Croix de Guerre, telling him that what he had done "was the greatest thing accomplished by any soldier of all the armies of Europe." WIKIMEDIA

On October 10, the 36th Division relieved the 2nd Division and, on October 13, moved on to the Aisne River. This advance by an American unit attached to the French army at last brought the French Fourth Army on line with the US First Army. On October 8, Pershing had ordered the French XVII Corps to attack across the Meuse near Brabant, east of Montfaucon. The two French and two American divisions in this corps forged ahead two miles and captured three thousand prisoners as well as a number of key observation points. Moreover, this operation also forced the enemy to divert its divisions away from the principal battleground between the Meuse and the Argonne, thereby accelerating the Allied advance.

•

On October 14, the First Army commenced a large-scale assault all along the German lines in its front. The III and V Corps once again set their sights on the elusive fortified hills of the Cunel-Romagne front. The US 3rd, 5th, and 32nd Divisions spent the next four days fighting to capture these strongpoints. This time, they prevailed. Simultaneously, on the western flank of the general assault, I Corps advanced as far as the southern half of the village of Grandpré, which it reached on October 16. Within another week, First Army had attained most of the objectives set out for the opening phase of the campaign. The American army had penetrated through the third of four German lines, and it had cleared the Argonne Forest of the enemy.

•

As the old saying goes: "Be careful what you wish for." By this point in mid-October, General Pershing, who had clamored for American military authority, now concluded that far too much of the operational and tactical direction of the war had devolved upon him. He was massively overworked. Not only was he the US theater commander responsible for everything concerning American forces in France but he was also tasked with coordinating the efforts of other national commanders. In addition, he was the active *field* commander of an army consisting of fourteen divisions currently fighting a complicated campaign in very difficult terrain.

His army—the US First Army—had become an unwieldy monster of more than a million men strung out along an eighty-three-mile front.

Clearly, reorganization was now an imperative. On October 12, General Pershing formed the US Second Army and entrusted it to the command of Robert Lee Bullard. Pershing turned over to the new army and its commander thirty-four miles of his eighty-three-mile front, a relatively "quiet sector" between the Meuse and Moselle rivers south of Verdun. Pershing retained control of the more intensely active Meuse-Argonne sector for the First Army, but he turned over field command of that force to General Hunter Liggett on October 16.

The rationale for this massive reorganization was to allow Pershing to direct all his attention to the big-picture strategic issues of theater command, but the fact was that Pershing, exhausted, was in a state approaching nervous collapse. As if that were not sufficiently alarming, Liggett immediately embarked on a tour of inspection of the First Army's corps and divisions. He judged them to be in a shocking state of depletion following weeks of unrelenting combat. Some divisions now possessed less than a quarter of their authorized strength, and these Liggett pronounced "combat ineffective." Part of their depletion was due to casualties, but a cause at least equal to battle losses was stragglers. Liggett estimated at least one hundred thousand men were not where they should be and therefore unaccounted for. Another urgent problem was a shortage of draft horses and mules. Animals were a big part of the early twentieth-century American army, and combat was extremely hard on them (figure 46). They succumbed in proportions even greater than human casualties. While many supplies could be transported by truck or train, draft horses were still the main motive force for moving artillery from place to place. For want of horsepower, a large portion of the First Army's artillery was, at the time, effectively immobilized.

Liggett ordered what Pershing may have been unwilling or even unable to do. He sent the entire First Army into a two-week period of rest and refitting. He called a virtual moratorium on its participation in the offensive, restricting operations to a few local attacks. Despite the fact that the First Army had performed wonders and had gained enormous battle

Figure 46. In France, gas masks were worn by both man and beast. NATIONAL ARCHIVES AND RECORDS ADMINISTRATION

experience, Liggett subjected select units of his infantry and artillery to training in the latest tactics for attacking strongpoints. This would become their specialty. The Second Army and that portion of the First Army that had not received the special training were instructed simply to bypass rather than engage German strongpoint defenses whenever possible.

Liggett focused on preparing key units of *his* First Army to kill German defenders. The war was now a struggle against an army on the defense. As Liggett saw it, everything had to be directed at suppressing enemy defenses. This meant isolating enemy infantry units and perfecting the tactics of counterbattery fire. Chemical warfare was also emphasized as an effective means of suppressing defense.

●

With his newly retrained First Army, Hunter Liggett embarked on the second phase of the Meuse-Argonne offensive. The first step was a series of limited attacks that would establish a suitable line of departure for the second-phase offensive. III Corps (now commanded by General John L. Hines) and V Corps (now commanded by General Charles Pelot Summerall) launched sharp local attacks to clear forests of the enemy and capture hills and other high ground in the center of the line. I Corps engaged in a major battle of ten days to take Grandpré, which fell to the US First Army on October 27.

While second-phase preparatory battles were fought, Liggett resupplied his army and sent engineers out to repair and widen roads. On November 1, Liggett led the First Army north, toward the Meuse River. His objective was the Barricourt Ridge, five miles ahead. After securing the ridge, Liggett intended to march west, maneuver around the Bourgogne Forest, tie in with the French Fourth Army, and then, together with it, drive northeast to Sedan and the Meuse River.

Summerall's V Corps took Barricourt Ridge on day one of the resumed offensive drive, as Hines's III Corps advanced to the Meuse. Only Dickman's I Corps, to the west of these operations, struggled to make any progress—before suddenly breaking through and clearing the French Fourth Army flank of Germans. This accelerated everything the First Army did, and Liggett now drove it hard, eager to push the enemy as far east as possible before the war, which was clearly approaching an end, finally ended. It was strategically critical to make Germany's defeat as complete as possible before any cessation of hostilities. Although fighting continued, much of the German army had ceased to be very effective, and Liggett began moving so rapidly that the First Army literally ran off the maps available at AEF headquarters.

By November 4, elements of the First Army were deployed along the heights overlooking the Meuse. The army's artillery used this position to interdict German rail traffic on the railroad from Sedan to Mézières. Officially, this was the final First Army objective of the Meuse-Argonne offensive.

•

And yet the First Army kept moving and fighting. Liggett drew on the special training to which he had subjected his army. His men now cut through one German strongpoint after another. Where strongpoints had yet to be neutralized, First Army staff officers figured out ways to move elements of the army past them without engaging. A new pattern developed. In the past, attacks by American forces tended to make significant, even spectacular, advances in the first day or two of an attack, only to rack up decreasing gains with each successive day of battle. Liggett had refashioned the First Army into a force capable of increasing its productivity, making successively greater progress with each passing day of the offensive.

There were not, however, many more days of combat left to fight. One week after the First Army reached the Meuse, the Armistice was concluded on November 11, 1918, ending both the Great War and the Meuse-Argonne Campaign. It was the single greatest battle the US Army had fought to that time. After forty-seven days of combat, nearly 1.25 million American soldiers had been instrumental in creating total victory. The cost was terrible—more than 117,000 killed, wounded, or missing. But the US First Army had pushed back no fewer than forty-three German divisions some thirty miles through some of Western Europe's most inhospitable terrain and despite the heaviest field fortifications the world had seen up to this point in history.

CHAPTER 17

Vittorio Veneto

October 24–November 4, 1918

SINCE 1882, ITALY HAD BEEN A MEMBER OF THE TRIPLE ALLIANCE with Austria-Hungary and Germany. When the Great War broke out in the early summer of 1914, however, Italy announced that it considered Austria the aggressor and therefore declared its neutrality in the conflict. Less than a year later, on April 26, 1915, Italy signed the secret Treaty of London, which promised the nation the right to annex the Austrian Littoral, northern Dalmatia, Trentino, and South Tyrol, all part of the Austro-Hungarian Empire, in exchange for participation in the Great War as an ally of France and Britain.

The Italian government and military counted on a rapid victory in a surprise offensive in the Austrian-Italian borderlands. Instead, the conflict between Italy and Austria-Hungary quickly became a stalemated trench war in which the poorly led and poorly equipped Italian forces suffered a catastrophic 1,598,000 military casualties, killed, wounded, missing, or captured.

The major Battle of Caporetto, which was fought from October 24 to November 9, 1917, cost the Italian Army more than three hundred thousand casualties and sent it into retreat. The only good to come of it was the removal from command of Supreme General Luigi Cadorna, who had led the Italian military from one defeat to the next. He was replaced by General Armando Diaz, a far more competent commander who radically reorganized Italy's forces and established a defense in depth backed by mobile reserves. This stabilized the new Italian front line on the Piave River. In a bid to overcome Italy's Piave defenses, Austria-Hungary mounted a major offensive in June 1918. Like the Russian Empire, the Austro-Hungarian Empire was tottering on the verge of revolution. The leadership of its army and the quality of its soldiers had been poor throughout the war, and now much of the army was roiled by anti-imperial discontent. With morale very low, the offensive failed miserably.

Encouraged by this positive development on what had been a losing front, the Allied commanders appealed to Diaz to mount a strong counteroffensive immediately. They believed Italy now was in a position to knock Austria-Hungary out of the war. Diaz, however, demurred, arguing that the Italian military had all it could do merely to defend what ground it held.

Early in 1918, Newton Baker, the US secretary of war, decided that it would be helpful to establish a US military presence on the Italian front by establishing an American military mission to Italy. President Wilson was eager to assess the attitude of the Italian people toward the Allies, and he wanted to obtain for his generals an objective analysis of the Italian military situation with respect to armament, organization, supply, command, and, perhaps most of all, morale. On February 18, 1918, General Pershing named Major General Eben Swift to head the mission.

On June 20, 1918, Secretary of War Baker directed General Pershing to send one regiment of US infantry to Italy. Pershing selected the 332nd Regiment of the US 83rd Division, together with the 331st Field Hospital and a Provisional Motor Truck Train, which boarded trains from France and headed for Villafranca di Verona, Italy, on July 25, 1918. On July 24, Brigadier General Charles G. Treat took over command of the US Military Mission, and Major General Swift was given command of all US troops in Italy. The regiment arrived on July 29 and commenced training.

Astoundingly, the one person who was kept in the dark about putting American troops in Italy was Eben Swift. In a message to General Pershing dated July 1, 1918,[1] eleven days *after* Secretary Baker's order to Pershing to send a regiment, Swift explained that he was "somewhat surprised to get an invitation to lunch with Lord Cavan [the Earl of Cavan, the British general commanding the Tenth British-Italian Army in Italy] yesterday.... He lost no time coming to the point. He stated that he would like an American division attached to his command. He would then be able to form 2 army corps, one consisting of 2 British divisions and he would like to have me personally command the other army corps consisting of one British and one American division." Swift went on to note that reports had come to him "from many sources about American troops being ordered to Italy. I have not credited them because I have had no official information that they were coming and felt sure that I would get ample notice beforehand." He then noted:

> *The Italian newspapers today contain the following article:*
>
> *Washington–June 29.*
>
> *A regiment of troops, belonging to the [American] Expeditionary Forces under the command of General Pershing, has received orders to proceed to Italy to complete the union of British, French and American forces with those of Italy on that front.*
>
> *Yesterday, Secretary of War Baker announced that General Pershing has been charged with the task of choosing the regiment. which is now in training in France. It is to be sent immediately to Italy.*
>
> *This sending of American troops to Italy again shows the unity of purpose of the Allied nations and the United States on all the fronts.*

"I have not supposed up to the present that it was proper for me to make recommendations as to the policy of our country with reference to Italy," Swift continued in his letter to Pershing.

> *I did not think that a policy would be adopted of using American troops for propaganda purposes only. It appears to me, however, after*

seeing the character of newspaper articles which are written in the
United States on this subject, that it is time to make a recommendation.
It is my opinion that American troops should be sent to Italy in
some force or not at all. Such a headline as appears on the enclosed may
be offensive to the Italians as well as mortifying to the American soldier.

Swift went on to quote Captain Fiorello LaGuardia. The future mayor of New York City, LaGuardia had, in 1917, left his seat in Congress to accept a commission in the US Army Air Service on the Italian-Austrian front. LaGuardia, Swift wrote, "says, 'The Italians themselves will be the first to despise us if we use our troops'" for mere propaganda. Swift continued, "If a regiment of American troops comes to Italy I should like to brigade them with troops at the front, if they seem to be suitable." On July 11, Pershing finally deigned to inform General Swift that the regiment was coming.

●

On September 4, General Treat reported to General Pershing:

The time since the American troops have arrived in Italy has been
taken up largely in perfecting their proficiency in target practice,
training in trench work and raids, use of bombs and hand grenades,
work with machine guns on an extended area where firing of all char-
acter can be actually practised; also the assigning of officers of various
grades to different points of the line to observe in detail the Italian
methods of administration and care of troops in the line. It is the
intention, within a week or ten days, to take over a sector of the line.[2]

In the meantime, General Armando Diaz had devised with the other Allies a plan for the offensive they had asked him to lead. Three of the five armies currently at Piave, lining the front from the Monte Grappa sector to the Adriatic end of the Piave River, would advance across that river toward Vittorio Veneto, in the process severing communications between the two Austrian armies opposing them. The Italian armies

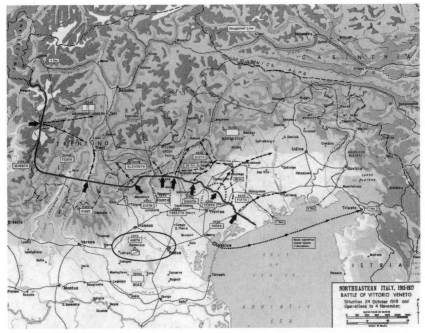

Map 12. Battle of Vittorio Veneto. US MILITARY ACADEMY

that were in the mountains would hold the front line there to prevent a flanking attack by the Austrians, and then pursue the enemy when he retreated (map 12).

Assigned to open the attack was the Italian Fourth Army (under Lieutenant-General Gaetano Giardino), on the Grappa River. The Franco-Italian Twelfth Army (one French and three Italian divisions, commanded by the English-speaking lieutenant general Enrico Caviglia), with the British-Italian Tenth Army (under Lieutenant-General Lord Cavan) protecting the right flank of the Twelfth, would also cross the Piave, breaking through Austrian defenses at Papadopoli Island. The Italian Third Army—with the 332nd US Infantry Regiment attached—was assigned to hold the lower Piave, crossing the river only after enemy resistance had been broken. The Italian Ninth Army, which included the 6th Czechoslovak Division along with two Italian divisions, was held in reserve. In addition to ground forces, the Allies had a force of six hundred aircraft (French and English), expected to readily achieve complete air superiority in the offensive.

In total, Allied forces consisted of fifty-seven infantry divisions, including fifty-one Italian, three British (23rd, 7th, and 48th), two French (23rd and 24th), one Czechoslovak (6th), and the 332nd US Infantry Regiment, along with supporting arms. Opposing these were forty-six infantry and six cavalry divisions of the Austro-Hungarian army. The Allies possessed a decided artillery advantage, 7,700 guns versus 6,030; however, influenza was epidemic throughout the armies of both sides.

The attack was launched on the one-year anniversary of the Caporetto disaster, October 24, shortly after midnight. Italian shock troops launched a sharp attack on Monte Grappa, which was intended to draw out the Austro-Hungarian reserves. At three in the morning, the artillery on the right wing of the Italian Fourth Army commenced a barrage intended to cover the positioning of its infantry. Two hours later, at 5:00 a.m., the rest of the available artillery joined in the preparatory barrage.

The Italian infantry had to scale steep slopes in this alpine region, which had been held by the Austrians through most of the war. Complicating the Allied attack was the fact that the Piave River was at flood stage, which forced the three central armies to advance serially rather than simultaneously; however, Earl Cavan's Tenth Army was able to capture Papadopoli Island downstream from the main attack and make a crossing quite quickly, gaining the left bank of the Piave on October 27. Indeed, by that same evening, the Allies had advanced so far that they were in peril of outrunning their lines of supply and communication. In this rugged terrain, that would leave them vulnerable to counterattack.

Fortunately, Earl Cavan's Tenth Army maintained its foothold on the left bank of the Piave and established a bridgehead 2.5 miles deep and 5 miles (8 km) broad, which accelerated the advance against the Austro-Hungarian positions on the far side of the river. The British divisions of the Tenth Army (commanded by General James Melville Babington) bagged 3,520 prisoners and 54 guns. At this point, the Austro-Hungarian commander on the Piave front, Field Marshal Svetozar Boroević von Bojna, ordered a counterattack on the Tenth Army bridgeheads. At this late stage of the war, the Austro-Hungarian regime was struggling to fend off revolution. To no one's surprise, the non-Austrian troops of Boroević von Bojna's army mutinied and refused to obey orders. The counterattack began to collapse before it had begun in earnest.

On the very next day, October 28, Czechoslovakia proclaimed its independence from Austria-Hungary. On October 29, the South Slavs followed suit. Two days later, on October 31, Hungary withdrew from its union with Austria. Austria-Hungary ceased to exist. Boroević von Bojna fell back with his remaining troops to Velden and fired off a telegram to the emperor, offering to fight the anti-Hapsburg revolution on the streets of Vienna. The emperor never replied. In fact, on October 28, the Austro-Hungarian high command ordered a general retreat.

Amid the withdrawal of Austrian forces, the Eighth Italian Army advanced toward the Tagliamento River. It approached Vittorio Veneto on October 29, engaged the defenders, and captured the town on the next day. The Eighth Army then launched an amphibious expedition, which captured Trieste on November 3.

In the meantime, the Italian Third Army, with the 332nd US Infantry Regiment (figure 47) attached, forced a crossing of the Lower Piave River in pursuit of withdrawing Austrians. The Americans now followed behind the Italian Tenth Army, pursuing the retreating Austrians from the Piave to the Tagliamento River. After a series of forced marches over difficult terrain, the 332nd made contact on November 3 with an Austrian rear-guard battalion, which was defending the crossings of the Tagliamento River near Ponte della Delizia. Early in the morning of the next day, the American regiment's 2nd Battalion crossed Tagliamento on a narrow footbridge. It engaged the Austrians and captured many on the far side of the river. After sending its prisoners to the rear, the 2nd Battalion continued its advance along the Treviso-Udine railroad, took the town of Codroipo, and appropriated a large store of abandoned Austro-Hungarian munitions and supplies.

Figure 47. Doughboys of the 332nd Regiment at the Battle of Vittorio Veneto on the Piave Front, Italy. NATIONAL ARCHIVES AND RECORDS ADMINISTRATION

Although the general Armistice ending the Great War would not take effect until November 11, a separate Armistice had been concluded between Italy and Austria–Hungary and was implemented at 3:00 p.m. on November 4. The advance elements of the 332nd Regiment were at Villaorba at the time.

●

The 332nd Regiment became one of many American units assigned to postwar peacekeeping duties after the general Armistice of November 11, 1918. The 1st and 3rd Battalions of the regiment were stationed at Cormons, near Gorizia, Austria. The 1st Battalion was subsequently ordered to Treviso, Italy, and the 3rd Battalion to Fiume, Austria (today, Rijeka, Croatia). The 2nd Battalion was stationed at Cattaro, in Dalmatia, and a detachment from it was sent to Cetinje, Montenegro. The 332nd Regiment received orders to return to the United States in February 1919, but

Figure 48. After the Armistice—"Gallant 15th Infantry Fighters Home with War Crosses. The French liner, *La France*, arrives with 15th Infantry—the Negro fighters who won honors in France." NATIONAL ARCHIVES AND RECORDS ADMINISTRATION

because its elements were widely broadcast throughout Italy, Austria, and Montenegro, it was March before they were reconstituted, which delayed the regiment's departure from Italy for the United States until March 29, 1919 (figure 48).

Part III

Marching into the American Century

CHAPTER 18

Hall of Mirrors

ASKED WHO WON THE GREAT WAR, PAUL VON HINDENBURG ANSWERED, "The American infantry in the Argonne."[1] That is certainly how it must have appeared to him. The First Army's campaign in the Meuse-Argonne offensive (chapter 16) was the biggest battle the US Army had ever fought to that time, and it made this offensive the culminating campaign of the Great War as well as the Allies' greatest victory in that conflict. Yet America's entry into what had been "the European War" had come more than a year earlier, in April 1917, at a very low point for the Allies, when they were ripe for final defeat under the relentless punishment of one Ludendorff offensive after another.

That America won the Great War is beyond argument—for the simple reason that, without American intervention coming when it came, the German army would have worn through French lines and captured Paris, as the German army had done in 1870–1871. This decapitating blow would have taken France out of the war. With France out of the war, the BEF would have left the continent, and Italy would have yielded disputed territory to Austria-Hungary. The Great War would have ended perhaps late in 1917 but more probably early in 1918, and Germany and the other Central powers would have declared a hard-won victory.

As is clear from the campaign summaries in part II, much of the American participation on the Western Front was on a small scale prior to the operations in Montdidier-Noyon and Champagne-Marne in the summer of 1918 (chapter 10). American participation in the Battle of Belleau Wood (June 1–26, 1918; chapter 9) also involved limited numbers but was of a character so heroic that the engagement created a strategic and emotional impact far beyond the numbers involved. Only at St. Mihiel (September 12–16, 1918; chapter 15) and Meuse-Argonne (September 26–November 11, 1918; chapter 16) did the United States fight on a very large scale and in an independent army. Belleau Wood earned accolades from the French military, but it was at St. Mihiel and Meuse-Argonne that the US Army earned among the Allies anything approaching the status of an equal (figure 49). The adulation French

"The Germans have gone!"

Baldridge
St. Mihiel

Figure 49. In this sketch by combat artist Cyrus Leroy Baldridge, two doughboys coax a woman out of the shell hole in which she has hidden by assuring her, "The Germans have gone." WIKIMEDIA

civilians showed to American forces came sooner and became increasingly intense as the war neared its end.

The French people saw in the American soldier their national salvation, and whatever Pershing's AEF gained the Allies militarily, its winning performance gained for Woodrow Wilson the commanding seat he wanted in the great peace conference that would shape postwar Europe and much of the postwar world.

•

What stopped the shooting at the eleventh hour of the eleventh day of the eleventh month of 1918 was not a treaty but an Armistice, a ceasefire pending the conclusion of a formal treaty. It was signed in a railway carriage that was part of Marshal Foch's rolling headquarters, parked on a siding in the forest of Compiègne, Picardy. There was nothing special or especially elegant about the railcar. In fact, after the war, it was returned to regular service with the Compagnie des Wagons-Lits—although it was later appropriated by the French president as part of his train. In April 1921, the car was put on exhibition at the Cour des Invalides, the courtyard of Les Invalides, the hospital and retirement home for French war veterans and the site of the magnificent Musée de l'Armée, the French military museum. The railcar remained there until April 1927. In November of that year, in a grand ceremony, it was returned to the siding where the Armistice was signed. The French government intended it as an enduring monument to the defeat of Germany—a defeat that the terms of the Armistice and the Treaty of Versailles that followed were intended to make utter, complete, and eternal. These things did not go unrecognized by Adolf Hitler. As a condition of the Armistice Germany dictated on June 22, 1940, after the ruinous Battle of France in World War II, Hitler demanded that the French offer their surrender in the same railway carriage in which the Germans had bowed to the French two decades earlier. Hitler, Hermann Göring, Wilhelm Keitel, and Joachim von Ribbentrop all gathered to receive the surrender. When it was done, the railway car was summarily coupled to a German locomotive and hauled back to Berlin, where it was parked in the city's celebrated Lustgarten, presumably to remain on exhibit for a thousand years.

Obviously, the differences between what happened in the railway carriage in November 1918 and June 1940 were many and profound. One of the most important was that the French surrender of June 22, 1940, was no more than the signing of a document, whereas the proceedings in 1918 were more complex and time-consuming—and, if anything, even more deliberately humiliating. The backstory began on September 29, 1918, when Kaiser Wilhelm II received a telegram from German Supreme Army Command announcing that the army now faced a hopeless military situation. Erich Ludendorff, in a panic, announced that his forces could not hold the front longer than two more hours. He called on the kaiser to authorize a request to the Allies for an immediate ceasefire. In a dramatic acknowledgment of the influence the American president now wielded, Ludendorff specifically advised Wilhelm to publicly accept the conditions for peace that Woodrow Wilson had promulgated in a speech to Congress on January 8, 1918—a set of principles that became known as the Fourteen Points. Wilson, with characteristic absolutism, had described them as "The programme of the world's peace . . . our programme . . . the only possible programme."[2] Furthermore, Ludendorff advised that the kaiser take some immediate steps to put the imperial government on the road toward democracy, a move, Ludendorff believed, that might coax from the Allies more favorable peace terms than otherwise.

Did Ludendorff really believe that the military situation was this dire at the end of September? The German historian Gerhard Ritter, who had fought in the war as an infantryman, later noted that by October 1, "Ludendorff was wiring [Berlin] every few hours demanding that peace be made immediately."[3] Many believe he did think the war had been lost but that his more pressing motive for bombarding the kaiser with telegrams was to give himself and the Imperial German Army an out. He wanted the defeat to be seen as a political failure rather than a military one, remarking to his staff officers on October 1, "They now must lie on the bed that they've made for us."[4] Moreover, with Germany teetering on the brink of revolution and the probable overthrow of the kaiser, Ludendorff may have been maneuvering to put the blame on an incoming liberal regime—hence his urging Wilhelm to make democratic reforms now.

Figure 50. The Big Three of the Big Four—(left to right), Georges Clemenceau, David Lloyd George, and Vittorio Orlando. WIKIMEDIA

Whatever Ludendorff's motives and intentions, the kaiser did accede to democratic reforms, quite possibly to curry favor with Wilson, whom he perceived as now the most influential of the Allies (figure 50) when it came to making peace. On October 3, Wilhelm approved the appointment of the liberal-leaning prince Maximilian of Baden as chancellor of Germany, an office equivalent to prime minister. Maximilian replaced the autocratic Georg von Hertling and would have the unenviable task of negotiating an Armistice. In the meantime, various German government officials met with Wilhelm to discuss available options. The conclusion? There were few options indeed. Revolution was in the air, and defeat was on the front. Thus, on October 5, 1918, the Reich government sent President Wilson—not President Raymond Poincaré or Prime Minister Georges Clemenceau of France or Prime Minister David Lloyd George of Britain—a message asking to negotiate terms on the basis of Wilson's Fourteen Points. The American president initially replied with hints that the kaiser would have to abdicate as a precondition of peace—hints that either failed to be comprehended or that were willfully ignored. On October 23, however, Wilson laid it all on the table. Before negotiations could even begin, Germany would have to withdraw from all occupied territories, immediately recall all submarines, and the kaiser would have to formally abdicate. These, he emphasized, were preconditions for negotiation. If Germany chose to retain its army in the field and its kaiser on the throne, the only way to end the war was by Germany's unconditional surrender.

This proved too much even for Ludendorff, the generalissimo who had been begging his government for capitulation. Pronouncing Wilson's conditions unacceptable, he announced his intention to continue the war. Perhaps the German government would have agreed—if the army had been willing to continue the fight. A vast number of soldiers, however, were verging on mutiny. Desertion became as great an epidemic as influenza. There was no possibility of rousing the troops to their own defense, let alone a new offensive. Chancellor Maximilian announced to Kaiser Wilhelm that he, together with the cabinet, would resign unless Ludendorff was removed. Maximilian insisted, however, that Otto von Hindenburg remain in sole command of the army—lest it dissolve or mount a coup d'etat. Accordingly, the kaiser summoned his officers. Both Ludendorff and Hindenburg tendered their resignations. The kaiser accepted Ludendorff's and refused Hindenburg's. Wilhelm Groener, a top army officer, was named chief of the German General Staff in Ludendorff's place. With this shake-up concluded, the Allies, on November 5, agreed to commence negotiating a truce. Wilson sent the Berlin government a note the next day, and on that very day, Matthias Erzberger, a politician who had earlier opposed the war, having become secretary of state (without portfolio) in the government of Maximilian von Baden, set off for France.

●

Having left Berlin late in the day on November 6, Erzberger and his delegation—which included Count Alfred von Oberndorff of the Foreign Ministry, Major General Detlof von Winterfeldt representing the army, and Captain Ernst Vanselow of the navy, none of them highly placed in either the government or military—crossed the French-German border and then the front line in a train of five railway coaches. The delegation was then escorted on a tortuous ten-hour journey through the cratered and ruined landscape of northern France. Their journey halted at a train station on the morning of November 8, and they boarded a train for an undisclosed location. It was Foch's private train parked in the seclusion of the forest of Compiègne.

For the next three days, the German delegation met in Foch's car with General Maxime Weygand, Foch's chief of staff; First Sea Lord Admiral Rosslyn Wemyss and Deputy Sea Lord Rear Admiral George Hope, both representing Great Britain; and Captain Jack Marriott, a British naval officer serving as assistant to the First Sea Lord. No American or Italian representative was present. Ferdinand Foch, the Allied supreme commander, appeared just twice during the three days of talks. On day one, he asked a single question of the German delegation: What do you want? On day three, he stopped in to examine their signatures on the document of Armistice-surrender, said nothing, and then departed.

On November 9, while the delegation argued and stewed, Kaiser Wilhelm II abdicated and fled into exile, after which Maximilian von Baden handed over the office of chancellor to Friedrich Ebert, a Social Democrat in the new republic, which had been proclaimed as a result of a brief revolution that had begun on October 29–30 with the revolt of German navy sailors.

In the railroad car at Compiègne, the delegates complained and protested, but there was no negotiation as such. The Allied representatives handed over a list of their demands and told the delegates that they had seventy-two hours to agree to them. The Germans discussed the terms with everyone but Foch. The most important of the demands were:

- Cessation of military hostilities within six hours of signature.
- Immediate withdrawal of all German troops from France, Belgium, Luxembourg, and Alsace-Lorraine within fourteen days.
- German demilitarization, consisting of the evacuation of all German troops from the west side of the Rhine and demilitarization of Mainz, Koblenz, and Cologne on the east side of the Rhine; the evacuated region was to be occupied by US and other Allied troops.
- Evacuation of all German troops on the Eastern Front from Turkey, the former Austria-Hungary, and Romania. They were to be back within the confines of German territory as it had existed on August 1, 1914. German soldiers in Russian territory were to be evacuated at some future undetermined time; given the instability of revolutionary Russia, the West was not speaking to the East.
- Renunciation of the Treaty of Brest-Litovsk with Russia (which gave Germany certain territories) and of the Treaty of Bucharest with Romania.
- Internment of the German High Seas Fleet.
- Surrender of all German U-boats.
- Surrender of a large amount of materiel, including armaments, aircraft, some 5,000 locomotive engines, and 150,000 railroad cars.
- Immediate release of all French, British, and Italian prisoners of war. The release and repatriation of German POWs was to be delayed until the conclusion of a full formal peace treaty.

And as for the strangling naval blockade of Germany, it would not be totally lifted until the conclusion of a treaty.

The demands were entirely nonnegotiable, and while the delegates registered a formal protest about the harshness of the terms, their own government had given them no option to decline agreement. On November 10, newspapers from Paris were delivered to the delegates to prove to them that Kaiser Wilhelm II had abdicated. Ebert, who had been named chancellor of the new Weimar Republic on November 9, sent Erzberger an order to sign the treaty. Even Hindenburg, representing the military in the new government, called for signing the Armistice regardless of whether the Allied terms could be improved.

The Armistice was signed between 5:12 and 5:20 on the morning of November 11, to come into effect at 11:00 a.m. (Paris time; noon, German time).

Fighting continued virtually unabated until 11:00 a.m. sharp. General Pershing was particularly insistent on this point. He wanted to claim every possible inch of German-held territory. In truth, the Armistice might have come more than a month earlier; it was delayed not because of any German obstinacy but because the French, British, and Italian leaders had come to resent some of Wilson's Fourteen Points, which did not limit demilitarization to the Central powers and which called for national self-determination—essentially the dismantling of all colonial empires, whether German, British, French, or Italian. The fact was that the Allies, when they were about to embark on the making of a treaty, were by no means unified on what they wanted and did not want. Grateful for America's role in the war, they nevertheless objected to much that Wilson made clear he intended to demand. If this lack of unity among the victors did not bode well, how much darker were the prospects of a treaty that was to be hammered out with neither the participation nor observation of any representatives of Germany or the other Central powers? As with the Armistice (figure 51), the treaty of peace would be unconditional and subject to no negotiation.

●

In Paris on January 18, 1919, twenty-seven Allied nations convened to draw up a definitive treaty of peace ending the war to end all wars. The "enemies"—Germany, Austria-Hungary, Bulgaria, and Turkey—were not invited. Their only role would be to sign whatever the victors handed them. And of those twenty-seven partner states in victory, only four had a significant voice in making the treaty: Britain, France, the United States, and—less significantly—Italy. These four major powers were represented by their political leaders, David Lloyd-George, prime minister of Great Britain; Georges Clemenceau, prime minister of France; Woodrow Wil-

Figure 51. The US 64th Regiment celebrates the Armistice, November 11, 1918.
NATIONAL ARCHIVES AND RECORDS ADMINISTRATION

son, president of the United States; and Vittorio Orlando, premier of Italy. The newspapers referred to them as the Big Four (figure 52).

Whatever animosity three of the Big Four harbored against Woodrow Wilson's idealistic vision for a world beyond the reach of war, none of it was reflected in the people of the Allied nations—especially the French. On the president's arrival in Paris on December 16, 1918, he was presented with "the great gold medal of the City of Paris" and his wife, Edith Bolling Wilson, with a diamond brooch. The president responded to the tumultuous welcome by speaking, he said, for the American people: "I know what they have thought, I know what they have desired, and when I have spoken what I know was in their minds it has been delightful to see how the consciences and purposes of freemen everywhere responded. We [Americans] have merely established our right to the full fellowship of those peoples here and throughout the world who reverence the right of genuine liberty and justice." Rarely in American history has an American president believed so absolutely that he knew the American heart and mind and that, when he spoke, he spoke that heart and mind unmistakably. Rarely in American history has a president

Figure 52. The Big Four at Versailles: from left to right, David Lloyd George, prime minister of Britain; Vittorio Orlando, prime minister of Italy; Georges Clemenceau, prime minister of France; and Woodrow Wilson, president of the United States. NATIONAL ARCHIVES AND RECORDS ADMINISTRATION

been so mistaken. But the people of France took him to their hearts. M. Autrand, the Prefect of the Seine (head of the administrative *département* of France encompassing Paris) addressed him: "Today we taste the deep joy of saluting in the person of President Wilson the nation whose valiant arms have contributed so brilliantly to the most magnificent of victories. Paris feels herself drawn irresistibly toward you by the force of all her affinities and convictions. . . . As the historic bulwark of liberty and justice she acclaims in you the disinterested servitor of these great moral ideas, the eloquent and inflexible apostle of the rights of humanity."[5]

President Wilson assumed absolute leadership of the American delegation to the Paris Peace Conference. As relentlessly as he had worked to mobilize his nation for war, he now battled to bring about the idea and image of peace that was in *his* mind. It was to be a perfect peace, a final and enduring peace, which would mean the end of war itself. Wilson's intense idealism, his determination that the sacrifice of so much life and treasure would not be in vain, combined with his absolute conviction that he and he alone understood what was right in this case, that he and he alone was not only the smartest man in the room but the smartest man in the world, blinded him to the imperatives of nationalism among the other Allies and the domestic political realities active in the United States he was convinced he knew so very well.

As Germany was to have no part in creating the final treaty of peace, neither was the US Republican Party. Pursuant to Wilson's Fourteen Points, the creation of a League of Nations, an international deliberative and arbitrative body that would settle disputes between nations without resort to war, was the keystone of the treaty. Wilson feared that Republicans—some of whom were isolationists, some of whom merely held a narrower view of US sovereignty than that of the president—would oppose the League. Wilson led America into war, he said, to make the world safe for democracy. But when it came to creating the treaty to end the Great War, Wilson arrogantly abridged democracy by appointing not a single Republican to the peace delegation. As if this omission did not sufficiently alienate Republicans, Wilson made the prospective treaty and the League of Nations specifically political issues by appealing to voters to reelect a Democratic Congress in 1918. In the end, the voters in the 1918 midterms responded by giving the *Republicans* a majority in *both* houses of Congress. It was one of the harshest midterm rebuffs in presidential history. Did Woodrow Wilson acknowledge a message in this? Did he not see that he was out of touch with the sentiments of his fellow Americans? No, he did not.

●

Nor was Woodrow Wilson in tune with Georges Clemenceau of France, David Lloyd George of Great Britain, and Vittorio Orlando of Italy. Without doubt, the United States had made sacrifices in the Great War. It had poured into it some two million of its sons, brothers, fathers, and uncles. Of these, 53,402 were killed in action and another 63,306 died in overseas military service from causes unrelated to combat; 204,002 were wounded—some maimed, disfigured, and disabled for life. Yet Americans had been at war for no more than nineteen months and had been engaged in intensive, massive combat for only the last hundred days of the war. As for the civilian population of America, they were protected by an ocean from the devastation that had visited France and Belgium. All the European Allies had lost far more of their boys and men than the United States: France, 1,150,000 combat deaths and 4,260,000 soldiers wounded; Britain, 774,000 combat deaths and 1,675,000 soldiers wounded; Italy, 460,000 combat deaths and 947,000 soldiers wounded. No wonder that the likes of Clemenceau, Lloyd George, and Orlando, each in his way, wanted to write a treaty that did little more than punish and humiliate Germany in ways from which (they expected and hoped) it would never recover.

For his part, Wilson wanted a treaty that would conciliate and heal all nations while removing incentives for more war. The Fourteen Points were uppermost in his mind, especially points one through five:

- A requirement that international agreements be "open covenants, openly arrived at"—not the kind of secret treaties that pulled Europe into war
- A guarantee of freedom of the seas
- Removal of economic barriers to international trade
- Radical disarmament worldwide, consisting of a reduction in armaments to the lowest point consistent with domestic security
- Modification of all colonial claims on the basis of the self-determination of peoples—in short, an end to empire

Eight additional points addressed specific postwar territorial settlements, and the fourteenth point was for Wilson the crown jewel of them all: a League of Nations.

Of the Big European Three, French premier Georges Clemenceau was the most bitterly at odds with Wilson's nonpunitive idealism. Except for Russia—which, having made a separate peace with Germany, played no part in the peace conference—France had suffered the greatest losses in the war, and Clemenceau burned with a passion to secure his nation against future German attack by destroying that nation's ability to make war—ever again. In addition, he made no secret about demanding a large measure of frankly punitive vengeance. The treaty would be the instrument by which he could exact it. The treaty would be France's instrument of righteous retribution.

Both Prime Minister Lloyd George and Premier Orlando had their own agendas. On a gut level, as it were, Lloyd George agreed with Wilson in adopting moderate conciliation toward Germany. He was, however, a politician, and he had been elected in large part on his pledge to punish Germany after victory had been won. More pressing to him were very real concerns that Wilson's insistence on self-determination for colonies would significantly conflict with British imperial colonial policy, for Britain was reaching the zenith of its imperial self. As for Orlando, he had but one nonnegotiable concern. Italy had entered the war on the side of the Allies from a narrow, straightforward motive of territorial acquisition. The promise of slicing off some of Austria and handing it to Italy had been the only relevant inducement to join France and Britain in making war. Both idealism and revenge were all well and good, but Orlando was determined only that Italy receive what it had been promised.

For six months from the convening of the peace conference, Wilson relentlessly chipped away at his counterparts as they hacked away at him. It was slow, exhausting, frustrating work—for all four of the Big Four. In the case of Wilson, who was never a man of robust health, it was physically ruinous. He had a history of what his physicians called "nervous exhaustion." Afflicted by runaway hypertension, he had suffered numerous minor strokes over some years. In Paris, as month after month went by, Wilson grew gaunt, gray-fleshed, irritable, and sickly. Nevertheless, he persuaded Clemenceau to abandon one of his chief demands, that the left bank of the Rhine be detached from Germany and put under permanent French military control. The price of this concession was Wilson's promise—made without consulting a single one of his advisors let alone a single Republican and much less the US Congress—that America would join Britain in future alliances and military support for France. In short, Wilson was coming perilously close to entering into the opposite of an open covenant openly arrived at. He was binding the nation to fight some future war.

The concession from Clemenceau was major, and, on balance, Wilson was able to get most of the gist of his Fourteen Points embodied in what became the Treaty of Versailles. Yet, to win inclusion of the letter of his principles, he had largely bargained away their spirit. He agreed, for the most part, to the punitive terms the other Allies imposed on Germany, including demands for monetary reparation as yet to be computed and specified but sure to be aimed at transforming Germany into a pitiably weak pauper state. Such is precisely what Clemenceau and, to a lesser extent, Lloyd-George and Orlando wanted.

Wilson was aware that he was giving up on vital points, but he consoled himself and sought to mollify his fellow American idealists by matter-of-factly rationalizing that the inclusion of the League of Nations as part of the peace was ultimately worth any compromise. When he presented the completed Treaty of Versailles to his fellow Americans—a huge document, much of which he wrote but about which he had consulted no other American political figure—he by no means proclaimed it a new Magna Carta. It was, he said, merely the best compromise obtainable. He explained that the League of Nations, the great forum and world deliberative body in which all nations would have an equal voice, would in the fullness of time correct and redress any injustices that had been thrust upon Germany or any other nation.

●

The Treaty of Versailles is a complex, highly detailed document—a tome, really—consisting of 440 articles. Edward Mandell House, better known as "Colonel House," Wilson's longtime confidant and advisor, a man instrumental in nudging the president toward entry into the "European War," had become increasingly estranged from Wilson in the course of crafting the Treaty of Versailles. At the end of the process, House wrote:

I am leaving Paris, after eight fateful months, with conflicting emotions. Looking at the conference in retrospect, there is much to approve and yet much to regret. It is easy to say what should have been done,

but more difficult to have found a way of doing it. To those who are
saying that the treaty is bad and should never have been made and
that it will involve Europe in infinite difficulties in its enforcement,
I feel like admitting it. But I would also say in reply that empires
cannot be shattered, and new states raised upon their ruins without
disturbance. To create new boundaries is to create new troubles. The
one follows the other. While I should have preferred a different peace, I
doubt very much whether it could have been made, for the ingredients
required for such a peace as I would have were lacking at Paris.[6]

The German delegation, led by Ulrich Graf von Brockdorff-Rantzau, the foreign minister of Germany's new—and very fragile—Weimar Republic, was summoned to Versailles for the signing of the treaty only after the document had been written by the Big Four and approved by the other Allies. On April 29, the Germans arrived in Versailles, where they were invited to study the document but not to debate or edit or change it. They reviewed it in the space of a week, and, on May 7, Brockdorff-Rantzau sent a reply to Clemenceau, Wilson, and Lloyd George. His focus was on the so-called War Guilt Clause, by which Germany was obliged to confess itself solely responsible for having caused the Great War. "We know the full brunt of hate that confronts us here," he wrote. "You demand from us to confess we were the only guilty party of war; such a confession in my mouth would be a lie."[7] With this, the German government formally protested against what it called the treaty's unfair demands, foremost among which was the hated War Guilt Clause. The demands, Brockdorff-Rantzau wrote, were unfair precisely because Germany had been excluded from negotiation. The Big Four rejected the protest, and the German delegation withdrew from the final proceedings of the Versailles conference.

The treaty—and especially the War Guilt Clause—caused outrage not just within the government but throughout Germany. In fact, during this chaotic period, it was one of the few issues on which Germans of all political stripes were united. Philipp Scheidemann, Germany's first democratically elected chancellor (February 13, 1919) addressed the new National Assembly on March 21, 1919, and called the treaty a "murderous plan," pleading to the legislators, "Which hand, trying to put us in chains like these, would not wither? The treaty is unacceptable."[8] Rather than sign his approval, Scheidemann resigned his office on June 20.

The Weimar government scrambled to cobble together a new coalition government, and now president Friedrich Ebert, broken-hearted and believing the treaty abhorrent, nevertheless argued that Germany was in no position to refuse to sign it. The Allies were still mobilized. Their forces, including many of those eager young American doughboys, were assembled in the Rhineland. They were ready to return to war at a moment's notice. Not only had Germany been barred from negotiation but it was now being given a take-it-or-leave-it ultimatum with a gun—multiple guns—aimed at its head. The Allies in Versailles had set June 28, 1919, as the day on which the treaty would be opened for signature. At the urging of Ebert, the National Assembly voted to sign the treaty, 237 to 138, with 5 abstentions. Ebert hurriedly sent a telegram to Clemenceau mere hours before the deadline. He dispatched Foreign Minister Hermann Müller and Colonial Minister Johannes Bell to Versailles, where the document, open for signatures, resided in the Hall of Mirrors, the central gallery of the Palace of Versailles. It was a magnificent space through which Louis XIV had walked daily between his private apartment and the chapel where he prayed. It was also the very room in which *King* Wilhelm I, of Prussia, declared himself, on January 18, 1871, *Kaiser* Wilhelm I, emperor of the German Empire, which was created as a result of Prussia's crushing victory over France in the Franco-Prussian War. Prime Minister Clemenceau was not unaware of the significance of the Hall. His point? This time, the shoe was decidedly on the other foot.

On the afternoon of June 28, 1919—which also happened to be the fifth anniversary of the assassination of Austro-Hungarian Archduke Franz Ferdinand and his wife the Grand Duchess Sophie in Sarajevo— the Allied powers signed the treaty, as did the delegation from Germany and those from the other Central powers. Upon signing, Müller and Bell lodged a formal protest against Britain's refusal to lift the Royal Navy blockade of Germany's ports. The starvation-inducing blockade was, the protest declared, "inhuman."

•

On July 9, the Weimar government's National Assembly ratified the Treaty of Versailles 209 to 116. The seeds of a new German nationalism, of the ultimate rejection of German democracy, and of the rise of a new militaristic absolutism were sown on that day. Those who approved the treaty were of two kinds. Some, like President Ebert, hated the document but could see no practical alternative to assenting to it. Others—liberals, socialists, and communists—accepted the treaty as necessary to German progress and reintegration into the family of nations. Those who led opposition to the treaty were nationalist conservatives, who condemned any support for the document as treason. Drawing on a tradition of German anti-Semitism, many of these conservatives lumped the specific political labels—liberal, socialist, communist—under one single scornful designation: Jew. They stirred the familiar malodorous stew of anti-Semitism and came up with a new ingredient: actual, outright treason. The Jews, they said, had deliberately sold out Germany. The German military had not been defeated by the Allies. It had been "stabbed in the back" by the Jews. The German armies, after all, had been on French and Belgian soil, not German soil, when the treasonous government surrendered. They were conquerors. Even more compelling was the fact that Germany, at the time of the surrender, stood unquestionably victorious against Russia, which had capitulated in the Treaty of Brest-Litovsk.

•

Upon Germany, the immediate effect of the Treaty of Versailles was economic devastation. Its more enduring effect was the spinning out of a myth of Jewish betrayal and the building of a foundation for a political program of anti-Semitic persecution that escalated to ethnic cleansing and then to genocide as key motives and objectives of a second world war.

The principle provisions of a treaty intended to end the war to end all wars were German territorial cessions, German admission of guilt for the war, German disarmament, and an assessment against Germany (and other Central powers) of extravagant monetary reparations. Most important geopolitically, the Treaty of Versailles dissolved the German Empire (reducing the population and territory of Germany by some 10 percent) and dismembered what had been Austro-Hungarian Empire. In more specific terms:

- Alsace and Lorraine, lost as a result of the Franco-Prussian War of 1870–1871, were returned to France.
- The coal-rich Saarland in southwestern Germany was placed under the supervision of the League of Nations until 1935.
- Three small northern areas were given to Belgium.
- Pursuant to a plebiscite in Schleswig, northern Schleswig was taken from Germany and returned to Denmark, which had lost it in the Second War of Schleswig (1864).
- The borders of Poland were radically redrawn to encompass most of what had been German West Prussia and Poznán (Posen), as well as a "corridor" connecting to the Baltic Sea. (Return of the "Polish Corridor" would be one of Adolf Hitler's demands in the run-up to World War II.) Pursuant to a plebiscite, Poland also acquired part of formerly German Upper Silesia.
- The formerly German city of Danzig (Gdansk) was declared a free city.
- Germany's modest overseas empire—colonies in China, the Pacific, and Africa—was taken over by Britain, France, Japan, and other Allied nations.
- The War Guilt Clause, which Germany was compelled to endorse, was not only an affront to "German honor," but made Germany liable under international law for reparations to the Allied nations. Those reparations were called for in the Treaty of Versailles as signed; they had not been computed in time for the signing. It was 1921 before they were fixed at a total of $33 billion (about $451 billion in 2017 dollars). Everyone who had signed the Treaty of Versailles understood that payment of anything approaching such a sum would destroy the German economy—and this would,

in fact, hit the global economy hard, especially in Europe. Nevertheless, the reparations went into effect, with punitive actions specified if Germany should fail to make payments on time.

- The treaty accused Kaiser Wilhelm II of having committed war crimes. He was guaranteed a fair judicial trial for these crimes, and the Allies specifically reserved the right to bring unspecified others before war crimes tribunals. As it turned out, neither the abdicated kaiser nor anyone else was tried for war crimes following World War I. Wilhelm fled to Holland immediately after abdicating and was granted asylum there by the Dutch government. He remained in comfortable Dutch exile until his death, which came early in World War II, on June 8, 1941. He was an enthusiastic supporter of Adolf Hitler and the Nazi Party.

- The treaty limited the strength of the German army to just one hundred thousand men, and the German General Staff (which had, in the Great War, functioned as a kind of shadow military dictatorship) was abolished and forbidden to be reconstituted. Surprisingly, this provision had little negative impact on German militarism. German military leaders turned the hundred-thousand-man limit into a rationale for creating an elite, all-volunteer force, which was called the *Fuhrerheer*, essentially an "army of leaders." The idea was that this small force would be the kernel around which a vast army could be raised by conscription, should the need arise. In the run-up to World War II, the *Fuhrerheer* would serve as the core of the Wehrmacht.

- Armament production was prohibited or curtailed. Germany was forbidden from manufacturing armored cars, tanks, submarines, airplanes, and poison gas. Production of munitions was drastically limited.

- Germany west of the Rhine and up to thirty miles east of that river was declared a demilitarized zone, with Allied troop occupation of the Rhineland set to continue for at least fifteen years, with an option for extension.

●

But then there was the League of Nations, in which Woodrow Wilson invested so much hope, including the hope of amending the Treaty of Versailles itself. The League of Nations was established by a Covenant separate from the Treaty of Versailles; however, at Wilson's insistence, membership in the League was obligatory for all signatories of the peace treaty. Of all the results of the Great War victory, Wilson believed that the creation of the League of Nations would do the most to truly make the world safe for democracy. Yet he made membership in the league not a matter of democratic choice but of coercion.

In twenty-six articles, the Covenant of the League of Nations set out three basic approaches to preventing war:

1. Arbitration for the resolution of international disputes

2. A specified, monitored program of general, worldwide disarmament

3. The establishment of collective security through guarantees of rights and sovereignty

Although all signatories to the Treaty of Versailles were obligated to join the League, League membership was open to all nations, whether they were party to the peace treaty or not. In the end, sixty-three nations joined and were represented in an assembly, which held regular sessions annually and additional emergency sessions as necessary. In a gesture of global democracy, the Covenant awarded each member one vote, regardless of the size of the country. The drawback was that no decision could be enacted without unanimous agreement. This assured that the League of Nations would accomplish virtually nothing and would be powerless to slow, much less prevent, the inexorable drift and then mad rush toward a new world war.

CHAPTER 19

Normalcy

As a global body that was to offer an alternative to war, the League of Nations was set up to fail. Requiring unanimity among all members before action could be taken virtually assured that no meaningful action would ever be taken. Democratic principles are based on majority will, not unanimity—which, in fact, is antithetical to the very idea of a democracy.

Yet the single greatest blow, which doomed the League of Nations from its inception, was not its paralyzing procedural requirement. It was Woodrow Wilson's failure to win both popular and Senate support for US membership in the League. The Republican-controlled Senate was, in fact, willing to substantially modify its opposition to the Treaty of Versailles and the League of Nations if Wilson would let it in on aspects of just how the United States would function within the League. The president's response to such reasonable requests was an irrationally petulant rebuff. He believed the Republicans intended to undermine both the League and the Treaty of Versailles, so he placed his hope in the American people. He believed he had their pulse. He could not conceive that anything less than a substantial majority supported the treaty and the League and would apply so much pressure to the Senate that it would not dare to withhold its unconditional consent to both the treaty and the covenant.

But Wilson had been away in Europe for nearly nine months in total. During this time, he devoted himself single-mindedly to the treaty and the League, drifting far out of touch with the restless mood of America. The truth was that a growing majority of people were tired of Wilsonian idealism—it was, after all, exhausting—and they felt too-long burdened with the world's problems. Wilson should have seen this even before he left for Europe. The "people" in whom he lodged his trust and reliance had, in 1918, put both the House of Representatives and the Senate into Republican hands. When the Republicans began to usher America off the global stage and back toward the comfortable iso-lationism associated with the "good old days" of the nineteenth century, the people made no protest.

"At last the world knows America is the savior of the world!"[1] Woodrow Wilson declared to an audience in Portland, Oregon. And, to be sure, the American triumph in France was greeted with joy in the United States (figure 53), but that jubilation was soon damped down by the misery of Europe, a growing postwar economic crisis at home (no jobs for millions of returning veterans), and an irrational fear of the rise of communism in Russia. In the wake of the Great War, America and Europe were swept by the "Spanish Flu" influenza pandemic *and* the so-called Red Scare, a fear that the fall of the czar in Russia and the kaiser in Germany had made way for a global communist revolution that, even now, was beginning to make itself felt in the United States. Indeed, while Woodrow Wilson was negotiating in Paris, at the start of 1919, US attorney general Mitchell Palmer launched a series of police raids on the headquarters of "red" organizations in a dozen American cities. Under the direction of a young federal agent named John Edgar Hoover, the "Palmer Raids" rounded up six thousand American citizens who were believed to be Communist "sympathizers."

Wilson, apostle of democracy, closed his eyes to the blatantly uncon-stitutional Red Scare and continued to tangle with the leaders of France, Britain, and Italy while deluding himself into believing that the League of Nation was above politics and therefore needed no support from carping and cynical Republican senators. On July 10, 1919, back in the United States, Woodrow Wilson personally delivered the Treaty of Ver-sailles to the Senate and addressed the body concerning the document. His faltering delivery of his speech—quite possibly a symptom of yet another stroke—did not bode well, but he did at least manage to finish

Within the image: *CLeRoy Baldridge · A.E.F.*

"Once upon a time."

Before leaving France
750.000 doughboys
contributed enough to
support 3.444 French
war orphans for one
year, and the "Stars
and Stripes" newspaper
left nearly three million
francs toward their
education

Figure 53. The handwritten inscription on this Cyrus Leroy Baldridge sketch, titled *Once Upon a Time*, notes: "Before leaving France 750,000 doughboys contributed enough to support 3,444 French war orphans for one year, and the 'Stars and Stripes' [US Army] newspaper left nearly three million francs toward their education." WIKIMEDIA

with his customary eloquence and fluidity: "The stage is set, the destiny disclosed. It has come about by no plan of our conceiving, but by the hand of God. We cannot turn back. The light streams on the path ahead, and nowhere else."[2]

It was a peroration crafted to evoke thunderous applause—for which Wilson waited. And waited. What applause came his way was polite, but it was confined to the Democratic portion of the chamber. Recognizing that both the treaty and the League were in trouble, Wilson again refused to bargain with his leading Republican adversary, Senator Henry Cabot Lodge of Massachusetts, or anyone else on Capitol Hill. He resolved instead to take his case directly to the people, and, against the protests of his personal physician, Rear Admiral Cary Travers Grayson, a US Navy surgeon—who had attended him throughout the Paris peace talks—Wilson boarded a train and embarked on an unprecedented 9,500-mile transcontinental speaking tour.

The president was gratified by the huge crowds who came to hear him. They seemed to greet his words on the League with the enthusiasm he had failed to find in the Senate. Yet instead of drawing an increase of strength from each audience, Wilson steadily declined. On September 25, 1919, he spoke to the people of Pueblo, Colorado. When he finished, he collapsed; he was bundled back into his private railway coach and rushed back to Washington. Dr. Grayson ordered strict bedrest, but Wilson's decline continued. On October 2, a week after he had returned to the White House, he suffered a massive stroke, which left him partially paralyzed. At this point, all the Republicans were asking for were certain "reservations" to be attached to their consent both to the Treaty of Versailles and membership in the League of Nations. Wilson had compromised on much more momentous points with Clemenceau, Lloyd George, and Orlando. But now he refused to budge on points that, in the great scheme of things, were fairly innocuous. Ill and partially disabled, he instructed Democrats in the Senate to accept no compromise of any kind on the League. The Senate rejected both the Treaty of Versailles and the League of Nations in November 1919. There was hope that both could be salvaged in March 1920, but Wilson gave no ground, and the Senate's rejection became final.

How bitter President Wilson's last months in the White House must have been we can only surmise. Hailed in Europe as president of the nation the whole democratic world knew as a savior, Woodrow Wilson was now a prematurely aged shell of himself, half paralyzed, exhausted in mind and body, and no longer engaged in the affairs of this world. In a secret arrangement, he turned over the day-to-day conduct of government business to his wife, Edith. Dr. Grayson conspired with her, the president, and White House staff to hide Wilson's condition from the public.

In the meantime, having rejected the Treaty of Versailles, the United States concluded separate, brief peace treaties with Germany, Hungary, and Austria in 1921. And in the general election of 1920—an election in which Wilson briefly considered running, despite his debilitation and the two-term tradition established by George Washington—Republican machine politician Warren G. Harding handily defeated Democratic Ohio governor James M. Cox and his vice-presidential running mate, former New York state senator and assistant secretary of the navy Franklin Delano Roosevelt. Harding ran on a platform that promised a "return to normalcy" and, in his inaugural address on March 4, 1921, declared flatly, "We seek no part in directing the destinies of the world . . . [the League of Nations] is not for us."[3]

●

Unsupported by the United States, the League of Nations did not instantly collapse. In fact, it convened regularly and, on a few occasions, even successfully mediated some relatively minor international disputes. Its first major test, however, was in response to the Japanese invasion of Manchuria in September 1931. All that could be agreed upon with the required unanimity was the formation and dispatch of a "commission of inquiry" in 1932. When the commission reported unfavorably on Japan, Japan responded by leaving the League. What could the League of Nations do to compel Japan to return the territory it had seized? Absolutely nothing.

The impotence of the League of Nations against Japan in 1931–1932 was repeated throughout the 1930s. In 1935–1936, Mussolini's Italy invaded Ethiopia, and, once again, despite an eloquent appeal by Ethiopian emperor Haile Selassie I, the League of Nations could do nothing to end or redress the aggression. When protests were lodged against Italian aggression, Italy walked out of the League as Japan had done before it.

The League of Nations was the instrument that was to enact the dream in pursuit of which Woodrow Wilson had led America into war—the final war, the war to end all wars. But the League proved powerless and rapidly descended into irrelevance. In 1943, at the Tehran Conference during World War II, the new Big Three—the Soviet Union's Joseph Stalin, Britain's Winston Churchill, and the United States' Franklin D. Roosevelt—would agree to create the "United Nations" as a deliberative body to replace the League. On April 18, 1946, the League of Nations convened its final session in Geneva, Switzerland. Its sole topic was its own dissolution. Lord Robert Cecil of Britain, who had been a leading proponent of the League, addressed his colleagues at the session. He concluded his remarks poignantly: "The League is dead. Long live the United Nations."[4]

As for the Treaty of Versailles, which created the League of Nations, it now figures in the eyes of history as a tragic document. Its deeply flawed purpose had been to disable Germany from ever disturbing the peace of Europe and the world again. Yet in demonizing Germany, it created the very demon it feared. Seeking to end war, the Treaty of Versailles made a second world war all but inevitable.

●

"Return to normalcy": It was what Americans wanted to hear in the 1920s, following the Great War, but it was a phrase as hollow as the Harding administration itself. It evoked a nostalgic fantasy of the good old days, before world war, revolution, and wicked American cities teeming with immigrant masses. Warren Gamaliel Harding was a beefy, hale, and handsome small-town Ohioan with a pleasant manner, a fine speaking voice, and an approach to Republican Party politics guided entirely by total compliance. He had been a state senator, Ohio lieutenant governor, and a US senator, serving in all three offices with unobjectionable mediocrity. When the 1920 Republican National Convention deadlocked,

Harding emerged as the ideal compromise nominee precisely because, as a political nonentity, he could become anything the party bosses wanted him to be. Harding hardly campaigned for the presidency. In contrast to Woodrow Wilson's man-killing transcontinental whistle-stop crusade for the League of Nations, Harding ran a so-called front porch campaign, mostly from his Ohio home. Public and press came to him, and the resulting image of an easygoing Midwesterner clicked with a public weary of idealistic demands. Harding won the election with 60.3 percent of the popular vote, the biggest presidential election margin to that time.

The Harding administration was as regressive with old-time Gilded Age corruption as the Wilson administration had been idealistically progressive. The rural minority managed to make Prohibition the new American reality, but the urban majority wanted to keep on drinking—therefore, Prohibition turned the United States into a nation of lawbreakers, a situation perfectly in sync with the corruption at the highest levels. On August 2, 1923, Harding died in the midst of the infamous "Teapot Dome" bribery scandal. The official cause of death was food poisoning, but rumors of foul play abounded. Harding's vice president, Calvin Coolidge, assumed the presidency and, apart from quietly cleaning house at the highest levels, thereby resolving many of the government corruption issues, he took a hands-off approach to both domestic and international policy, prompting presidential historians Sidney M. Milkis and Michael Nelson to observe, "Coolidge raised inactivity to an art."[5] When he ran for the presidency in his own right in 1924, he did so—with great success—on the laid-back campaign slogan, "Keep Cool with Coolidge."

As the mass of Americans sleepwalked through the 1920s, at least part of Europe was roiled in ferment. Russia was torn by revolution followed by bloody civil war. In Italy, on October 28, 1922, Benito Mussolini led his Fascist Party in a march on Rome. This demonstration of paramilitary strength won for Mussolini "temporary" dictatorial powers through a mandate from King Victor Emmanuel III to form a coalition government.

Born in 1883, the child of a blacksmith with strong socialist and antichurch beliefs, Mussolini grew up reading Machiavelli and Nietzsche, worked briefly as a schoolteacher, and then became a socialist journalist. At first an ardent opponent of Italian entry into the Great War, Mussolini suddenly became a passionate advocate for it. This turnabout earned him expulsion from Italy's socialist party, an event that prompted him to start his own newspaper. He used it to promote a political movement he called *Fascism*, a form of government that, defining the state in terms of "race," put the state at the center of life and gave the leader of the state absolute authority. After the Great War, Mussolini grew his party quickly and used the authority the king had given him to boldly remodel Italy's ruinous economy, reform government bureaucracy, forge a "statist" partnership with big business and industry, and build a formidable military. "All within the State; nothing outside the State; nothing against the State" was his one-sentence formulation of Fascist rule.[6]

In a brilliantly staged feat of public relations, Mussolini relinquished his dictatorship in 1924 and called for new elections—the outcome of which he had carefully predetermined through passage of legislation guaranteeing his party a two-thirds parliamentary majority—regardless of the popular vote. When the popular socialist leader Giacomo Matteotti strongly opposed Mussolini's candidacy, Fascist agents murdered him. This brought down an avalanche of anti-Fascist attacks in the opposition press, to which Mussolini responded by banning all parties except for the Fascists, abolishing trade unions, and imposing general press censorship. Loyalty was enforced by an army of thuggish "Blackshirts," and Mussolini co-opted the Catholic Church by concluding the Lateran Treaty of 1929, which established the Vatican as a city-state within the city of Rome under the absolute sovereignty of the pope. Militaristic totalitarianism in a cult of personality had displaced any trace of democracy in Italy.

Among those who watched the man the Italians now called *Il Duce* ("the Leader") was Adolf Hitler. An Austrian-born frustrated artist and an all-around shiftless youth who sometimes eked out a living by painting postcards, Hitler had found his calling as a soldier in the Great War. Although he never rose above the rank of corporal, he proved his bravery in action and was decorated with the Iron Cross, Second Class, in 1914, and, in 1918, the Iron Cross, First Class—a decoration almost never bestowed on an enlisted soldier. In his best-selling political memoir and manifesto, *Mein Kampf* (*My Struggle*), published in 1925, Hitler wrote of the day the news reached him that the Great War had begun: "Even today I am not ashamed to say that, overpowered by stormy enthusiasm, I fell down on my knees and thanked Heaven from an overflowing heart for granting me the good fortune of being permitted to live at this time."[7]

When the war ended, Hitler remained in the army as a "political agent," assigned to spy on the radical revolutionary movements then taking shape in an economically and spiritually bankrupt Germany. In 1919, Hitler joined the embryonic German Workers' Party, in Munich. He turned from spy to enthusiastic member; for this party was determined to undo the humiliation of the Treaty of Versailles. Hitler, the former nonentity, discovered in himself an uncanny political charisma and rapidly rose within the party, which was renamed, in 1920, the *Nationalsozialistische Deutsche Arbeiterpartei*—abbreviated as the Nazi Party.

Hitler and the Nazis began to find traction in Bavaria, a populist hotbed that resented the elitism of Berlin and, in particular, the pallid and ineffectual democracy of the Weimar Republic. Munich, the provincial Bavarian capital, became headquarters for disgruntled veterans. Here, legions of unemployed former soldiers joined the *Freikorps* ("Free Corps"), a homegrown "militia" organized in 1918–1919 from entire units of the German army that simply refused to demobilize after the Armistice.

With an eye toward Mussolini's skyrocketing success, Hitler joined arms with Freikorps members like Ernst Röhm to recast the Nazi Party as a private army of street fighters. Hitler and Röhm modeled their force after Il Duce's Blackshirts but put them in brown uniforms instead of black. Officially called the SA (*Sturmabteilung*, "storm detachment," or "storm troopers"), they were popularly known as the Brownshirts, and they violently intimidated and suppressed all opposition. Like Mussolini, Hitler combined brute-force tactics with savvy propaganda, and, in November 1923, he approached none other than Erich Ludendorff to join him in a national revolution to overthrow the despised Weimar Republic.

In what he hoped would be the beginning of an overwhelming political movement—the equivalent of Mussolini's March on Rome the year before—Hitler led his Brownshirts into a right-wing political meeting in a Munich beer hall on November 8, 1923. He took over the meeting and won the agreement of those in attendance to join a mass march on Berlin.

Alas for Hitler, on the very next day, the column of three thousand Nazis was confronted by squads of police, which opened fire on them. In the resulting melee, sixteen Brownshirts and three policemen were killed. Hitler's revolution died aborning, and both Hitler and Ludendorff were arrested and tried. While Ludendorff, the war hero, was released, Hitler was convicted and sentenced to five years in prison, which was the minimum sentence for treason—not that this ended what the so-called Beer Hall *Putsch* ("push," that is, violent action intended to overthrow the government) had begun.

Hitler was consigned to Landsberg prison, a comfortable receptacle for political prisoners. His "cell" was really a kind of study/bedroom, and Hitler used his sentence—of which he would serve only nine months—to write the first volume of *Mein Kampf*. He was free to see visitors, including his followers as well as new political admirers, and to talk politics with the other political prisoners. By the time he was released, he had distilled into *Mein Kampf* his doctrine of Nazism. Like fascism, Nazism was based on race. Hitler believed that Germany's destiny was to rise to world supremacy, driven by its racial identity as the "Aryan people." All other races, Hitler wrote, were inferior to the Aryans, who were, in fact, the "master race." He claimed that the Weimar democracy sought to extinguish the rightful expression of Aryan supremacy and elevate in its stead "Marxism": socialism and communism, the politics of the Jews, who had in 1918 stabbed the army in the back, forcing the ignominious surrender enshrined in the Treaty of Versailles. "I set the Aryan and the Jew over against each other," Hitler declared in a speech early in the 1930s, "and if I call one of them a human being, I must call the other something else. The two are as widely separated as man and beast. Not that I would call the Jew a beast. He is much further from the beasts than we Aryans. He is a creature outside nature and alien to nature."[8]

In *Mein Kampf*, Hitler posed the question of what and who would redeem Germany and restore its people to possession of their birthright as members of the master race. The answer to the *what* was the destruction of the democratic Weimar Republic. The answer to the *who* was the gathering of the German people under the absolute rule of a masterful leader: a *Führer*—an infallible guide, an Adolf Hitler.

Once released from Landsberg, Hitler set about becoming *Der Führer*. He worked to reorganize the Nazi Party, which had largely fallen apart in his absence. Unfortunately for him, the Weimar government had grown in strength and had actually managed to restore a modicum of economic stability to Germany. Hitler had his work cut out for him. But the same improved economic conditions that bolstered Weimar also helped the Nazi Party to recover and grow. Then, with the onset of the worldwide economic collapse signaled by the crash of US stock-market crash in 1929, Hitler was able to point to the spectacular failure of Weimar and paint himself and his party as the means of Germany's salvation. Inspired partly by the economic success of fascism in Italy, the German elector-ate catapulted the Nazi Party to the number two position in the 1930 election. Two years later, in 1932, Hitler ran against President Paul von Hindenburg. Although the war hero was widely revered, he was ancient and infirm. Hitler did not defeat him, but he captured more than a third of the vote. This was a sufficient showing to force Hindenburg to name Hitler—a man he both feared and detested—chancellor, the equivalent of prime minister, the number-two man in the German government.

●

One of paradoxes of World War I is that the principal European victor, France, suffered by far the worst material and human devastation in the conflict, whereas the principal loser, Germany, was intact within its bor-ders. To be sure, like the other combatant nations, it had suffered terrible military losses, but no great battles had been fought in Germany. Ger-many had fought the war on the Western Front in France and Belgium, leaving great swaths of ruin in both nations.

The German army had surrendered while it still held territory in nations it had devastated. When, having surrendered, the soldiers marched back to Germany, they found their homeland to be physically whole. Yet the Treaty of Versailles—that treasonous, democratic, Jewish document (as many Germans regarded it, even before the emergence of Hitler)—had imposed pauperism on Germany while simultaneously emasculating it through forced disarmament. With more than a quarter of German workers unemployed, the nation was brought to the verge of a communist revolution led by the Spartacus League, a Marxist guerrilla organization. The Weimar government was too feeble to oppose the communists decisively, but the Freikorps handily extinguished left-wing revolts in Berlin, Bremen, Brunswick, Halle, Hamburg, Leipzig, Silesia, Thuringia, and the Ruhr. Freikorps members assassinated Karl Lieb-knecht and Rosa Luxemburg, Germany's most prominent communist leaders. These actions had the unintended consequence of bolstering the Weimar Republic, which gave the Nazis and the Freikorps a common enemy. As Hitler rose in influence, the Freikorps merged with and was finally absorbed by the Brownshirts, and thus the paramilitary arm of the Nazi Party grew.

On February 27, 1933, fire destroyed the Reichstag, the German parliament building. Most historians believe that the fire was set by the Nazis themselves; however, Chancellor Hitler did not hesitate to ascribe the arson to communists, and almost immediately Marinus van der Lubbe, who was a Dutch communist, and three Bulgarians were arrested. Georgi Dimitrov, Vasil Tanev, and Blagoy Popov were all known to the Prussian police as operatives of the Comintern, the Soviet-based Communist International, an organization dedicated to the global spread of communism. Ernst Torgler, chairman of the German Communist Party, was also arrested. All were tried, but, in the end, only van der Lubbe was convicted—and subsequently beheaded. As for Hitler, his only concern was to use the fire as a pretext for securing the authority to outlaw and abolish the Communist Party in Germany. The very next month, on March 24, 1933, Hitler pushed through the parliament the Enabling Act, which endowed him with dictatorial authority for four years. Now Hitler in Germany was on equal footing with Mussolini in Italy.

The Führer was not shy about exercising his new authority. He outlawed all political parties, except for the Nazi Party. He issued edicts purging all Jews and other "undesirables" from all government posts (including the civil service) and from all government-controlled institutions, including the universities. Then he focused on the Nazi Party itself.

Ernst Röhm, leader of the Brownshirts, had been instrumental in Hitler's rise. Now Hitler saw him—quite rightly—as a rival to his absolute rule. He therefore, on June 30, 1934, unsheathed what became known to history as the "Night of the Long Knives," a sudden purge of Röhm and that portion of the SA leadership loyal to him. By July 2, eighty-five (and perhaps as many as seven hundred to one thousand) men were killed. Most of the bloody work was carried out by two new organizations, Hitler's personal bodyguard, called the *Schutzstaffel* ("protection squadron") or the SS; and the Gestapo, the Nazi regime's secret police. Röhm was not killed during the raid but taken to Stadelheim Prison, thrown in a cell, handed a pistol, and left to shoot himself. When no shot was heard, his jailers went to his cell. In the doorway stood Röhm, his shirt unbuttoned, chest bare and puffed out defiantly, daring the jailers to shoot him. They shot him.

The action against the Brownshirts was a purge. The Night of the Long Knives was also a coup d'etat, in which conservatives still in government were either forced out or murdered. Hitler's final step was to disband the Brownshirted SA and replace it with the Blackshirted SS, which, over succeeding days, weeks, and months, led by Heinrich Himmler and aided by the Gestapo, began rounding up prominent Jews and other political adversaries. On another track, Hitler's propaganda minister, Josef Goebbels, formulated and implemented propaganda campaigns designed to bring all of Germany in line behind the Nazi program of political and economic recovery based on massive rearmament and the complete abrogation of the Treaty of Versailles. Some aspects of the rearmament were carried out covertly, but, as Hitler increasingly realized that the democratic powers in Europe, primarily Britain and France, were bent on disarming themselves, he acted more overtly and even brazenly. He gambled on Germany's Great War enemies being so gun-shy that they would not threaten Germany for its violations of the peace treaty. Hitler's gamble paid off.

France was aware of what Germany under Hitler was doing and therefore embraced an idea put forth by André Maginot, a politician who, after the Great War, became minister of war. Maginot proposed a system of fortifications running along the French side of the nation's borders with Switzerland, Germany, and Luxembourg. The system of fortifications was intended to delay—not stop—a German invasion of France. Maginot's belief was that such a delay would buy time for the French army to get into position when and where it was needed to massively repel an invasion. Construction of what came to be called the Maginot Line began in 1929. Maginot himself died early in 1932 and did not live to see the completion, in 1938, of what was, in fact, a marvel of modern military engineering. The Maginot Line was a great chain of fortresses connected by a network of tunnels through which troops and supplies could be transported by rail. Exposed defenses were built of thick ferroconcrete capable of withstanding bombardment from any artillery known at the time.

"Maginot Line" has become a historical punchline applied to any instance of obtuse head-in-the-sand thought or policy. In fact, it was a reasonable idea that was misused. Intended to slow, not stop, an invasion, the Maginot Line was to be used in conjunction with a French counter-attack. The fortifications were so impressive, however, that they had the unintended consequence of making the people and politicians of France feel as if they were protected by an impregnable wall. The Maginot Line engendered complacency within both the government and the military. It actually made France more vulnerable.

As for the British, they did without any meaningful defensive provisions at all. Eager to demobilize and disarm, in the belief that this would set an example for the rest of the world, the Brits closed their eyes to the fact that Germany, in increasingly open defiance of the Treaty of Versailles, was forging swords and fashioning cannon.

●

Adolf Hitler continued to take the measure of the democracies. The more provocative his actions, the less they pushed back. Early in his chancellorship, Hitler spoke of a concept called *Lebensraum* ("living space"). It was a term introduced by the German geographer and ethnographer Friedrich Ratzel in 1901. States, he wrote, expanded or contracted their boundaries according to their ability to do so. Strong states expanded; weak states contracted. Hitler appropriated this term and declared it both natural and right that the German people, the master race, should have all the

Lebensraum that the military and economic might of the state could win for them. In the mid-1930s, an alarmed Britain and France—even joined by Italy—issued a statement of opposition to any policy of German expansion. The French also entered into a defensive alliance with the Soviets in 1935, and the Soviets concluded a similar pact with the Czechs.

Somewhat surprisingly, it was Italy, not Germany, that made the first blatantly expansionist move very much in defiance of the League of Nations. Mussolini sought to expand Italy's foothold in Africa by invading Ethiopia. The British response came from the government's foreign secretary, Sir Samuel Hoare, who attempted to "appease" Il Duce by trading Britain's acquiescence in Italy's annexation of most of Ethiopia for Mussolini's agreement to preserve the existing defensive alliance—Italy, Britain, and France—against Germany. Considered a betrayal of British honor, Hoare's offer created a scandal that ended his government career. As for Mussolini, he waged his war against Ethiopia, bombing and even using chemical weapons against the virtually defenseless nation until it could resist no longer.

The Hoare-Mussolini episode added a new word to the lexicon of modern diplomacy: appeasement. Hitler now discovered that the democracies were willing to trade states and peoples for anything that avoided an immediate shooting war. On March 7, 1936, Hitler unilaterally ended the demilitarization of the Rhineland specified in the Treaty of Versailles; he marched twenty-two thousand German soldiers across the bridges of the Rhine. It was no more than a token force that Hitler intended to withdraw if France or Britain intervened. But neither country so much as protested. Famously, a *Times* of London editorial asked, "It's none of our business, is it? It's their [Germany's] own back-garden they're walking into."[9]

There was a lesson in this for both Hitler and Mussolini: neither Britain nor France would fight for the Treaty of Versailles. For his part, Mussolini decided to make a pact with Hitler. He began by assenting on July 11, 1936, to Hitler's proposition that Austria should be deemed "a German state," thereby clearing the way for Germany's annexation of Austria. Later that same year, on November 1, Italy and Germany signed the Rome-Berlin Axis, which was followed on November 25 by the

German-Japanese Anti-Comintern Pact—an alliance ostensibly against communism, but, in fact, a treaty of general military cooperation. The forces opposed to democracy—that sacred value America had fought to save in the Great War—were joining hands.

In May 1937, Neville Chamberlain replaced the retiring Stanley Baldwin as British prime minister. Baldwin and his predecessor, Ramsay MacDonald, had presided over a long period of British disarmament. Chamberlain entered office seeing very good reason to begin rearming. Therefore he proposed, with regard to Germany, a policy he called "active appeasement": find out what Hitler wanted and then give it to him. His motivation was not simply to run away from war (as some have charged) but to buy time to rebuild Britain's defensive capability to defend not just against Germany but against the nations Chamberlain believed were even more immediately dangerous, Italy and Japan.

On March 13, 1938, Hitler finally invaded Austria. Unopposed by either Austria or Mussolini's Italy, the Führer declared Austria a province of the German Reich. This annexation, or *Anschluss*, positioned Germany to make its next move: into Czechoslovakia. Chamberlain, who had not attempted to interfere with the *Anschluss*, admonished Hitler to negotiate with the Czechs. Hitler refused, and Chamberlain journeyed to Berchtesgaden, Hitler's Bavarian chalet. There, Hitler demanded cession of the Sudetenland, the German-speaking region of Czechoslovakia, a nation created by the Treaty of Versailles and whose sovereignty the Allies were bound by that treaty to defend. Aware that Britain was still in no position to fight a war with Germany, let alone with Germany *and* Italy, Chamberlain offered Hitler what he demanded. He asked only that the Führer delay invading Czechoslovakia until he, Chamberlain, could persuade both Paris and Prague to accept the cession.

The French government was appalled by Chamberlain's appeal and, in turn, communicated with US president Franklin D. Roosevelt, asking that he declare American opposition to the German annexation of a piece of another sovereign nation. The United States had come to the aid of Europe in 1917. Perhaps it would come again. But, like both Britain and France, the United States had rushed to demobilize and disarm following the Great War. Reduced now to a few hundred thousand men, the US Army was in no position to intervene militarily and, even more, the American people were in no mood for involvement in a second "European war." Besides, the United States was not a party to the Treaty of Versailles. It had made no guarantee to Czechoslovakia or anyone else. President Roosevelt declined to offer assistance or even take a stand. Warren Harding had died in 1923, but "normalcy" as he had envisioned it was still the desired state of American affairs.

Unwilling to stand alone, France agreed to hand the Sudetenland to Hitler. The Czechs, however, proposed to fight. This would put France and Britain in a most awkward position, for it would be almost impossible for those nations not to aid Czechoslovakia if a war broke out. "How horrible, fantastic, incredible it is that we should be digging trenches and trying on gas masks here because of a quarrel in a far-away country between people of whom we know nothing," Chamberlain observed.[10]

In fact, more than a piece of a "far-away country" was at stake. Czechoslovakia was one of Europe's strategic crossroads. Its location was critical in military terms, and the Sudetenland was rich in mineral wealth, was home to the major Skoda arms works, and domiciled thirty Czech army divisions. Nevertheless, Chamberlain scrambled to arrange the Munich Conference on September 29–30. Here he agreed to give Hitler the Sudetenland in exchange for the Führer's pledge to make no more territorial demands in Europe. The deed done, Chamberlain flew back to London, stepped off the plane, waved a scrap of paper in the air, and proclaimed to Britain and the world that he had returned from Munich bearing "peace for our time." He closed his brief remarks with this: "And now I recommend you go home and sleep quietly in your beds."[11]

Britain and France—and doubtless many people in the United States—cheered Chamberlain. Franklin Roosevelt sent the prime minister a two-word cablegram. "Good man," it said.[12] The Czechs wept in the streets of Prague. Winston Churchill, who held no leadership post at the time, addressed fellow members of the House of Commons: "I will begin by saying what everybody would like to ignore or forget but which must nevertheless be stated, namely, that we have sustained a total and unmitigated defeat, and that France has suffered even more than we have."[13]

●

It was a defeat sustained without a shot having been fired, and it was the prelude to a new war, a war that would force the renaming of the "war to end all wars" from the *Great War* to *World War I.* The democracies of Europe—and the great democracy across the Atlantic—having won World War I, showed themselves unwilling to take the steps now necessary to win the peace.

The march to World War II began with the Treaty of Versailles, framed with every good intention by Woodrow Wilson, who proved unable to prevail against the leaders of France, Britain, and Italy to obtain the just document he wanted. To correct the many injustices of the treaty, he trusted to the League of Nations, which, thanks in no small measure to his hubristic conviction that he and he alone knew the right and how to achieve it, he could not even sell to his fellow Americans.

The Treaty of Versailles ended one war but made enduring peace all but impossible. Clearly, even the victors, France and Britain, lacked sufficient faith in the treaty to enforce it. The victorious nations gave Germany a reason to embrace Adolf Hitler and, with that embrace, to wage a genocidal war of universal destruction. Then those same Allied nations offered Hitler and Germany no opposition in the march to war—until it was too late to avert the conflict.

There can be no doubt that the United States won the Great War in 1918. There is, however, ample room for a great deal of doubt as to whether that victory was a good thing. Had Germany, in the absence of fresh and brave and healthy American soldiers on the Western Front, prevailed, would Adolf Hitler have ever amounted to anything more than a failed postcard painter?

We cannot know. All we know for certain is what did happen: a second world war for which none of the democratic nations was prepared either materially or emotionally. France collapsed quickly. Thanks in no small measure to the leadership of Winston Churchill, the British—nearly too late—realized the existential threat that was upon them and rose up against Hitler. As for the United States, realization of the existential threat posed by World War II came only with the shock of a massive attack on the US territory of Hawaii and on the Pacific Fleet domiciled at Pearl Harbor. It was the very attack that the most important air force commander of World War I, the American Brigadier General Billy Mitchell, had predicted.

All of the democracies paid a ghastly price in World War II. Alone among them, the United States also realized a gain. As a result of World War I, it had won acclaim as the savior of Western democracy and attained the status of a world power. In the twenty short but momentous years between World War I and World War II, America squandered that status, relinquishing it much as King Lear foolishly and selfishly relinquished his crown. In the course of World War II, the United States regained its position of global power and responsibility. In large measure because of its role in both world wars—and then for its role in the years following World War II—the twentieth century has been called the American Century. Will history bestow that same name on the twenty-first century?

Notes

Introduction

1 All quotations and details of the assassination are taken from John S. Craig, *Peculiar Liaisons: In War, Espionage, and Terrorism in the Twentieth Century* (New York: Algora Publishing, 2005), 19–27.

2 Quoted in Alan Axelrod, *Profiles in Folly: History's Worst Decisions and Why They Went Wrong* (New York: Sterling, 2008), 175.

3 Anthony Lejeune, ed., *The Concise Dictionary of Foreign Quotations* (London: Stacey London, 1998), 182.

4 Craig, 19–27.

5 Quoted in Barbara Tuchman, *The Guns of August* (1962; reprint ed., New York: Ballantine Books, 1994), 21.

6 George Seldes, *You Can't Print That! The Truth Behind the News 1918–1928* (New York: Payson & Clarke, Ltd., 1929), 32–40.

Chapter 1

1 NPR Staff, "WWI: The Battle That Split Europe, and Families" (April 30, 2011), http://www.npr.org/2011/04/30/135803783/wwi-the-battle-that-split-europe-and -families.

2 Woodrow Wilson, Message to Congress, 63rd Cong., 2nd Sess., Senate Doc. No. 566 (Washington, DC, 1914), 3–4, https://wwi.lib.byu.edu/index.php/President _Wilson's_Declaration_of_Neutrality.

3 Jo Fox, "Atrocity Propaganda," *World War One* (British Library, January 29, 2014), https://www.bl.uk/world-war-one/articles/atrocity-propaganda.

4 https://www.bl.uk/world-war-one/articles/atrocity-propaganda.

5 Hajo Holborn, *A History of Modern Germany: Volume 3, 1840–1945* (Princeton, NJ: Princeton University Press, 1982), 459–60.

6 Quoted in NPR Staff, "WWI."

7 James D. Ciment and Thaddeus Russell, eds. *The Home Front Encyclopedia: United States, Britain, and Canada in World Wars I and II* (Santa Barbara, CA: ABC-CLIO, 2007), 379.

8 See *Lusitania Online*, http://www.lusitania.net/.

9 Lusitania warning, WikiMedia Commons, https://commons.wikimedia.org/wiki /File:Lusitania_warning.jpg.

10 G. J. Meyer, *The World Remade: America in World War I* (New York: Random House, 2017), 100.

11 Meyer, *The World Remade*, 100.
12 Woodrow Wilson, "Address to Naturalized Citizens at Convention Hall, Philadelphia, May 10, 1915," The American Presidency Project, http://www.presidency.ucsb.edu/ws/?pid=65388.

Chapter 2

1 Poll cited in Alan Axelrod, *Selling the Great War: The Making of American Propaganda* (New York: Palgrave Macmillan, 2009), 56.
2 George Creel, *How We Advertised America* (New York: Harper & Brothers, 1920), 5.
3 George Creel, *Wilson and the Issues* (New York: Century Co., 1916).
4 Creel, *How We Advertised America*, 5.
5 David R. Woodward, *The American Army and the First World War* (Cambridge: Cambridge University Press, 2014), 46.
6 Quoted in Walter Millis, *Arms and Men: A Study in American Military History* (New Brunswick, NJ: Rutgers University Press, 1986), 233.
7 Creel, *Wilson and the Issues*, 25 and 29.
8 Woodrow Wilson, quoted in *Congressional Record LIII* (Washington, DC: Government Printing Office, 1916), 3156.
9 "The Zimmermann Telegram: Decoded Message Text," National Archives, https://www.archives.gov/education/lessons/zimmermann/decoded-text.html.
10 Quoted in Byron Farwell, *Over There: The United States in the Great War, 1917–1918* (New York: W. W. Norton, 1999), 34.
11 Thomas H. Greer, "Ben Tre's Destruction," *New York Times*, February 20, 1968.
12 Quoted in Farwell, *Over There*, 34.
13 Ibid., 35.
14 "Wilson's War Message to Congress, 2 April, 1917," https://wwi.lib.byu.edu/index.php/Wilson's_War_Message_to_Congress. Accessed January 22, 2018.
15 Woodrow Wilson, "Address Supporting the League of Nations," Sioux Falls, SD, September 8, 1919.
16 H. G. Wells, *The War That Will End War* (London: Frank & Cecil Palmer, 1914); Wells shortened the phrase to "the war to end war" in his *In the Fourth Year: Anticipations of a World Peace* (1918; reprint ed., N.p.: Read Books Ltd., 2016), preface. The phrase became associated with Woodrow Wilson, who used it only once, however; see Kathleen Hall Jamieson, *Eloquence in an Electronic Age: The Transformation of Political Speechmaking* (New York: Oxford University Press, 1988), 99.

Chapter 3

1 George Creel, *Rebel at Large: Recollections of Fifty Crowded Years* (New York: G. P. Putnam's Sons, 1947), 157.
2 George Creel, *How We Advertised America* (New York: Harper & Brothers, 1920), 17.
3 Creel, *Rebel at Large*, 157.
4 Creel, *Rebel at Large*, 158.
5 Ibid.
6 Woodrow Wilson, "Executive Order 2594—Creating Committee on Public Information, April 13, 1917," The American Presidency Project, http://www.presidency.ucsb.edu/ws/?pid=75409.

7   "Primary Documents—U.S. Espionage Act, 15 June 1917," http://www.firstworld
    war.com/source/espionageact.htm.

8   *Philadelphia Public Ledger* and *Hartford Courant* quoted in James R. Mock and
    Cedric Larson, *Words That Won the War: The Story of the Committee on Public Infor-
    mation 1917–1918* (Princeton, NJ: Princeton University Press, 1939), 32.

9   "Primary Documents."

10 "Primary Documents—U.S. Espionage Act, 7 May 1918," http://www.firstworld
    war.com/source/espionageact1918.htm.

11 Robert Lansing, *War Memoirs* (Indianapolis: Bobbs-Merrill, 1935), 322–24.

12 Mock and Larson, *Words That Won the War*, 48–49.

13 Mock and Larson, *Words That Won the War*, 6.

14 Ibid.

15 Creel, *Rebel at Large*, 160.

16 Mock and Larson, *Words That Won the War*, 65.

17 Mock and Larson, *Words That Won the War*, 66.

18 George Creel, *How We Advertised America*, 21–23.

19 Creel, *Rebel at Large*, 161.

20 Mock and Larson, *Words That Won the War*, 68.

21 Nancy Derr, "The Babel Proclamation," *Palimpsest* 60, no. 4 (July/August 1979):
    98–115.

22 Byron Farwell, *Over There: The United States in the Great War, 1917–1918* (New
    York: W. W. Norton, 1999), 34.

Chapter 4

1   Center of Military History, *American Military History: The United States Army and
    the Forging of a Nation, 1775–1917* (Washington, DC: Center of Military History,
    US Army, 2009), 378.

2   Byron Farwell, *Over There: The United States in the Great War, 1917–1918* (New York:
    W. W. Norton, 1999), 50.

3   Frederick Funston obituary, *Omaha World-Herald*, February 20, 1917, 1.

4   Newton Baker, quoted in David Fromkin, *In the Time of the Americans: FDR,
    Truman, Eisenhower, MacArthur—The Generation That Changed America's Role in the
    World* (New York: Vintage Books, 1996), 182.

Chapter 5

1   Newton Baker, quoted in David Fromkin, *In the Time of the Americans: FDR,
    Truman, Eisenhower, MacArthur—The Generation That Changed America's Role in the
    World* (New York: Vintage Books, 1996), 182.

2   Max Boot, *The Savage Wars of Peace* (New York: Basic Books, 2002), 191.

3   Quotations from Gene Smith, *Until the Last Trumpet Sounds* (New York: John
    Wiley & Sons, 1998), chapter 3.

4   Alex Horton, "Trump Said to Study General Pershing. Here's What the President
    Got Wrong," *Washington Post*, August 18, 2017, https://www.washingtonpost.com
    /news/retropolis/wp/2017/08/18/after-barcelona-attack-trump-said-to-study-gen
    eral-pershing-heres-what-the-president-got-wrong/?utm_term=.6d0db78f335c;

Linda Qiu, "Study Pershing, Trump Said/But the Story Doesn't Add Up," *New York Times*, August 17, 2017, https://www.nytimes.com/2017/08/17/us/politics/trump -tweet-pershing-fact-check.html?_r=0; David Mikkelson, "General Pershing on How to Stop Islamic Terrorists," Snopes, October 31, 2001; updated, August 17, 2017, http://www.snopes.com/rumors/pershing.asp.

Chapter 6
1 Brevet-Colonel J. F. C. Fuller, *Tanks in the Great War 1914–1918* (New York: E. P. Dutton, 1920), 19–20.
2 "Engineers Praised by Field Marshal Haig," *Railway Age Gazette* 63, no. 25 (January 11, 1918): 1138.
3 Center of Military History, *Military Operations of the American Expeditionary Forces* (Washington, DC: Center of Military History, US Army, 1989), 4:8.
4 Center of Military History, *Military Operations*, 4:10.

Chapter 7
1 Center of Military History, "Critical Condition of British Front: Sir Douglas Haig's Order to the Army," *Military Operations of the American Expeditionary Forces* (Washington, DC: Center of Military History, US Army, 1989), 4:60.
2 Reports from US engineer officers, April 21–May 1, 1918, *Military Operations*, 4:63–64.
3 "The 28th Aero Squadron in the Lys Operation," *Military Operations*, 4:64–65.
4 Quoted in "German Offensives and the AEF's First Battles," in Richard W. Stewart, ed., *The United States Army in a Global Era, 1917–2008* (Washington, DC: Center of Military History, 2010), 30.

Chapter 8
1 Center of Military History, *Military Operations of the American Expeditionary Forces* (Washington, DC: Center of Military History, US Army, 1989), 4:270–336.

Chapter 9
1 Albertus W. Catlin, *With the Help of God and a Few Marines* (1919; repr., Nashville: The Battery Press, 2004), 4.
2 Lloyd Williams, quoted in Robert B. Asprey, *At Belleau Wood* (1965; repr., Denton, Texas: North Texas University Press), 120.
3 Clyburn O. Mattfeldt, comp., *Records of the Second Division (Regular)*, vol. 6 (Washington, DC: Army War College, 1925–1927), quoted in Asprey, *At Belleau Wood*, 111.
4 Mattfeldt, *Records of the Second Division*, vol. 6, cited in Asprey, *At Belleau Wood*, 345.
5 James G. Harbord, *Leaves from a War Diary* (New York: Dodd, Mead, 1925), 294–95.
6 Bliss, quoted in Richard Suskind, *The Battle of Belleau Wood: The Marines Stand Fast* (New York: Macmillan, 1969), 75; Robert Lee Bullard, quoted in Anne Cipriano Venzon, ed., *The United States in the First World War: An Encyclopedia* (New York: Garland, 1995), 77.
7 Matthew Ridgway quoted in Suskind, *The Battle of Belleau Wood*, 75.

Chapter 10

1 Center of Military History, *Military Operations of the American Expeditionary Forces* (Washington, DC: Center of Military History, US Army, 1989), 4:745.
2 Center of Military History, *Military Operations*, 4:745.
3 Center of Military History, *Military Operations*, 4: 745–46.
4 Center of Military History, *Military Operations*, 4:746.
5 Center of Military History, *Military Operations*, 4:746.
6 Center of Military History, *Military Operations*, 4:747.
7 Center of Military History, *Military Operations*, 4:752.
8 Center of Military History, *Military Operations*, 5:81–82.
9 John J. Pershing, quoted in Vernon Williams, "Château-Thierry Sector," in Anne Cipriano Venzon, ed., *The United States in the First World War: An Encyclopedia* (New York: Garland, 1995), 140.

Chapter 11

1 Center of Military History, *Military Operations of the American Expeditionary Forces* (Washington, DC: Center of Military History, US Army, 1989), 5:684–85.

Chapter 12

1 US Army Center of Military History, "U.S. Army Campaigns of World War I," http://www.history.army.mil/html/reference/army_flag/wwi.html.
2 Philip Gibbs, "The Battle of Amiens," August 27, 1918, http://www.firstworldwar.com/source/amiens_gibbs.htm.

Chapter 13

1 Center of Military History, *Military Operations of the American Expeditionary Forces* (Washington, DC: Center of Military History, US Army, 1989), 6:5.
2 Robert Lee Bullard, *Personalities and Reminiscences of the War* (Garden City, NY: Doubleday, Page & Company, 1925), 234.
3 Bullard, *Personalities and Reminiscences of the War*, 235–36.
4 Bullard, *Personalities and Reminiscences of the War*, 236–37.
5 Bullard, *Personalities and Reminiscences of the War*, 238.
6 Quoted in Edward M. Coffman, *The War to End All Wars: The American Military Experience in World War I* (Lexington: University Press of Kentucky, 1998), 258.
7 "The Capture of Juvigny: A Dashing Achievement," *Mercury* (Hobart, Tasmania), September 4, 1918, Trove, http://trove.nla.gov.au/newspaper/article/11407988.
8 "U.S. Army Campaigns of World War I," U.S. Army Center of Military History, http://www.history.army.mil/html/reference/army_flag/wwi.html.

Chapter 14

1 Center of Military History, *Military Operations of the American Expeditionary Forces* (Washington, DC: Center of Military History, US Army, 1989), 6:304–5.
2 Center of Military History, *Military Operations*, 6:306–7.
3 Center of Military History, *Military Operations*, 6:313.

4   Ian McCollum, "Granatenwerfer 16," ForgottonWeapons.com, http://www.forgotten weapons.com/granatenwerfer-16/.
5   Center of Military History, *Military Operations*, 6:313.
6   Center of Military History, *Military Operations*, 6:320.
7   Center of Military History, *Military Operations*, 6:321.
8   Center of Military History, *Military Operations*, 6:324.
9   George Thompson, "American Military Operations and Casualties in 1917–18," KU Medical Center, http://www.kumc.edu/wwi/index-of-essays/american-military-op erations-and-casualties.html.

Chapter 15

1   Richard W. Stewart, ed., *The United States Army in a Global Era, 1917–2008* (Washington, DC: Center of Military History, US Army, 2010), 41.
2   Douglas Waller, *A Question of Loyalty* (New York: Harper Perennial, 2004), 20.
3   "Pershing Reports 13,000 Prisoners Taken; Enemy Destroying Vast Stores in Flight," *New York Times*, September 14, 1918.

Chapter 16

1   Quoted in Karl H. von Wiegand, "Interview with the Crown Prince," in *Current Misconceptions about the War* (New York: The Fatherland Corporation, 1915), 3; accessed at https://archive.org/details/currentmisconcep00vonw.
2   This account is based on Alan Axelrod, *Patton's Drive: The Making of America's Greatest General* (Guilford, CT: Lyons Press, 2009), 245–49.

Chapter 17

1   Center of Military History, *Military Operations of the American Expeditionary Forces* (Washington, DC: Center of Military History, US Army, 1990), 6:528–30.
2   Center of Military History, *Military Operations*, 6:538.

Chapter 18

1   George Seldes, *You Can't Print That! The Truth Behind the News 1918–1928* (New York: Payson & Clarke, Ltd.., 1929), 32–40.
2   Woodrow Wilson. "President Woodrow Wilson's Fourteen Points, 8 January 1918," Avalon Project, http://avalon.law.yale.edu/20th_century/wilson14.asp.
3   Hunt Tooley, *The Great War: Western Front and Home Front* (New York: Palgrave Macmillan, 2016), 328.
4   Erich Ludendorff, quoted in World Library, "Armistice with Germany (Compiégne)," http://www.worldlibrary.org/articles/armistice_with_germany_(compi %C3%A8gne).
5   "Made a Citizen of Paris. President Receives a Gold Medal from the Municipal Council. Tells Why We Fought," *New York Times*, December 16, 1918, http://query .nytimes.com/mem/archive-free/pdf?res=9C0DE7D81031E03ABC4F52DFB4678 383609EDE.
6   "Edward Mandell Houses's Diary: 1919," quoted in George E. Stanley, *An Emerging World Power 1900–1929* (Milwaukee, WI: World Almanac Library, 2005), 26.

7   ConnectUS, "10 Foremost Pros and Cons of the Treaty of Versailles," *ConnectUS: The Global Issues Blog*, http://connectusfund.org/10-foremost-pros-and-cons-of-the-treaty-of-versailles.

8   Alan Woods, "The Treaty of Versailles—The Peace to End All Peace," In Defence of Marxism, April 13, 2009, https://www.marxist.com/treaty-of-versailles-to-end-all-peace.htm.

Chapter 19

1   Woodrow Wilson, speaking on the League of Nations to a luncheon audience in Portland OR. US Senate, *Senate Documents: Addresses of President Wilson* 11, no. 120 (May–November 1919): 206.

2   US Senate, "Woodrow Wilson Addresses the Senate, July 10, 1919, https://www.senate.gov/artandhistory/history/minute/Woodrow_Wilson_Addresses_the_Senate.htm.

3   Warren G. Harding, "Inaugural Address," March 4, 1921, Avalon Project, http://avalon.law.yale.edu/20th_century/harding.asp.

4   United Nations Office at Geneva, "The End of the League of Nations," https://www.unog.ch/80256EDD006AC19C/(httpPages)/BA9387B56BFAAFB-4C1256F3100418C75?OpenDocument.

5   Sidney M. Milkis and Michael Nelson, *The American Presidency: Origins and Development, 1776–2014*, 7th ed. (Los Angeles and London: Sage/CQ Press, 2016), chapter 9, Kindle ed.

6   Benito Mussolini, "The Doctrine of Fascism," in Michael J. Oakeshott, *The Social and Political Doctrines of Contemporary Europe* (Cambridge: Cambridge University Press, 1939), 164.

7   Adolf Hitler, *Mein Kampf*, quoted in Jeffrey Verhey, *The Spirit of 1914: Militarism, Myth, and Mobilization in Germany* (Cambridge: Cambridge University Press, 2000), 225.

8   Quoted in Dan Stone, *The Holocaust, Fascism and Memory: Essays in the History of Ideas* (New York: Palgrave Macmillan, 2013), 49.

9   Quoted in William L. Hosch, ed., *World War II: People, Politics, and Power* (New York: Britannica Educational Publishing, 2010), 27.

10 Quoted in Colin S. Gray and Geoffrey Sloan, *Geopolitics, Geography and Strategy* (London and New York: Frank Cass, 1999), 212.

11 Christopher Klein, "Chamberlain Declares 'Peace for Our Time,' 75 Years Ago," *History Stories* (September 30, 2013), http://www.history.com/news/chamberlain-declares-peace-for-our-time-75-years-ago.

12 *Newsweek* Staff, "Presidents and the Mythology of Munich," June 14, 2008, http://www.newsweek.com/presidents-and-mythology-munich-91361.

13 Winston Churchill, "The Munich Agreement," address to the House of Commons, October 5, 1938, https://www.winstonchurchill.org/resources/speeches/1930-1938-the-wilderness/the-munich-agreement.

Index